Golda Meir:
WOMAN WITH A CAUSE

MARIE SYRKIN

G. P. PUTNAM'S SONS
NEW YORK

© 1963 by Marie Syrkin

Library of Congress Catalog
Card Number: 64-10403

MANUFACTURED IN THE UNITED STATES OF AMERICA

CONTENTS

ON THE ROSTRUM, 9

CHILDHOOD, 12

THE REASON, 31

ON THE POCAHONTAS, 58

FIRST YEARS IN PALESTINE, 69

WITH THE HISTADRUT, 93

THE STRUGGLE STARTS, 110

MA'AVAK, 127

HEAD OF THE POLITICAL DEPARTMENT, 149

THE ARABS ATTACK, 169

MISSION TO AMERICA, 183

TRYST WITH ABDULLAH, 192

THE STATE, 203

IN MOSCOW, 219

MINISTER OF LABOR, 235

PLENTY OF JEWS, 247

THE ROAD TO REVIVIM, 265

THE FOREIGN MINISTER, 275

AT HOME, 306

Illustrations will be found
following page 160

Golda Meir:
WOMAN WITH A CAUSE

ON THE ROSTRUM

When Mrs. Golda Meir, Foreign Minister of Israel, walks to the rostrum of the General Assembly to present her country's case during any one of the recurring crises that beset her small land, she is a formidable advocate. As she speaks in her homespun American style—so unlike the Churchillian elegance of Mr. Abba Eban who preceded her as Israel's chief spokesman at the United Nations—the delegates listen with attention if not agreement. Reactions may vary with the political orientation of the auditor but they are never perfunctory.

The delegates of the Arab bloc wait impatiently for their hour of rebuttal. They are not deceived by Mrs. Meir's simplicity, for she is a dangerous opponent capable of swaying some uncommitted representatives from South America or the African countries by her direct plea for peace in the Middle East and by her disconcerting offers to negotiate.

The British know Mrs. Meir from the troubled days of the Mandate when she defied all British officialdom, from the high commissioner down, for the right of Jewish refugees

to enter Palestine. Even then the British paid her the deference due a valiant foe; now they recognize a familiar mettle.

The Americans cannot escape a proprietary interest in
Mrs. Meir, who represents a beguiling variant of the American success story. Raised in Milwaukee, she had once been
an American librarian and schoolteacher. The Russians, too,
have their memories. This commanding woman, as disdain-
ful of powder and lipstick as any old-time Soviet feminist—
her hair severely parted in the middle and coiled at the nape
of her neck—had jolted their complacency in 1948 when she
had come to Moscow as Israel's first minister. Her dramatic
encounter with Soviet Jewry had brought home the unpal-
atable truth that after decades of revolutionary propaganda
the Jews of Russia still stubbornly remembered Zion.

The delegates from the young African states have recent
affectionate associations with the speaker. When she offers
Israel's fraternal help—that of one small state with the experience of newly won independence to other small emerging states—they do not dismiss the words as a transparent
maneuvering for a foothold in Africa. Not that the newcomers are politically ingenuous. They have been well
briefed on the menace of Israel by hostile fellow Moslems
and Africans. Nevertheless, no matter what shifts the power
struggle between Moslem and non-Moslem, white and col-
ored, East and West, may subsequently dictate, they trust
her personally. Was she not made a paramount chief in full
regalia on one of her several journeys to the heart of Africa?
Though eventual votes may waver, now they cheer her
warmly.

For the women of the Assembly, whether they wear saris,
veils or Western dress, whatever their nationality or political
affiliation, Mrs. Meir has a special significance. With rare

exceptions, women delegates generally find themselves relegated to committees where they discuss social welfare, child health, the status of women and kindred themes—all worthy and major subjects. But their debates take place in rooms filled with a disproportionate number of female delegates. For a woman to be the chief representative of her country and to participate on equal terms in the political debate of the General Assembly is unusual. Consequently the presence of Mrs. Meir is encouraging even to her bitterest female antagonists from the Arab countries. A woman can make the grade; a mother and grandmother, not the child of a wealthy aristocratic family like Mrs. Pandit but the daughter of penniless immigrants who had fled from Czarist Russia to America.

For those in the visitors' gallery who have come specially to see and hear her, she is already a legend: the American girl who became one of the founders of Israel; the heroine of Jewish national independence.

The man of action, the individual who does not merely suffer history but presumes to shape it, always exerts a special fascination. Where does he get his faith or effrontery? What makes him tick? A woman of action is even more intriguing. In the modern world, despite several generations of emancipated women gifted in the arts, successful in the professions, a woman who plays a major political role is rare. What inner checks and outer handicaps did the imposing woman at the rostrum have to overcome before she reached her present place at the center of events, expounding her people's case as an equal among equals?

CHILDHOOD

GOLDA MEIR is unique among Israeli leaders: no other prominent Israeli of the pioneer generation came from America; only Golda was brought up in the United States and left its security for a precarious vision.

Goldie Mabovitch was born in Kiev in southwestern Russia on May 3, 1898. Most of Russian Jewry lived within the Pale of Settlement—the Russian districts in which Jews were permitted to reside under the Czarist regime. Within or without the Pale, the Jew was a second-class citizen. In addition to the oppression of a despotic government from which all suffered, Jews were harassed by a host of anti-Jewish laws which defined their inferior status. Discriminatory legislation subjected Jews to heavy economic and social disabilities from which only the most resourceful could escape. Even within the Pale, only a strictly limited quota of Jewish youth could attend high school. Those who dreamed of higher education had to make their way to the universities of Western Europe. In Switzerland, France and Germany, eager young Russian Jews, avid for secular culture, acquired the degrees forbidden at home. These were the few. For the masses of Russian Jewry the only hope of deliverance lay in political change or emigration. Worst of all, to the misery of daily persecution by edict was added the terror of sporadic pogroms when mobs of drunken peasants inflamed by anti-Jewish propaganda would start breaking into Jewish homes, looting and killing.

Kiev lay outside the Pale. Moshe Mabovitch, the head of the family, was a skilled carpenter and cabinetmaker who had won the right to live there because special dispensations were given to superior craftsmen. In her childhood Golda had more than once heard that they lived in Kiev, not as of right but on sufferance. Yet even the privilege of residence in Kiev was of little help to the wretchedly poor Mabovitch household. Moshe was an excellent artisan: he had been among the first in Kiev to make an icebox, an innovation in those days. However, neither skill nor industry served to keep his family from want. Of eight children only three survived: Shana, the oldest, Golda, and a younger sister Zipporah. Five boys born in the ten-year interval between Shana and Golda died in infancy; the vigorous girl broke the spell of death.

Since there was little chance of improvement in Kiev, it was decided that Moshe should try his fortune in the New World. From all over Russia, Jews who could scrape together the fare were escaping to America. Perhaps a good carpenter, even a Jew, would prosper in one of its great cities. Moshe left alone in 1903, planning to send for his wife and children when he could. The family would have to move back to Pinsk, a small town within the Pale, since the right to live in Kiev was forfeited by Moshe's departure.

Of her first five years in Kiev, Golda was to retain one

sharply etched memory from the blur of early impressions. She is four years old. Her father and the neighbors are putting boards across the doors and windows of their house while she and the other children on the street watch silently. They have been told a pogrom is expected. The child knows that when the peasants surge through the town crying "Christ-killer," they will beat and stab every Jew who does not manage to hide. Her father is hammering the planks for the family to cower behind.

It was a false alarm. Although the pogrom did not take place, Golda carried the sound of the hammer and the sight of the planks with her through life. Here, perhaps, was the origin of her rebellion against the cravenness of passive suffering. Half a century later, when accepting public honors, she offered a memory of the little girl in Kiev, hiding helplessly behind boarded doors and waiting for a violent mob to smash the thin wood, as the explanation of all that she had tried to do in the course of her life.

Pinsk, her mother's home town to which the family returned while waiting for Moshe to send for them, had a population of some 30,000 of whom two thirds were Jews living in the tight *statdl* community immortalized by Sholem Aleichem. For the most part small shopkeepers and petty tradesmen, they struggled ingeniously to exist, hoping that somehow their children would escape. Even the innkeeper, licensed to sell whisky to the peasants when they came to market, scraped together a niggardly livelihood that was little better than that of his envious patrons.

Although almost all the streets were unpaved and *Pinsker blotte* (Pinsk mud) has become a Yiddish byword, there was nothing stagnant about the intellectual life of the town. A surprisingly high percentage of eminent Russian Jews—the families of Chaim Weizmann and Moshe Sharett, for example—sprang from this malaria-ridden town near the Pripet Marshes.

Golda was never to forget the muddy alleys of Pinsk, no more than the house in Kiev. Once Cossacks on horseback came dashing through the street where she was playing. Not bothering to rein in their horses, they leaped indifferently over the children, the hoofs of the steeds flashing above the small heads. Perhaps the Cossacks were skilled enough horsemen not to hurt the children, but Golda would always believe that they would as soon have crushed her as not. To the sound of the hammer were added the hoofs of the rearing horses.

In time an abiding indignation replaced the panic of childhood. Pogroms, mud, the hoofs of the Cossacks' horses—that was Jewish life in the *Galuth*, the Diaspora. Other five-year-old Jewish children suffered similar experiences without such shock, or at any rate without such anger. But Mrs. Meir, addressing an Israel bond conference in 1959 among the lush surroundings of Miami, could declare in all honesty: "If there is any logical explanation necessary for the direction which my life has taken, maybe this is the explanation—the desire and the determination to save Jewish children, four or five years old, from a similar scene and from a similar experience."

How many times in the years to come, prodded consciously or unconsciously by that childhood anguish, would she strive to give meaning to suffering by making it purposeful? The mud of the rain-soaked fields of the Palestine Emek in winter would be deeper even than the mud of Pinsk, but the pioneers sloshing through the grime would make roads. As Minister of Labor, she herself would one day have the joy of building so many roads that they would be known as *goldene wegen* (golden roads). And no children along those roads would watch their fathers ignominiously wait for the hand of the killer; whatever the outcome, the fathers would fight back.

One way of fighting back was taking place in Pinsk. The Pale was deeply stirred by the revolutionary currents agitating Russia. Many young Jews pinned their hopes on the overthrow of the Czar; the Jewish problem would be solved by the victory of democratic ideas when special Jewish woes would vanish in the melting pot of international brotherhood. Eager, idealistic Jewish boys and girls, breaking loose from their orthodox moorings, held the same kind of secret revolutionary meetings as their Russian counterparts; with the zeal of outcasts, they joined the dangerous revolutionary struggle.

Sixteen-year-old Shana and her teen-age friends were among those who conspired to bring about the day of liberation. They gathered cautiously in the Mabovitch home to discuss "plans" while Shana kept an ear cocked for the possible tread of a policeman from the nearby police station. The whispered debates of the "big ones" fascinated the six-year-old Golda, who would climb unseen to the top of the coal stove (every reader of Russian novels is familiar with this favorite spot in the kitchens of the poor) and try to hear what was being hatched. Once Shana and her comrades were startled by the sudden emergence of the previously unnoticed Golda, who threatened: "Look out, or I'll tell the police what you're saying."

Sometimes the child was wakened by screams coming from the police station where the police were beating youths caught taking part in forbidden meetings. Those cries heard in the night were also to leave their mark. What did the beaten students want?

The Russian revolutionary songs that Shana sang fascinated her. In the years to come Golda would dream of a new society, no less than of a new land. One day, recalling her sister's schoolgirl plotting, she was to declare proudly: "If one is privileged in one's lifetime to go all the way from that small room in Pinsk to the State of Israel where there are great and humane workers' enterprises and workers' settlements—if a child in that little room grows up to be blessed with a daughter and grandchildren who live in a kibbutz, under a system unsurpassed for justice and respect for human dignity—for what more can a daughter of Israel ask?"

Not all was dour in Pinsk. The pretty, precocious little girl was a general favorite. Shana was frankly jealous of her "because she was so beautiful and everyone spoiled her." Opportunities for spoiling did not include toys or sweets. The family was too poor for such nonsense, but the child aroused admiration for her looks and brightness. Despite the inadequate diet—sometimes there was literally no bread in the house—she thrived. The mother, mourning for five small sons, delighted in this active, buoyant child, and the little girl derived assurance from love and approbation.

Yet the mother had cause for complaint. Goldie early displayed an unholy stubbornness. Later this quality might flatteringly be described as strength or will power, but in the Pinsk days it struck troubled relatives as plain cussedness. "There's a *dybbuk* in her."

One of the childhood anecdotes is impressive even outside the family circle. The Kishinev pogrom took place in April 1903; forty-five Jews were murdered. The post-Hitler world, numbed by the carnage of millions, would find the universal horror aroused by the Kishinev massacre puzzling: heads of states protested, and Jewish communities everywhere declared days of fasting. In Pinsk, too, the community mourned: Every adult Jew fasted in the synagogue. Children were naturally exempt, but Golda, not yet five years old, insisted on joining the fast. If Shana and her mother could fast, so could she. Little attention was at first paid the childish whim, but Golda, whose appetite was ordinarily excellent, showed no sign of capitulating. As the day wore on, the family begged her to eat something. The stubborn child refused until the elders returned from the synagogue. Sheer willfulness or a presage of a formidable will?

Perhaps the streak of stubbornness came from the *Bobe* Golda, the great-grandmother whose namesake she was. *Bobe* Golda had been a striking figure, a matriarch to whom the whole village came for counsel, who died at the age of ninety-four. During the last years of her life the iron-willed *Bobe* had eaten abstemiously and taken castor oil daily because, "I don't want to feed the worms." She had habitually used salt instead of sugar in her tea, saying, "I want to take the taste of the *Galuth* into the other world."

It may have been the *Bobe* Golda or the *dybbuk*. There would be more fasts in the future, notably the solemn fast in Jerusalem forty years later for Jewish refugees held on an "illegal" ship in La Spezia—a hunger strike before which Great Britain would give way.

Even in Pinsk there were plenty of lighthearted hours of play in the summer fields and the winter alleys, though the mysterious agitations of the adult world were never too far in the background. The little girl was not morbidly obsessed by what she heard and saw, but no matter how wholesome her disposition, no spirited child could ignore what kept happening. That day in 1905, for instance, shortly after "Bloody Sunday."

On Bloody Sunday, a large parade of Russian workers marching peacefully to the Czar's palace to petition for a constitution had been ruthlessly shot down by the Cossacks lined up before the gates. Russia was aroused to fever pitch. Demonstrations, which the government met with increased repression, took place everywhere. In Pinsk, too, were mass meetings in which bold orators clamored for *freiheit* (freedom), and the town was agitated by rumors of imminent pogroms. The peasants, befuddled by the excitement and incited by the authorities, were looking to their usual scapegoat. On one such tense day a neighboring peasant came up to seven-year-old Golda and another little girl in the yard, knocked their heads together playfully, and announced: "That's what we will do with the Jews. We'll knock their heads together and we'll be through with them." Golda never forgot the joke.

Impatiently the family waited for the magic ticket from America. Finally, in 1906, like thousands of other Russian Jews fleeing from want and persecution, the mother and her daughters emigrated to the United States to join Moshe. The land of hunger and pogroms was behind them.

In the three years that had elapsed, Moshe Mabovitch had not made his fortune; he was not even making a modest living adequate for a household of five. In New York, the first stopping place of penniless immigrants, he had not managed to earn more than three dollars a week. Finally, HIAS, the immigrant aid society—in the hope that his skills would serve him better farther from the crowded seaboard—had shipped him to Milwaukee. There he had gotten work as a carpenter. Despite his family's imminent arrival, he had failed to find an apartment, as much from lack of enterprise as from lack of funds. The first American home the mother and daughters knew was the shabby furnished room to which he took them. Eight-year-old Golda looked wide-eyed at the one dingy room where all were to sleep. So this was America.

Some kind of apartment had to be rented. The only place the Mabovitches could discover was a little store with two rooms in the back located on 10th Street, then a poor Jewish section of Milwaukee. More than one moneyless family settled the problem of living quarters by unexpectedly going into business. Mrs. Mabovitch undertook to run a little grocery store, not more ambitious than the familiar hole-in-the-wall *kreml* (little store) of Pinsk.

Moshe had objected to the dreary little store with its barrel of flour, half-penny candy and few supplies of cheap groceries for customers little more affluent than the owner. Though it provided the family with two rooms instead of one, not to mention the hope of increased income, a grocery store was beneath his craftsman's dignity. He would work as a skilled carpenter whenever he could get a job; let his obstinate wife and the girls worry about the store.

Economically, life at first proved little better than in Pinsk. The mother tried to master the complexities of American business. How many loaves of corn bread and how much unsalted butter should you buy on credit? If the bread grew stale or the butter spoiled before someone bought it, the financial loss might run to a couple of dollars. Yet who could rely on the wages Moshe might bring? Odd jobs were too irregular. The daughters, too, were of little use, the mother thought as she stood behind the counter waiting for someone to buy a couple of rolls or half-a-pound of loose sugar.

The process of a Russian Jewish family with capable children taking root in American soil is a familiar one. At the turn of the century the success story generally followed a stereotyped pattern. The Mabovitch household deviated from the rosy norm. Neither parent had the initiative or acumen which enabled many a Jewish peddler recently arrived from Europe to thrive financially before too many years had passed. Nor did they understand the longings of their children. Sons required an education, not females. The Mabovitches had the traditional Jewish reverence for learning, but it is sometimes forgotten that this reverence did not include higher education for girls.

Yet this was one of the two great blessings the New World had to offer even to its poor. Running water in the house, gas illumination instead of an oil lamp, a flush toilet—these were significant improvements on Pinsk, to be sure. One wore one's indigence with a difference in America. But what really mattered were first, freedom—the *freiheit* for which daring souls had clamored uselessly in Pinsk—and the education in public schools without quotas.

It took a little while to get used to the notion that police were no menace to a well-behaved Jewish child. On the first Labor Day after their arrival, Moshe grandly had his family watch him march; Zipke, the youngest, screamed in terror when she saw men in uniform at the head of the parade: "Cossacks!" Golda knew better. There were no Cossacks in Milwaukee. Freedom came easily here, like the water which flowed at the turn of a faucet or the light piped into the shabbiest dwelling.

Seventeen-year-old Shana no longer had to hatch adolescent plots against a tyrant. Now she dreamed of studying. But Mother Mabovitch had no patience with this curious female passion for knowledge. Shana should help at home till she married. What else should a respectable Jewish girl do? Shana, imaginative, intelligent and strong-willed like her redoubtable little sister, would not settle for life in the shabby grocery store. Defiantly she left home and started her career by working long hours for small wages under poor hygienic conditions. Slight, of delicate physique, the young girl paid dearly for her independence. She developed tuberculosis, the shop worker's occupational disease at the turn of the century. Fortunately a boy from Pinsk, Sam Korngold, gave her the moral and physical support she needed. Together they went to Denver where Shana entered the Jewish sanatorium for consumptives. Upon her recovery the young pair married and settled in Denver.

The younger Mabovitch daughters attended the public school in the Milwaukee Sixth District. It is difficult for a generation accustomed to reading about the decay of the public school system and the reluctance of its scholars, to appreciate the hungry expectation of these immigrant young. Golda learned English quickly and within two years was at the head of her class, a record which she was to maintain until graduation. However, from the first grade there was a daily tug of war at home. The usual morning pattern was reversed. Instead of shooing the children off to school, her mother told Golda to wait in the store until what she optimistically called the "morning rush" was over. The child would be late to school, spoiling an otherwise admirable record. When she wept, the mother would say tartly in Yiddish, *"West sein a rebbetzin mit a tog speter."* ("You'll be a learned dame a day later.")

Lack of sympathy at home could not effectively mar the joy in fresh experiences so unlike the nightmarish memories of Kiev and Pinsk. The Yiddish-speaking little girl was petted and encouraged by teachers charmed by her quick intelligence and prettiness.

In addition to the pleasure of learning, there were other thrills. In the assembly, one pledged allegiance to the flag and recited the words "with liberty and justice for all." This was the treasure, denied by the Czar and offered by the buck-toothed President Theodore Roosevelt. And there was the Declaration of Independence. In her history class, Golda learned how the colonies had declared their independence from England. That, too, seeped in. One day when Golda Meir would sign her name firmly to a later Declaration of Independence, she would for the first time fully understand what Jefferson and Washington had undertaken.

In Milwaukee, before World War I, German was a compulsory language in the elementary schools. The German teacher used to sing "Deutschland über alles" and "Die Wacht am Rhein" with inspiring patriotic fervor. Golda dutifully learned German. Even the teachers who prophesied a promising future for their able student could hardly have foreseen that French, in view of Israel's close ties with France, might prove a more useful language for a foreign minister of Israel. Because of Milwaukee's devotion to its Germanic antecedents, Mrs. Meir would one day have to converse in German with a French ambassador who knew no English.

In the second grade, Golda made a lifelong friend—Regina Hamburger—who would accompany her to Palestine and who eventually would become the private secretary of Moshe Sharett and Abba Eban. In the second grade, Regina did not suspect her own destiny though she early realized that her chum was not only the smartest girl in the class but

[23]

the leader of the group as well. Once, having gotten free tickets for a performance of *Uncle Tom's Cabin*, they played truant. It was their first visit to a theatre. During the all too realistic beating of Tom, Golda screamed aloud in outraged horror.

In the meantime Golda maintained contact with Shana in Denver. The child, forbidden to write to the rebellious sister, carried on a clandestine correspondence through a sympathetic neighbor. Regular letters of advice and exhortation came from Shana, and just as regular answers from the little sister, composed in secret, reached Shana. These letters, preserved by Shana, throw light on the early years in Milwaukee.

Although Regina, the chum from elementary school, says, "Golda was always the brightest girl in the class," and the school record bears out the praise, there is no evidence of precocity in the neat, badly spelled letters which remain. In 1908, Golda wrote: "I am very good in school I am now in third high and in June I am going to pass in fourth low. I haven't got what to write if you write me a letter I will write you more. Yours Truly your lovingly sister." Another letter of the same period explains: ". . . I can tell you that Pa does not work yet and in the store is not very busy and I am very glad that you are out of bed."

Apparently Shana's economic conditions were no brighter than those of the family in Milwaukee, because Golda writes reassuringly: "I am not surry because Sam did not buy me a present because he does not work. I am very very obliged for the ribbon and is enough for me . . ." Another letter, written a few weeks later, offers condolence because Shana "spits blood" again and because she (Shana) lacks two cents for a stamp; it concludes with the discouraging, "Pa isn't working."

For a bright ten-year-old, neither the style nor the orthography is impressive. Of course Golda had been in the United States only two years and had mastered neither English spelling nor idiom. But however feeble the manner of expression, the content is grimly mature. She was involved in sickness, poverty and family conflict, and accepted responsibility in each situation. She kept the correspondence secret. She saved some pennies to send her sister stamps, and she worked industriously in school and in the store.

By 1909, the grosser errors had been eliminated. Golda was sufficiently Americanized to be able to write glibly, if inappropriately: "Your letter on hand . . ." Her use of other expressions, obviously learned in a recent lesson on business letters, was equally lavish.

Her gifts for public leadership manifested themselves early. In 1908, she organized the American Young Sisters' Society, whose purpose was to provide textbooks for needy school children. The Milwaukee schools did not furnish free books. Apparently the society was a success, because a Milwaukee paper devoted an emotional column to its activities: "A score of little children who give their play time and scant pennies to charity, and charity organized on their own initiative too . . . And it is worthy of comment that this charity is itself a loud comment on the fact that little children may go to the public schools without proper provision of books. Think what that means . . ."

The accompanying picture showed a group of earnest little girls with tight braids. Only the notation: "President Goldie Mabovitz is in top row, fourth from right," distinguished the moving spirit of the enterprise.

[25]

A letter to Shana, dated August 2, 1909, related the further progress of the association: ". . . Now, dear sister, you asked me about the Ball which was given by the American Young Sister Society of Milwaukee. I can tell you that I took part in it but everyone's name was not on the program. I said a speech from my head in which I explained the purpose of the Society. Then I said two Jewish poems, "Der Schneider" and "Die Zwei Korbones" ["The Tailor" and "The Two Sacrifices."] Dear sister, now I can tell you that we had the greatest success that there ever was in Packen Hall. And the entertainment was Grand. . . ."

From Denver, Shana kept a critical watch on Golda's activities. Apparently a photograph of Golda in a folkdance costume displeased the puritanical sister, because in 1910 Golda feels constrained to explain: ". . . You wrote that you don't like my picture. I am glad of it because I see how dearly you love me. But don't take it so hard. You think that I changed into a girl that I never dreamed to be but don't take it so hard. I am still the same old Goldie that you left here pretty near 3 years ago." The letter continued with assurances that "nice girls" started the dancing class, and concluded: "As far as I can see, I don't see any harm in it and I hope you don't either but if you do I would be glad if you would write me. . . ." Then came reassuring details about high marks in school.

Golda was valedictorian of her graduating class at P. S. 1. She had matured early and looked older than many of her classmates. Fair-skinned, with long chestnut braids and deep-gray eyes, she was strikingly pretty. Acquaintances surveying her coloring, perfectly straight nose and regular features, often told her that she "didn't look a bit Jewish." The supposed compliment never pleased. When she took the part

of Queen Esther in a Purim play, she had longed for the
dark tresses and brilliant eyes of Jewish heroines of fiction.
As she stood earnestly urging her class to march bravely
to life's battles, nothing foretold the future orator except perhaps an unusual assurance in her voice and bearing. There
was no trace of foreign accent in the valedictorian's clear,
fluent English. The teachers on the platform had the satisfaction of knowing that they had guessed right.

Both Golda and Regina planned to enter high school together in the fall. Going to high school was still something of
a distinction in 1912. The children of the poor, unless they
were inordinately ambitious, took out working papers and
started fending for themselves. The Mabovitches, who had
not prospered in the eight years since the family's arrival in
the United States, could ill afford the luxury of idle scholar-
ship for their promising daughter. Not that Golda was a
complete financial drag on her parents. For the past year on
Saturdays she and Regina had worked as messenger girls
in a department store on the South Side. The hours were
from nine in the morning to nine in the evening, and the pay
was one dollar for twelve hours. This last vacation before
high school the two girls worked in the department store
daily all summer. Despite the distance to the South Side,
they never ventured to spend a nickel for carfare except on
Saturday nights when it was too late to walk home. Even the
tantalizing bags of salted peanuts which the street vendors
beguilingly offered for a few pennies would only be purchased in a rare moment of weakness. While the hours were
long, the job was not taxing: wrapping parcels, running er-
rands. It was more amusing than the grocery store, and besides, there was the expectation of high school in September
when the world of adult learning would open its doors.

Golda's stay in the North Side high school which she entered that fall barely lasted one term. She wanted to be a teacher, not for the long vacations and stable pay which are often the profession's chief attraction to its acolytes, but because a teacher's vocation was "intellectual and socially useful." Both attributes mattered to the young American girl with her memories of Pinsk. Unfortunately Mother Mabovitch had heard an ugly but correct rumor that married women could not teach in the local school system. Was Golda planning to embrace spinsterhood? "You want to be an old maid?" she asked her daughter bitterly. While the prospect was too remote to alarm fourteen-year-old Golda, her parents continued to insist that she transfer to a business school to be trained in skills less hazardous to matrimony.

Mrs. Mabovitch's experience with her older daughter had not made her more tolerant. And apparently she had forgotten the *dybbuk* in Golda and her talent for immediate action when her sense of justice was outraged. Golda, docile enough in school and in the grocery store, did not meekly accept her parents' dictates. Besides, she was not alone. Shana, now recovered from tuberculosis, helped her. The secret correspondence with Denver had never slackened, and in this crisis inflammatory counsel was forthcoming without hesitation. Shana was not going to let the bright little sister be deprived of that much dreamed of "education." Plans were hatched for Goldie to "run away" to Denver.

A letter from Sam (Denver, November 15, 1912) urged Goldie to leave home secretly. "No, Goldie, I say that you shouldn't stop school. You are too young to work; you have good chances to become something. My advice is that you should get ready and come to us; we are not rich either, but you will have good chances here to study. We will do all we can for you." Shana added a few words: "Have not much to add to Sam's letter . . . first you'll have all the opportunities to study; second, you'll have plenty to eat; third, you'll have the necessary clothes that a person ought to have. . . ."

Successive letters developed the scheme of flight. An elaborate conspiratorial plan was evolved. Goldie was gradually to get her clothes out of the house and into the hands of her confidante Regina. When she had money for the ticket, she was to leave with her books, supposedly for school. Instead, she was to go to the railroad station and take a train to Denver. On the way she was to send her parents a post card announcing her departure, so that they would not worry. Above all, not a soul except Regina was to know anything of the proposed events. Shana's final injunction read: "The main thing is never to be excited; be always calm and act coolly. This way of action will always bring you good results. Be brave."

It was not easy to amass the money for the fare. Goldie and Regina gave English lessons to immigrants for ten cents a lesson; Shana sent a part of the required sum, and Goldie managed to borrow the rest from an older friend. Finally the money was scraped together. The flight went off as planned. True, when the post card arrived at the Mabovitch household in the late afternoon, Goldie was still sitting in the station in Milwaukee, waiting for a train, but fortunately the parents were no better versed in the mysteries of timetables and railroad schedules than their daughter. For her complicity, Regina got a few stern smacks from her outraged mother, who sympathized with Mrs. Mabovitch: "What children can do!"

A letter from Regina dated March 1913, reported the speculation aroused by Goldie's flight. "You asked of the opinion you have in Milwaukee. Well, to be truthful, I hope I won't hurt your feelings, everybody thought you had eloped with an Italian. How they got the idea I can't get at. . . . Now, dear Goldie, don't get angry at me for writing this but I can't help it, you asked . . . I burned with anger and resentment, but what could I do?"

THE REASON

THE sister who abetted Golda's flight and received her warmly in Denver was herself only in her mid-twenties. Tiny and fragile, except for her masses of red hair, she looked like a miniature version of Golda, and in her way she was just as strong-willed. Barely recovered from tuberculosis, Shana was not going to play the invalid, nor was she going to worry about the responsibility she and Sam had assumed in encouraging Golda's departure from Milwaukee.

They had precious little in the way of material comfort to offer. To support his wife and child, Sam worked nights as a janitor in an elevator building. He had just opened a small dry-cleaning store and hoped that the business would develop sufficiently to permit him to drop the night job. Shana, neat, efficient and thrifty, was an ideal poor man's helpmeet. Her marriage, begun gallantly in sickness and poverty, was to prove deeply happy in all the hard years ahead. Though an extra mouth to feed was no slight strain on the home's carefully calculated economy, Sam was as delighted with Golda's arrival as was his wife.

Golda promptly entered the local high school. The term began auspiciously. As in Milwaukee, Golda proved to be an excellent student. After school she would stand by the ironing board in the Korngold cleaning establishment, faithfully pressing shirts and dresses. She ironed with the same deftness and competence that she displayed in all household arts. At no time in her life would Golda, whatever her office, scorn domestic tasks, or would she ever tolerate the slipshod or untidy. If in years to come an astonished soldier bearing a message would surprise Madam Minister on her knees, scrubbing woodwork neglected by her maids, he would not be witnessing a momentary aberration nor would the unexpected intrusion cause Golda embarrassment. The lad might look flustered as he saluted his crouching superior, but the lady rising from the floor would return the salute with rolled-up sleeves and complete serenity. There was no point in prating about the dignity of labor if one was ashamed to be caught laboring. That had been one of the never-to-be-outgrown lessons of youth in America.

In Denver, there was a colony of Jewish intellectuals who had been, or still were, patients at the Jewish Hospital for Consumptives. For the most part immigrants uprooted for the second time by illness, they waited for the complete recovery which would enable them to return to their familiar urban communities. Isolated in the mountain city, unmarried, they often congregated in Shana's house for glasses of tea with lemon and much talk. Mainly East European in origin, they reflected the ideological currents of the countries they had left. Socialists, anarchists, Marxists, Zionists, they sat in Shana's house quarreling feverishly about their various social creeds with an animation that bore no relationship to the concrete possibilities of their programs or to their immediate environment.

Fifteen-year-old Golda was enchanted by the political debates and charged atmosphere. One young man was a disciple of Kropotkin; another expounded dialectical materialism. Hegel and Schopenhauer were bandied about with more audacity than formal knowledge. And of course there was the eternally intriguing woman question. How free should women be? The double standard? Suffrage? All questions of intense and instant urgency.

The Zionists were in the minority. Zionism, with its concentration on the Jewish problem, was too narrow and parochial for the cosmopolitan tastes of most of the tea drinkers. Shana, with her memories of adolescent revolutionary activities in Russia, listened sympathetically to the radical panaceas offered by her guests. Golda, too, found the generous programs which proclaimed the brotherhood of man wonderfully appealing. Unlike her classmates, she was already genuinely drawn to political ideas, not as academic expositions but as ways of life to which she would have to assume definite commitment.

There was no danger of the pretty young sister's being overlooked by the debaters. Soon Golda was eagerly going to meetings and lectures, escorted by equally eager expositors of new truths. Inevitably, strict, strait-laced Shana began to look askance at late hours, no matter how ideologically inspired. Running around to lectures or concerts and not getting enough sleep would lead to no good.

As the first year in Denver drew to a close, Golda's impatience with her sister's "bossiness" reached the breaking point. She had not left her parent's home to be hectored by another relative. A girl of fifteen was no child to be ordered about. Shana meant well but she did not respect her sister's adult independence.

One evening after a sharp quarrel, Golda said, "Very well, I'll leave." Too proud to take any of the clothes which Shana had purchased, she stalked out with only the blouse and skirt she was wearing. She sought refuge with a tubercular couple who lived in a furnished room with an alcove. There she stayed until she could pay the rent for a cheap room of her own.

The equally stubborn Shana, indignant at Golda's high-handed behavior, made no move to patch up the rift. Golda gave up school, and benefiting from her experience in Sam's shop, took a job in a laundry which specialized in the washing of lace curtains. She would stretch the curtains on a wooden frame and pin them in place until her hands bled. Finally she obtained a job in a department store where she sold linings and took measurements for skirts. The hours were long—nine a day—but the work was easier. Fortunately she looked older than her age, and her employers had no worries about violating child-labor regulations.

Independence came hard but was worth having. The breach with Shana went unhealed, and if the older sister watched Golda's willful emergence into womanhood with concern, she was no more prepared to yield than Golda. The girl enjoyed her freedom. Plenty of energy remained at the end of the day's work for exciting friendships and pursuits of knowledge other than those offered by a high school curriculum. She met Morris Myerson, a young Russian-Jewish immigrant a few years older than herself, and a romance soon blossomed. Morris, penniless as she, self-educated and with no prospect of acquiring professional training, made a pre-

carious living as a sign painter. Not that this bothered Golda.
No one in her circle had as yet made the ascent, characteristic of her immigrant generation, from working class to petty
bourgeois. The young men who buzzed around her, new in
the country, worked at any menial job they could get. If they
could not enter the universities to which their children and
grandchildren would throng, they all the more hungrily went
to the public libraries.

Omnivorous readers, passionately advocating some political utopia, they spent their evenings at meetings or lectures.
In time many of them would become successful businessmen
solidly rooted in the American scene, proudly watching their
children become the physicists, social scientists or artists
that they had dreamed of being; some, less worldly, would
remain perpetually disoriented, with unrealized strivings
and no financial security. Morris belonged to the latter group.

Quiet, reticent, he hardly seemed a fitting match for the
vivid attractive girl who aroused perfervid admiration wherever she went. Golda was drawn to him by what she conceived to be his superior erudition and what she called his
"beautiful soul." He supervised her reading and drew up
long lists of works meriting special consideration. The romantic poets, particularly Byron, enjoyed a high priority.
Morris took her to concerts when he could raise the money.
Sometimes there were public concerts in the park, and
Golda, who had acquired a ten-cent red straw hat at Wool-
worth's, prayed for clear weather lest rain make the color run.

Regina, aware of her friend's predilections wrote sagely
at this time: "I suppose you meet high intellectual people
who always talk about books and dry subjects." She added a
few thoughtful warnings about distinguishing between passing fancies and true love, but by 1915 she was already con-

gratulating Golda on her "blissful happiness"—a reference to Morris.

Was she blissfully happy? Very early in their relationship their differences in temperament began to emerge. The introspective Morris was aware of the potential conflict between Golda's boundless vitality and his passive, retiring nature. In 1915 he wrote: "Have you ever stopped to think whether your Morris has the one attribute without which all other refinements are worthless, namely, 'the indomitable will'?" And a few weeks later he wrote: "Are you still worrying about me and the meaning of the strain of sadness you discern in my letters . . . ? My sadness is not due to any personal discomfort. It is only a part of that universal sadness that is bound to permeate every person endowed with the least bit of sensibility and clarity of vision. Can any thinking being be altogether happy and satisfied? Therefore, don't worry. Be the same happy smiling Goldie you were heretofore. . . ." This vein, which might be dismissed as self-conscious youthful melancholy, sounded an elegiac note that was to deepen with time.

But Golda had no gift for futile worry; the injunctions were superfluous. Morris' delicate sensibility was part of his attraction for her. Besides, he was mentor as well as lover. A boy of twenty who had read widely, he seemed a well of profundity to a teen-ager unable to finish high school. After the day's work in the department store, the walks with Morris, the long conversations, were intimations of the intellectual life she seemed unable to achieve. As yet she had no realization of her own attractiveness. Morris, in a rare moment of self-assertion, wrote to her peremptorily: "I have repeatedly asked you not to contradict me on the question of your beauty . . . you pop up every now and then with these same timid and self-deprecating remarks which I cannot bear. . . ."

Her parents in Milwaukee had no inkling of the turn of events in Denver. Golda, who corresponded with her mother, was much too proud to admit the defeat of her scheme. She had defiantly run away from home, and though formal education seemed further away than ever, she did not ask for help. Somehow Mother Mabovitch learned that her sixteen-year-old daughter was living alone and fending for herself in a department store. At this point even Papa Mabovitch, who had refused to have any truck with his disobedient child, capitulated. He wrote to Goldie, imploring her to come home; he would let her finish high school. She would even be permitted to go to normal school.

With the prospect of deliverance, Golda admitted how repugnant drudgery in the department store had become. Morris would have to remain in Denver where he was his mother's sole support; Golda would return to Milwaukee to resume that much interrupted and long deferred education.

Back in Milwaukee, Golda energetically made up for lost time. In less than two years she had graduated from high school as vice-president of her class and had entered the Milwaukee Normal School for Teachers. Presumably the career she had dreamed of in public school and for which she had precipitated the dramatic break with her family was at last launched. But other impulses were to appear.

The young girl who returned home was no repentant prodigal. Despite her age, she was not a restless adolescent rejecting authority. During the two years in Denver she had matured emotionally and intellectually. The young men who had delighted in instructing her might have filled her head with half-assimilated theories, but independent convictions already were beginning to take shape in her thoughts.

The philosophic anarchism so innocently proclaimed in the Denver circle had made no appeal to her orderly, responsible mind. Once she had seen the anarchist leader Emma Goldman and been repelled by her "coarseness." Nor had the Marxists, with their materialistic interpretation of history, attracted her. Despite her ignorance of the texts under discussion, she had had the audacity to debate with lecturers who expounded materialism as a doctrine. On one occasion young Golda had made a tremendous impression on a hostile audience by maintaining that a labor movement had to be motivated by ideal quests as well as by economic goals. Naturally her girlhood hero was Eugene Debs, the American socialist leader whose nobility of person and humane socialism seemed to her to augur a regenerated society where man would not be wolf to man. And the influence of Victor Berger, the socialist Congressman from Milwaukee, gave substance to the socialist movement just before World War I.

So far she had not been actively drawn to Zionism. True, advocates of Jewish nationalism in its several variations had offered their panaceas in Denver, and even back in Pinsk, Shana's friends had advanced the thesis that perhaps Jews would be wiser to create a land of their own instead of dreaming of emancipation through an eventual Russian Revolution. But the processes of growing up, of striving for an education, of falling in love, were absorbing enough. The pogrom in Kiev, the Cossacks in Pinsk, had become remote.

The anti-Jewish excesses of World War I roused her. As the war progressed, reports of pogroms came from every part of Eastern Europe. In Pinsk, Jews were lined up and shot near the wall of the church Golda used to pass as a child. On the

Eastern front, wherever the rampaging armies went—Russian or Austrian—the Jewish populations in their paths were deported or massacred. As early as 1914, the American Jewish Joint Distribution Committee had been organized to aid the millions of Jewish refugees uprooted by mass deportations. Through the offices of the State Department and the intervention of neutral countries, aid reached the persecuted.

American Jewry had to be stirred to pour forth its donations for the ravaged Jewries across the sea. At first Golda, returning to Milwaukee, threw herself into relief work. She collected, she spoke, she agitated with amazing effectiveness for one so young. But as the campaign progressed, the appeals for philanthropy began to appear increasingly inadequate. Did one solve a problem by relief? Or by indignant speeches? There had been plenty of indignant speeches twelve years ago about the pogrom in Kishinev: what had the exclamations of outrage achieved? A little over a decade later the same miseries and indignities were being suffered on a vaster scale. Now she was making the speeches.

There had to be a radical solution, she thought. There had to be one country in the world to which Jews could come without quotas, where they would command their destinies, where they would not cower behind planks or be kicked by the horses of Cossacks. Zionism provided the answer.

The fact that she was in America, at last finishing high school and on the threshold of a successful future, as all her teachers assured her, did not alter the need of her people. Her own ease and contentment were no measure of the fearful necessity. On the contrary, the freedom and richness of opportunity she had found made an equal freedom for the sufferers in Poland, Russia, Galicia and Rumania more indispensable. She knew from personal experience what it was not to cower, not to be afraid. Her humiliated people should know this, too. And who better fitted than the young, the strong, the happy, for the realization of this old-new dream?

At the age of seventeen she had found her cause and she was never to waver. A measure of her intellectual independence can be gathered from the fact that she opposed Morris. Only a year before, he had seemed the source of all wisdom. Now she was complicating her personal life by a serious difference, since the boy to whom she was engaged was not a Zionist. He made that clear in a letter dated August 1915: "I do not know whether to say that I am glad or sorry that you have joined the Zionist party, and that you seem to be so enthusiastic a nationalist. I am altogether passive in the matter, though I give you full credit for your activity, as I do to all others engaged in doing something toward helping a distressed nation." He went on to belabor all forms of nationalism, and wrote: "The idea of Palestine or any other territory for the Jews is, to me, ridiculous. Racial persecution does not exist because some nations have no territories but because nations exist at all." He added: "The other day I received a notice to attend one of the meetings . . . but since I do not care particularly as to whether the Jews are going to suffer in Russia or the Holy Land, I did not go. . . ."

This was no academic difference of opinion. For Golda, even in early girlhood, an intellectual conclusion without its correlative of action was meaningless. In 1915, many Jewish boys and girls argued abstractly about the merits of Zionism. They belonged to ill-attended Zionist clubs, read magazines called *The Young Maccabean* or *New Judea*, and periodically stood on the streets with the blue-and-white boxes of the Jewish National Fund. Some even spoke vaguely of one day settling in Palestine, but with no sense of urgency or serious commitment. Their future was too promising, America too intimately dear, for the love of Zion to be other than safely abstract. Should an occasional zealot, after a spiritual crisis, feel called upon to uproot himself, a sensible counselor could generally reassure him with the soothing reflection that an American Jew could best serve the cause on the blessed soil of the United States. Pioneering was for the unlucky Europeans.

Golda was one of those to whom questions present themselves in their clear essence, not in their befuddling complexities. Having decided that she was a Zionist, she had no doubts about the next step. She would go to Palestine as soon as possible, without heart-searchings or breast-beatings; a self-respecting person could not live vicariously.

While the opposition of Morris presented a personal difficulty, it did not alter her resolution. He and her other pedagogues, male and female, were to discover the vein of iron which no amount of gray-eyed raptness and girlish softness could obliterate for long. The same intellectual and moral qualities which in future years would lend such force to Golda's encounters with British high commissioners and such persuasiveness to her appearances at the United Nations were already clearly defined in the Milwaukee schoolgirl. At no time would she indulge in hypersubtle or overelegant examinations of an issue; the kernel of truth without the adorning husks was enough. That would be her strength; critics would call it her deficiency—she would never be adequately aware of the "if's" and "or's" which preclude action.

In 1915, she formally joined the Poale Zion, the small, uninfluential, largely Yiddish-speaking party of the Labor Zionists. Characteristically, she made no organizational commitment until she had made a personal commitment. In a reversal of the usual process, she refused to become a member of a movement whose supposed goal was pioneering in Palestine until she had firmly decided that she would fulfill the goal herself. She chose the Labor Zionists rather than the larger general Zionist movement or Hadassah—already founded by an older American woman, Henrietta Szold—because the Poale Zion program called for the building of a cooperative commonwealth in Palestine without the economic inequities of capitalism. Her sense of outraged Jewish dignity had made Golda a Zionist; her sense of outraged human dignity, a socialist. In the platform of the Poale Zion, she found the synthesis of both her ideals. The ultrasecular brochures of the party quoted the pious saying of Hillel, the sage: "If I am not for myself, who will be for me? But if I am for myself only, What am I? And if not now, when?"

The future was now clear in its essentials. Golda was determined to go to Palestine to become a member of a kibbutz or cooperative settlement that was engaged in draining the swamps of the Emek, the Valley of Esdraelon. Her decision was made two years before the Balfour Declaration, at a time when the notion of creating a Jewish homeland in the barren Turkish-held territory of Palestine seemed purely visionary.

As for Morris, who had followed her to Milwaukee, she would not marry him unless he promised to go to Palestine. And Morris, torn between love and dread, trusted that the girl who so recently had been a respectful pupil would calm down and change her mind. After all, precious few Zionists actually left America. There was plenty for her to do right here in Milwaukee if she insisted. Why, of all girls, did she have to be so headstrong?

Not that Golda was lost in her mission. Sociable as well as socially minded, she had a large number of admiring friends. "Four out of every five boys we met fell in love with her," Regina related. Her engagement to Morris in no way interfered with these friendships. The package of letters from a philosophical chum, Yossel Kopelov, beginning "Dear Sister Goldie," indicates the tone of these relationships. Yossel even wrote to Morris about Goldie. Though his English was sometimes a bit shaky, his attitude was clear:

> [June 1915] This race of humanity, I mean girls, are already perfect ladies when we think they are only children. . . . They embody the life principle, they are the riddle of the universe, and that is why we are craving to solve them. And as for care and tenderness, don't worry, plenty of it. Always know that if a girl is loved by one, she is cared for tenderly by others too. . . .
>
> She is primordially good and she cannot be stuffed with base matter. She has a natural inclination towards the good and noble. . . . Meanwhile I may tell you that I am very glad of my stay in Milwaukee. I am very happy if I can contribute something to her mental store. She is real, young, energetic and studious and, from a non-partisan point of view, she is not only a treasure but a kingdom. . . . I am reading *Job* with Goldie. . . .

The letters to Golda are equally high-flown:

> You ask me if hearts are made to be broken? With our minds we cannot see why it should be that way; in reality it is so, and the greater the heart, the more it breaks, the more it suffers. . . . You also asked me in your letter what books you should read about mysticism. From my article you could see that Emerson is one; Carlyle, another. . . .

Golda Meir: Woman with a Cause

Golda's vigor and warmth had a special fascination for
emotional young people, both male and female. It is obvious
from various letters full of adolescent anguish that she inspired crushes as well as love. The following declaration
from a girl is typical of many similar outpourings:

> I do need a friend in whom I can confide all my longings
> and desires, and I am sure that I have found it in you. . . .
> Yet it is probably true that you do not need me. You have
> many true friends who really admire you for your true worth;
> you have various organizations and doings to keep you busy;
> and, best of all, you have the courage of your convictions.
> You see, all qualities which I lack.

The anonymous writer—anonymous in the sense that
thirty-five years later Golda could barely decipher the signa-
ture or recall the individual—had, despite her emotionalism,
shrewdly enumerated the crucial differences between Golda
and most of the other intense young girls of her circle. Golda
already had "doings" and the "courage of her convictions."
From this point on it became almost impossible to disentan-
gle the personal and private from the impersonal and public
in her contacts. There was no dichotomy; both types of experience became intimate and absorbing. Almost no letter
or human relationship in future years would be free from the
stress of the "doings" and "convictions."

She quickly attracted attention as a speaker for the People's Relief and for the American Jewish Congress, organized to safeguard the civil and ethnic rights of whatever European Jewish communities survived the war. Bilingual from
the first, the girl made fiery speeches in Yiddish and English
on street corners and in halls. Perhaps the most impressive
tribute to the oratorical talents of her youth was provided by

her father. Papa Mabovitch, horrified at the notion that his daughter appeared at street-corner meetings, had ordered her "never to do it again." When word reached him that Golda was going to speak at a neighborhood rally, he went to the meeting determined to pull her off the soap box. Golda knew of his intentions, but she went anyway. During her speech she noticed her father in the audience. She expected an explosion but he listened quietly. When she got home, he looked at his daughter wonderingly. "What a tongue," he said, "what a spirit." There were no further family efforts to keep Golda from speaking.

When a parade of protest against pogroms in Poland and Russia was planned, the respectable Jewish community leaders of Milwaukee called on the eighteen-year-old girl to urge her to use her influence against "unwise" demonstrations. The call was the first of a long series of pleas she was to encounter to lie low, accept, and above all, make no noise. Naturally she was among the first to march.

Golda taught in the *folk schulen* (folk schools) which were conducted in Yiddish and which advocated Labor Zionism. She proved to be a capable teacher of Yiddish and the usual subjects in the curriculum of an elementary day school. A fellow teacher recalled that she was "inspiring" and that despite her youth she was an excellent disciplinarian.

Hebrew, too, was taught in the folk schools, but the emphasis was on Yiddish. If a few years later Golda and her group were to find themselves sailing to Palestine without a knowledge of Hebrew, this was due to no oversight or lack of diligence. In that period, debates as to whether Hebrew or Yiddish was to be the language of the Jewish renascence still raged among Diaspora nationalists. In Palestine, the question had been settled in favor of Hebrew from the outset. In the

United States, however, Labor Zionists advocated Yiddish on the grounds that it was the actual language of the Jewish working class and consequently preferable to the dead sacred tongue. Many a young secular Jewish nationalist of the time discussed Schopenhauer rather than Jeremiah to demonstrate his emancipation from the religious orthodoxy of his parents, and deliberately spoke in Yiddish rather than in English as a protest against assimilation. As a result of this insistence, Golda's Yiddish was always to remain richer and more supple than the Hebrew she learned after she settled in Palestine.

At this time Golda met the man who was to exert a profound influence on her political development and with whom she would work in the close partnership of a common struggle for a common victory. David Ben-Gurion, aged thirty, banished from Palestine by the Turkish Government together with his friend Itzhak Ben-Zvi for "Zionist conspiracy," arrived in America in 1915. Both young men sought to kindle in the hearts of American Jews a desire to reclaim the wastelands of Palestine. The future first prime minister of the State of Israel and its future second president traveled up and down the United States, urging young American Jews to train for settlement in the arduous collective farms of Palestine. Sitting up nights, since Pullman berths were bourgeois luxuries for which no money was available, they brought their message to every town with a sizable Jewish community.

No pair could have been less alike in appearance and manner than Ben-Gurion, short, stocky, blue-eyed and dynamic, and Ben-Zvi, tall and thin, who even in youth had the withdrawn air of a scholar more familiar with bookish theory than revolutionary politics. Members of the legendary

Second *Aliyah,* the Mayflower of Palestinian settlement, both had gone to Palestine as pioneers in 1906 and had labored since then in its fields. After their banishment they engaged in the singularly unrewarding task of bringing the light of Zion to American Jewry. It was easy enough to arouse fraternal compassion. With unprecedented generosity, rich and poor Jews wrote checks and gave pennies. To persuade them to start training for physical work in a kibbutz after the war was another matter.

Ben-Gurion attracted scant notice on his first journey to America. Even the American Zionist movement found this Palestinian, with his extreme ideas of "back to the soil," alien and uncouth. His sole disciples were the largely working-class Poale Zion, few in numbers, first-generation immigrants who theoretically embraced the tenets which the doughty Palestinians practiced and propounded. Needless to say, few listened to Ben-Gurion more devoutly than Golda. This was different talk from that of her American comrades who had a gift for long-winded, dreary discussions which seemed to evade the issue. Ben-Gurion spoke in crisp, staccato sentences; he was sure, clear and "inspiring." But neither Ben-Gurion nor Ben-Zvi had any inkling of how closely allied their destinies would be with that of the refreshingly good-looking eloquent young *havera* (comrade) in Milwaukee who was to be the only American among the founders of the Jewish state on the day of its proclamation.

Golda once lost a chance for closer acquaintance with the admired leader. Ben-Gurion was coming to Milwaukee for a much-heralded meeting. It was to take place on a Saturday night at the same time as a concert by the Chicago Symphony Orchestra. Morris, too often obliged to accompany Golda to meetings he detested, balked at a further sacrifice.

He wanted to hear the concert instead of Ben-Gurion. And Golda, feeling guilty for constantly dragging Morris to Zionist meetings, weakly agreed to go to the concert.

The next day the question arose as to where Ben-Gurion should have lunch. This was in the ascetic days when the poorest restaurant would have been considered criminally luxurious and when traveling comrades were put up by the local disciples, no matter how meager the accommodations. Golda suggested her house. She received a curt answer: "A *havera* who does not attend Ben-Gurion's meeting does not deserve to have him for lunch." Years later, when Golda recounted the anecdote, she laughingly referred to the incident as "the most heartbreaking event of my youth." Though not quite that, at the time it was a serious matter. She had failed her own code.

A decision in her private life had to be made at this time. Was there any sense in finishing the course in normal school? The individual subjects of the curriculum were interesting enough, and she applied herself conscientiously to such notably dull offerings as pedagogy and the history of education. However, if she was in earnest about settling in a kibbutz, then a teacher's license would be of precious little use as a preparation for physical work on the soil. And there was something else. Intuitively she realized that any achievement not contributing to her purpose might prove an obstacle. She had seen it happen. First you got your degree; then an appointment with a regular salary, long vacations and security, and you began to postpone the break. It was wiser not to forge these pleasant links and to spend her time on things that led directly to her goal. She needed a quickly acquired skill that would enable her to support herself till her departure for Palestine and that would not engage her energy as exactingly as teaching.

On the basis of this reasoning she left the Milwaukee normal school—one day the University of Wisconsin would give Mrs. Meir an honorary degree—to take a course as a librarian. That career proved brief. After a few months she agreed to devote her full time to the Labor Zionist movement. As a speaker who could be equally rousing in English and Yiddish, she was a rare treasure for the impecunious, obscure Poale Zion. Golda would have attracted attention in any circle; among the small band of Yiddish-speaking Labor Zionists she was something of a marvel. Who better than she would be able to bring the Labor Zionist gospel to a strangely impervious American Jewish youth? Her salary was far less than even the modest earnings of teacher or librarian, but she managed on the fifteen dollars a week the party scraped together.

Still another problem had to be settled at approximately the same time. If Morris persisted in his refusal to go to Palestine after the war, the relationship should be severed. To achieve the break and to rouse Chicago Jewry, Golda left for Chicago. She was soon back. Chicago Jews continued to slumber, but Morris, alone in Milwaukee, had been stirred to action. Unconvinced as before, he nevertheless yielded to Golda's demand: he would go to Palestine. There was no longer any reason to postpone the marriage for which he pressed. They were married on December 24, 1917.

By the age of nineteen, the girl had taken the two major steps of her life: one would lead her to her arduous but unswerving ascent to national and political eminence; the other to the tortuous, tormented role of a wife whose basic values

[49]

clashed with those of her husband. In time, Morris would change his views about Palestine and Zionism, but he would never make peace with his wife's imperious need for a wider sphere of action than the home. Yet he should have been forewarned. In the three years of their engagement, the reverential little girl had become a personality. She commanded attention and respect, as well as masculine admiration. Already overshadowed, he was wholly, helplessly in love.

The girl, too, might well have had misgivings. No longer dazzled by his greater learning, with wider contacts she had lost her schoolgirl humility. However, her appreciation of his essential goodness and devotion had not wavered. There was perhaps another element which remained unvoiced: she could not bear to hurt the youth to whom she had "pledged her troth"—old-fashioned phrase—and who had finally agreed to follow her to Palestine. Bound by his love, she would continue to be bound while the conflict between them about the central issue of her young womanhood—where is a woman's place—deepened. In his meek, persistent way, the husband and father would never cease pressing the case of home and hearth versus the public arena, a case whose most powerful advocate would be her own maternal solicitude, never convention.

Just as the outline of her future misery could already be detected, so was the paradox of Golda's character already apparent. The girl who displayed such singular clarity of direction, fixity of purpose, and strength of will in her social and national ideals showed no such awesome resolution in her personal life. There she hesitated, pitied, and endured confusion like any ordinary woman. In one respect, however, she was to differ profoundly from a familiar feminine pattern. For Golda, public achievement was never to be the anguished fruit of private frustration. Henrietta Szold, the only American woman whose contribution to Zionism can be measured with Golda's, was an austere spinster who turned a defeated passion into a victorious life, but Golda would know the fullness of womanly experience although neither its joy nor its pain would be her springboard of action. What is called public life would always be as intimately a part of her as the personal, and would spring from as deep a source.

All this was in embryo in 1917 when Golda made her twin decisions. Marriage in no way curtailed her activities. After all, Morris was no hidebound reactionary opposed to the emancipation of women on principle; implicit in his agreement to go to Palestine had been acquiescence in her continued work for Zionism. The issuance of the Balfour Declaration in 1917 had transformed Zionism from a vague dream into a political reality. Some months earlier Great Britain had finally agreed to the formation of a special Jewish military unit, the Jewish Legion, to fight for the liberation of Palestine with the battalions of the Royal Fusiliers. After America's entry into the war, when the American Government permitted enlistment in the Jewish Legion, many young Labor Zionists volunteered. Ben-Zvi and Ben-Gurion returned to Palestine with the legion. Golda had offered to serve in any capacity, but women were not taken; besides, she was too young.

The first American Jewish Congress—representing all Jewish groups from assimilated non-Zionists to extreme nationalists—was to convene in Philadelphia in December, 1918. It was to formulate a program for the protection of Jewish civil and ethnic rights in Europe to be presented at the forthcoming Peace Conference in Versailles. Despite her youth, Golda was among the delegates, rubbing shoulders with both the affluent magnates of the American Jewish Committee and the East Side labor leaders. Her eloquence made a great hit, but she was thinking of no personal triumph when she ecstatically wrote to Morris, who had not accompanied her: "I tell you that some moments reached such heights that after them one could have died happy." The congress adopted a resolution favoring the establishment of a Jewish homeland in Palestine, a motion the passage of which had by no means been assured in view of the serious ideological rifts among the delegates.

When Golda traveled for the Labor Zionists, her letters to Morris were usually matter of fact, briefly describing some meeting she had to address or some new project for which she had been selected. Only the changing postmarks— Bangor, Philadelphia or New York—showed the swift pace back and forth. A reassuring number of "I long for you's" occur in every letter, as well as circumstantial directions as to what her husband should eat and how much he should rest. Apparently Golda was seriously troubled by the frequent separations and the fear that perhaps she was not fulfilling her wifely duties; her explanations stressed the necessity of what she was doing rather than her desire for these activities. She was even ready to assume domestic financial responsibilities. In one letter she wrote, touchingly and probably unwisely: "Don't worry if you have no work. Don't worry about money. Only take care of your health."

Not that Golda did not have moods of discouragement. In her contacts with older comrades, she was often to find more apathy than vision, more readiness for interminable rehashing of the same ideas than willingness for action. In moments of disillusionment she determined to abandon her party work and devote herself solely to the problem of getting to Palestine. Even when in Milwaukee, her fiery young soul felt "chilled" by the lack of genuine response. A letter from a friend exhorted her to continue the unrewarding party work: [October, 1919] "I hate cynicism, and particularly those who think they know everything. In the presence of such people I want to shriek 'corpses.' So you see I sympathize with you, and yet I say you must not leave the work. . . . Dear friend, must we not pay with something for the fact that we are in America and not with the massacred downtrodden Jews of the Ukraine? Will you be able to escape from your conscience which will ask what you are doing to show your relationship to the great people which is perishing in blood across the sea?"

So urged, Golda continued her efforts to organize party branches and galvanize the lethargic. Her formidable talent in this direction was not lost on any of her associates. Regina encouraged her to return to Chicago because: "I am sure if you came Chicago would wake from its deep sleep. You are a good motor." While Yossel, now engaged to Regina, lamented about his erstwhile pupil's "overactivities."

In 1920, the Poale Zion daringly undertook the publication of a Yiddish daily, *Die Zeit* (*The Times*). To launch the project, shares had to be sold to the faithful in various cities. Golda, full of zeal, engaged on this mission. Allowed the customary fifteen dollars a week and expenses, she never stayed in a hotel. She put her carefully calculated meals on the expense account—all items except dessert. Ice cream was not to be charged, because she had decided that the party "did not owe me ice cream."

Her abstemiousness did not affect her persuasiveness. Full

[53]

of honest indignation at every Labor Zionist who ventured
to question the solvency of *Die Zeit,* she was sometimes too
successful. In Minneapolis, she convinced a shoemaker who
had been saving his money to bring his family from Russia
to invest in the paper. Doubt was a heresy Golda would not
condone. *Die Zeit* lasted exactly twenty months—a record
of longevity in view of its financial backing. Forty years
later Mrs. Meir, recalling the shoemaker, admitted half smiling: "I have him on my conscience." There were no such
qualms in 1920.

In the meantime the rift with Shana had been patched
up. From Denver, Shana kept a worried eye on her younger
sister's emergence into the public light. Golda's intemperate
espousal of her cause, her insistence on going to Palestine,
her disregard of her husband's unwillingness, were bound to
create domestic difficulties.

Deeply troubled, Shana wrote:

> I don't want to shatter your dreams. I know what it means
> but, Goldie, don't you think there is a middle field for ideal-
> ism right here on the spot? Oh, my! Oh, my! How much work
> there is to be done by those who believe. And as far as per-
> sonal happiness is concerned, grasp it, Goldie, and hold it
> tight. There are not many who can speak about happiness.
> You behold happiness without much effort and don't grasp
> the real value of it. . . . The only thing I heartily wish you
> is that you should not try to be what you *ought* to be but
> what you are. If everybody would only be what they are, we
> would have a much finer world. . . . find your own self.

The most complacent of husbands could hardly have
been expected to view unprotestingly his bride's growing
absorption in activities which took her away from home a
good deal of the time. Besides, Morris did not want to go

to Palestine. As the time approached for the promise to be made good, inevitable doubts arose.

But the one dilemma that Golda was by nature saved from facing was that of discovering "a middle field for idealism." With the end of the war there were no longer any major obstacles to departure for Palestine. The problem was to raise money for passage. Regina, fired by Golda's example, worked in a shoe store in addition to an office job. Yossel worked as a barber and read philosophy; in Palestine he would be known as the "philosopher barber" till his death. Morris painted signs when work was available, and Golda rejoiced that at last she would be through with speeches. In 1921, tickets for the S.S. *Pocahontas* were finally purchased.

Only the farewell with Shana remained. The Korngolds had left Denver for Chicago. Life was easier now; Sam was making a living and Shana was well. Though Shana's girlhood sympathy for Zionism had become more pronounced in recent years, she presumably was much too level-headed to go off on adventures to unknown Palestine with two small children. Perhaps someday when conditions in Palestine were more settled, her children older, she and her family might join Golda in the Jewish homeland still to be created. Even the uncompromising younger sister exacted no greater commitment. Then something peculiar happened. When Golda arrived to make her farewells, Sam made a mistake. He turned jokingly to his wife and said, "Perhaps you'd like to go, too?" And Shana answered at once, "Yes, if you give me the money for expenses."

Shana, telling the story thirty years later in her flowering garden at the village of Holon, near Tel Aviv, commented at this point: "Then Sam was sorry but it was too late."

Even Golda was startled when Shana announced that she

would leave the husband whom she loved, to accompany her sister. Sam would have to stay behind and work to send the meager funds required for the support of his wife and children.

Little in Shana's character or previous behavior could account for such a rash decision. She was neither erratic nor ecstatic. Neither a dedicated young girl like Golda nor a romantic one like Regina, she had always shown a strong sense of responsibility toward daily tasks. Above all, she was a devoted wife for whom even a temporary separation from her husband would mean genuine suffering. Neither whim nor impulse could account for her act. Somehow the whole moral content of her life had telescoped itself into that instant when she arose in her simple Chicago apartment, looked at her children, and said, "I am going." Suddenly, duty and responsibility had assumed a more exacting form.

On May 1, 1921, shortly after her decision, violent Arab riots broke out in Palestine. Physical danger was now added to the other hazards of the journey. Nobody knew when the disturbances would subside or how readily they might flare up again after a respite. When Sam, reinforced by agitated friends, begged her to consider the fresh perils, she answered, "Then I must go."

As Shana reached this part of her story while we ate sweet purple plums fresh-picked from the trees in her orchard, she did not elaborate. "Then I must go" was self-evident and self-explanatory. Any embellishments would have sounded like a speech. By then her children were already grown, with farms of their own near the road to Beersheba, and Sam had been dead a year, buried in a grave in Israel. The necessity and logic of her act had become obvious over the years. But Shana wept as she spoke of Sam who had understood the necessity of the action in 1921, and had continued to under-stand it in the thirty years to come.

The elder Mabovitches temporarily stayed in Milwaukee till Golda and Shana were able to send for their parents, who died in Palestine. The only member of the family to remain permanently in the United States was the youngest daughter, who married and settled in Connecticut. An energetic worker for the United Jewish Appeal and the Israel Bond Campaign, Mrs. Clara Stern would devote her life to American Zionism in her own way.

For Golda, the fifteen years in America were at an end. What had they meant to her? She had come as a frightened child of eight and was departing a confident young woman of twenty-three. Her girlhood had been spent among poor, Yiddish-speaking first-generation immigrants like herself. She would never look back on Milwaukee with the longing of a Henrietta Szold for the flowers of Baltimore. There would be no nostalgia, no regrets. Yet she had been shaped as much by America as by Pinsk. By a fortunate alchemy, she had been able to transform the privations of Europe and the opportunities of America equally to fit her purpose. America's pioneer past, its struggle for independence, its present liberties, were all signs of what might be possible in Palestine. She was not abjectly fleeing from persecution but freely leaving a good land. The splendor of the American dream had strengthened the Zionist vision. In the years to come, her proud independence without truculence, her quiet assurance in the presence of titled adversaries, would owe something not only to her character but to the democracy in which she had grown up. Golda was bringing to Palestine more of America than she herself suspected.

ON THE POCAHONTAS

On May 23, 1921, the S.S. *Pocahontas* left New York bound for Naples. Because of a mutinous crew, sabotage and arson, the ship took forty-four days to reach its destination instead of two weeks. On the way, the engineer committed suicide and another member of the crew died of something mysteriously referred to as "fright" in the ship's records. The exact causes were not to be discovered till months later when the United States Shipping Board held an inquiry into the extraordinary circumstances of this journey.

Among the several hundred passengers who found themselves involved in this turbulent voyage was a group of twenty-two young American Jews bound for Palestine—among them Golda, Morris, Shana, Regina and Yossel. Most of the party consisted of boys and girls in their early twenties; in addition, there were several "older" people a little past thirty, including three women with small children. One of the women—a Mrs. Kaplan—was in the seventh month of pregnancy when the S.S. *Pocahontas* set out.

Getting on the *Pocahontas* was to prove almost as trouble-

some as getting off it. Passengers were to embark in New
York, but when they arrived they discovered that departure
had been postponed because of a strike. The ship finally left
port with the strike apparently settled, but got no farther
than twelve miles out to sea when it stopped. The unlucky
passengers were not too clear as to what was happening. The
ship was to make a stop at Boston; it took the *Pocahontas*
nine days to cover the distance between New York and that
port. Just before reaching Boston, a fierce fight broke out
among the crew in the course of which one sailor shouted
at the startled passengers, "Your ship will sink in mid-ocean."

The trip to Boston had been so harrowing that three members of the Palestine party left the boat, having gotten no
farther than Massachusetts. They were naturally viewed as
weaklings by their hardier fellows who did not propose to be
stopped by fires or broken pumps. Sam kept receiving telegrams from alarmed friends who had read of the boat's singular progress and who urged him to "take them off the ship."
But Shana was not to be dissuaded. In Boston, all the engineers except the chief engineer were dismissed, and after
eight days devoted to repairs, the ship set out again. From
all accounts, the eight days in Boston were very gay. There
were no conscious heroics. As soon as the Poale Zion comrades in New York learned that their friends were becalmed
in Boston, they promptly took the train for further farewells. Each evening until the *Pocahontas* finally got going,
there were moonlit rides on the Charles River and similar
merrymaking. The ladies with small children presumably
found things less jolly, but Golda and Regina had a wonderful time.

In addition to the friends who urged caution, a greater
number applauded. Shana and Golda have kept the letters

they received in those days with messages such as: "I congratulate you on having the strength to go. You are the heroes of our times. . . . In the name of Zion, the holy earth of our fathers, may you be blessed in your mission. . . ." There was no lack of rhetoric among those who stayed behind.

After the *Pocahontas* left Boston, presumably repaired and seaworthy, sabotage was renewed. The firing of the engineers had not remedied the situation. Pumps and boilers started to break down, as did condensers and refrigerators. Food spoiled and had to be thrown overboard, leaving only bully beef and brackish water for the passengers. Fires broke out in two of the bunkers.

The captain's report, submitted to the American Consul in Naples, gave a clearer account of what happened than the confused memories of the passengers. Some of the highlights of the report included the following mishaps: on June 5, the engine room was flooded and the ship listed; Seaman G. was put in irons; two portholes were mysteriously opened, ruining a quantity of supplies; suspicious ashes were discovered, and the dynamo men were put in irons; on June 14, all boiler pumps stopped and all fires but one were out; water continued to flood the engine room; more members of the crew were put in irons.

When the captain put in at Ponta Delgada in the Azores on June 16 for repairs, an attempt to burn the ship was discovered. As an added fillip, four engineers were overheard boasting on shore that they would sink the *Pocahontas* between the island and Naples. The captain clapped them into irons.

After the ship left the Azores, the chief engineer, maddened by his troubles, supposedly threw himself overboard.

According to the captain's record, the recovered body revealed that the man's hands had been tied with a large pipe
between "so he was unable to swim." The death was listed as
suicide.

Despite these tribulations, a good time was apparently
had by all the young folk, always excepting the two women
with small children and Mrs. Kaplan, the birth of whose
baby was becoming alarmingly imminent. Golda studied
Hebrew and—to quote Regina—"when the women with
kids got downhearted, she kept them chipper." During the
enforced delay at the Azores, the Jewish community of
Ponta Delgada learned of the Zionists aboard and proceeded
to wine and dine them. Americans going to Palestine as
settlers appeared as exotic to them as did the Sephardic rites
of the Azores Jews to the Americans.

Even after the voyagers disembarked in Naples on July 5,
their troubles were not over. In Italy they discovered that
because of the disturbances in Palestine, Jaffa boatmen were
refusing to take Jews off the ships. (At that time Palestine
had no adequate harbor. Passengers disembarked at sea
and were rowed ashore by Arab boatmen.) Consequently
no ship line was willing to book Jewish immigrants for
Palestine. The only way left was to go by ship to Egypt and
continue the journey by train from Alexandria. Here there
was another hitch. Those of Russian descent who were
not American citizens could not get visas to Egypt; this applied to several of the party. Fortunately one of the group
was more worldly wise than his fellows and a Mason, to boot.
The American Consul whom he approached for help turned
out to be sympathetic and a fellow Mason. Thanks to the
consul's intervention, Egyptian visas were procured for
all and passage on a ship from Brindisi to Alexandria was

arranged. This stroke of good fortune came just in time, because the funds of the party were running low and the problem of meeting the Naples hotel bill was becoming increasingly complicated.

But even at this point a fresh calamity arose. When the group reached Brindisi just in time to embark, it made the horrifying discovery that the baggage which was supposed to be on the train was missing. All the trunks, suitcases and bundles of the nineteen people, containing most of their earthly possessions, had failed to show up. The ship was leaving in a couple of hours. Despite the assurances of the steamship company that the baggage would promptly be despatched on the next ship, many in the group showed an understandable reluctance to set out without their belongings. There was little time for discussion. Golda announced decisively: "You can wait for baggage; I won't." Others supported her stand, and the hesitant were persuaded. They went on board minus their luggage.

On the way to Alexandria, Shana wrote to Sam, graphically describing this stage of the trip:

> Everything is like a dream. It's hard to understand the situation. Everything is mixed up in my head—hotels, trains, baggage, halutzim [pioneers], big and small, the lack of food, no places to sleep—a chaos and a *mishmash*. It's hard to understand it all, so my letter won't be clear either. But let me start at the beginning so perhaps I'll be able to give you an idea of our present life or rather wanderings.
>
> You know about our arrival in Naples. A man died on board so we couldn't get off the ship till the next morning. Hotel agents are like dogs and each one says his hotel is cheapest and best. . . . Why should I drag this out? It cost us $15 merely to get to the hotel (with baggage). We realized that if we would not be more economical we would not

get far . . . Nor could we take board at the hotel because
of the cost, so we cooked for ourselves. But to remain for
three weeks in a hotel which charges $1.50 a day is very
expensive. Besides food is far from cheap. Milk is dearer and
worse than in the United States. The strangest thing is that
the milk is fresh, straight from the cow. I mean this literally.
You go out on the street and see a woman with a cow and
calf. You stop her and she milks a pitcher full for you right
on the spot. . . .

A few went out to find out when a ship goes and when we
can proceed. And they came back with this report. It seems
we can't go farther. They don't sell tickets. We got a funny
answer from the companies, really something to laugh at.
Christians and Moslems can go to Palestine but they can't
sell tickets to Jews. They do this for our own sakes because
the Arabs throw the Jews into the sea. So here you have a
sad joke—no Jews can enter *Eretz Israel*.

But I told you that we have a real fixer in our midst. He
started running around and somehow managed that we
should get visas to Egypt. . . .

Shana continued with an account of the difficulties of getting passage and of the hardships of the train ride from
Naples to Brindisi, even permitting herself a note of doubt:
"Hayim doesn't understand any tricks and wants to eat and
sleep. Had you seen with what greed he grabbed a piece of
bread? He is terribly thin. I think that you alone know that
sometimes a doubt steals into my heart. I look at my children
and ask myself, God, what am I doing to them? To whom
and to what do I lead them? How are they guilty? And yet
perhaps this is really better for them. . . ."

Life on the voyage from Brindisi to Alexandria had its
complications, though of a less dramatic nature than that
of the *Pocahontas*. In Brindisi, the Americans learned that
a large group of Lithuanian halutzim, organized Zionist

pioneers prepared for kibbutz life, would be on board. The Lithuanians had no money for cabins and were going to travel on deck, a kind of Mediterranean steerage. Golda promptly suggested that the comradely and honorable thing for the American group was to give up their aristocratic third-class cabins and join the Lithuanians on deck. Though a number in the group were beginning to balk at Golda's "moralistic" leadership, none had the courage to deny idealism. Conditions on deck were particularly trying for the women with children, and Golda had pangs of conscience. Though sleeping quarters for the children were subsequently made available in some of the public rooms, it was tough going. Furthermore, the sacrifice had been in vain. The Lithuanians declined to establish bonds of friendship with the Americans. Unlike the Americans, they were members of a halutz group; they were "real" pioneers, trained in agriculture and with an excellent knowledge of Hebrew. Only two of the American contingent knew Hebrew and none possessed agricultural skills. The Lithuanians scorned them as bourgeois and dilettante.

The Lithuanian halutzim were young, stern and dogmatic. Not only did they decline to let the American group join them, they made no attempt to ease the blow. To Golda's warm offer, "Let us be a part of you," they answered uncompromisingly: "We don't want Americans." But they accepted money from affluent European-Jewish passengers on the ship.

After World War I, American Jewry had become identified in the minds of some East European Jews with a supercilious philanthrophy, a readiness to buy exemption from personal responsibility for their people's fate by cash donations. As a result, the Lithuanians obstinately refused to be impressed by this American group's demonstration of true faith. Apparently the Americans accepted the situation without indignation. Since they had enjoyed a comfortable life in the United States, were ignorant of Hebrew and untrained in pioneering skills, they were prepared to be viewed as a lesser breed. They would have to prove their worth before they could gain admission into this spiritual aristocracy. A letter from Yossel to Sam (July 1921) revealed their touching, rancorless admiration:

> Shana wants me to add something to her letter. What can one write when there is such a *mishmash* in one's head, such a mixture of East and West? When I see the hundreds of halutzim who are on the same ship I feel small and unworthy. They are new Jews for us—grown up in the seven years of fire and need. Many of them worked in German mines—young people with hard muscles, who can sleep on hard decks, who eat hard bread made of bran, and who speak Hebrew with the hard Sephardic accent. Real Hercules who are ready to build a land on just foundations with their backs. And not only a land but a new language. Fine young fellows, splendid human material which would be the pride of any people. . . . The ship goes swiftly; we are approaching Egypt. I have strange feelings of excitement and uncertainty. . . .

Though life on deck had not resulted in closer ties with the Lithuanians, it certainly added to the discomfort of the journey. Shana allowed herself a heretical outcry in a letter to the patient Sam: "I can't bear to stand in line and wait till something is handed out. I can't bear to see how Haimke has to eat out of the same dish with another child. We were

[65]

raised in another country in another manner." Had a Lithuanian halutz been privileged to read this last sentence, he
would probably have considered his doubts amply justified.

On board ship was an immigration officer of the Mandatory Government whose function it was to examine the pass-
ports of immigrants to Palestine. He delighted in discouraging Golda and Regina. "How will you make a living?" he
asked the girls teasingly, and mocked their enthusiastic:
"We will go on the land." Regina remembered this particular
British official because he, too, never left Palestine and remained to become a functionary in the Israel Department of Trade and Industry where he no doubt received directives from Mrs. Golda Myerson, Minister of Labor.

The journey which had started on May 23 came to an end
on July 14 when the train from Alexandria reached Tel Aviv.
It was a blazing hot day. Sand stretched as far as the eye
could see. The only reception committee consisted of a
hotelkeeper who owned a wretched little hotel on Rehov
Lilienblum, then the center of the new town.

The first night in the promised land was dispiriting. The
beds were full of bedbugs. And Morris, who now that he was
among brethren had confidently left his precious American
razor on the window sill, discovered in the morning that it
was gone.

Nothing was going to be easy. The first weeks and months
were the test. Even Regina wavered. If her mother had not
made the tactical error of writing, "I suppose I'll have to
send you money for a ticket home," she might have returned,
unable to endure the hardships of the new life.

Golda had no regrets, at least none that were voiced.
After a few weeks (August 24, 1921), she wrote a letter to

Sam which is the best comment on her character and state
of mind:

I'd like to write a long letter and *podrobno* [in detail]
about everything, but Shana wants to mail the letter, and we
must see about our baggage, so I'll write briefly.

Our group from the first day on divided into two sections.
As soon as we arrived, in fact as we got off the train, Yossel
wanted to return [Yossel died in Palestine in 1942] at once.
Not for political reasons but simply because sitting in America and talking about hard work is easier than doing the
work. To deny oneself various comforts is also easier in talk
than in deed. I am sure this is the only reason. The question
is a quite different one for him who is a genuine Zionist, for
him who does not come to Palestine to remain if it is good
or to leave if it is bad, but who comes to remain and to
suffer, yes, suffer a great deal under all conditions.

Today what do we see? First the political situation. I am
no politician and cannot exactly describe to you the politics
of England. But one thing is clear to me. If we will not go
away, then England will help us. True, one feels the English
government quite heavily in the country but this does not
frighten me. England will not choose the Arabs instead of
us to colonize Palestine. . . .

Shortly after the pogrom [the Arab riots of 1921] the Arabs
were great heroes, but now halutzim are again arriving regularly. But as I said, not one of us can foretell the future,
neither you nor I and not even Yossel. There is only one way:
he who is a Zionist, he who cannot rest in the *Galuth* must
come here, but he must be ready for anything.

Economic conditions have gotten worse since the pogrom,
but even for the brief while that we are here we can already
see some improvement. All say that the last winter was a
period of bloom and everything would have been marvelous
if not for the riots.

Another fact is important for me. Those who talk about

returning are recent arrivals. An old worker is full of inspiration and faith. I say that as long as those who created the little that is here are here, I cannot leave, and you must come. I would not say this if I did not know that you are ready to work hard. True, even hard work is hard to find, but I have no doubt that you will find something. Of course, this is not America, and one may have to suffer a lot economically. There may even be pogroms again, but if one wants one's own land, and if one wants it with one's whole heart, one must be ready for this. When you come I am sure we will be able to plan. Perhaps you will come with us to Merhavia. Get ready. There is nothing to wait for.

FIRST YEARS IN PALESTINE

Morale was low among the newcomers. Yossel threatened to return as soon as he had tasted the delights of the Hotel Barash and the heat of the Tel Aviv sand dunes, but stayed, complainingly it must be admitted. Regina's bad time lasted a few months. The lack of sanitation, the squalid, fly-ridden streets where she was forced to live, the first oppressive sense of a primitive and hostile environment, made Palestinian reality very unlike the jolly adventure she had envisaged in Milwaukee. Whether Regina survived the first crucial year because she would not give her mother the satisfaction of sending her a ticket home or whether her endurance sprang from nobler motives hardly matters. At any rate, it was not long before she was in Jerusalem, working in the offices of the Zionist Organization and later of the Jewish Agency. The vivacious girl who loved fun and excitement was sensitive enough to appreciate the adventure of pounding a typewriter conscientiously in Jerusalem, at the center of the Jewish struggle, despite the physical and eco-

[69]

nomic hardships suffered. "I've worked with such wonderful people and seen such wonderful things," she was to tell me, years later, eyes shining.

Shana had a wretched time of it. Golda, recalling this period, described her older sister as the "real heroine" of the group. In a sense the praise was merited. Shana had immediate problems. She could not experiment. She had to make a home for her children, find some work for Sam so that he could join his family, and discover some way of eking out the small sum Sam was able to send her. This would have been a full program in the best of circumstances; in the Palestine of 1921, it was a gigantic enterprise. First of all, the three-year-old Haimke proceeded to contract a variety of local afflictions, the worst of which was trachoma.

Then there was the problem of an apartment. A calculatedly chipper letter to Sam announced the final arrival of the lost baggage and showed the devices employed to furnish the rooms:

> [September, 1921] . . . We just learned that the baggage came. We were overjoyed and Golda, Yossel and I went for the baggage. To tell you all the details about the baggage is impossible; I'll tell you the story briefly. Instead of sending the baggage to Jaffa, it went to Beirut, Syria. When the Syrian government saw thirty-three trunks, they didn't like the business. They wanted to open them all and have us pay duty for everything, new and old. Can you imagine? But we are not just ordinary folks but Americans and American citizens, so Golda and M. went to Jerusalem and there was a great to-do. The American Consul and the High Commissioner sent telegrams and, finally, with God's help, the baggage came.

The letter continued with a catalogue of missing articles and proceeded to describe how the trunks were transformed into house furnishings:

> There was a lot of work but now the apartment looks quite livable. Out of so many trunks we made various things. A table which looks like a platform nicely draped with curtain goods. With another two trunks we made a sofa, with another two we made a dresser. From a high case we made a stand nicely draped with a statue on top. There are pictures on the walls; we have bedspreads on the beds and a tablecloth. On the shelves we put dishes and pots. I tell you it's pleasant now; only you are lacking. There's little lacking in the pots. Everything is dear and there isn't much choice, but we eat and have enough of everything. We also have a lot of acquaintances because of Golda's lessons [Golda was giving English lessons], and today we celebrate the arrival of the baggage.

If Shana had any qualms as she looked at Hayim's eyes and the trunks, she kept them to herself. Hardest of all was the separation from Sam. It took a special kind of dedication to amplify the concept of homemaking to include a home for her people. The boys and girls who had come with her, most of them still vagrant in impulse, were in a different situation. Shana did not want to merge her family in the cooperative existence of a kibbutz. The new life would have to be fashioned in her own way.

Golda had no worries about work or apartments. Her decision to go to Palestine had included the complete program of the Labor Zionist—a program whose ideal fulfillment could only be found in membership in an agricultural cooperative settlement, a kibbutz. The slogans of the movement called for the personal participation of the individual in the redemption of the land, and the creed allowed no substitutions. The land would have to be rebuilt, acre by acre, by the believers; and labor—"self-labor" as distinct from hired labor—would be the measure of devotion. Only a few months before Golda's arrival, Jabneli, a young halutz speaking at a workers' conference in Tel Aviv, had called on Jewish youth to become workers in Palestine:

> [December 1920.] The four thousand Jewish workers living by their labor in *Eretz Israel* constitute a force for the revival of the nation that has no equal in the lands of the dispersion. We, children of middle class families, who never in all our days have known physical labor but who are coming to Palestine and becoming successfully adapted to all types of work, whether it be constructing roads and highways, plowing in the plains, stone-clearing or planting in the hills—we are living proof that the marrow of our nation has not run dry. . . . It is for us to proclaim to the Jewish people that there is the possibility of rescuing the Jews of Poland and Rumania and settling them in Eretz Israel. And with full consciousness we shall all declare that even before our hair has turned gray, they shall be citizens of Eretz Israel here with us, for so it shall be . . .

Jabneli's vow was to be fulfilled, but not quite as he had anticipated. His hair was to be gray, and most of the Jews of Poland were to perish before they could become citizens of the land. But the young people of the Third *Aliyah*, the wave of immigration which came in the early twenties after World War I and the Russian Revolution, shared his hope. They formed kibbutzim or entered those already established.

In 1921, the Jewish National Fund had purchased large tracts of land in the Valley of Jezreel known as the Emek.

First Years in Palestine

The region was swampy and ridden with malaria and black-water fever. It had to be drained and cultivated. Merhavia, the kibbutz which Golda chose because some Americans who had come over with the Jewish Legion had settled there, was one of the oldest cooperatives in the Emek. Originally founded in 1909 by members of the legendary Second *Aliyah*, it had proved to be a difficult spot to colonize. After ten years most of the marshland was drained, but the original group had been physically broken in the process. Fresh blood and courage were needed. The new group, among them many American legionaries, found comparatively better physical conditions.

In the twenties the kibbutz as a social form was still in the process of development. The halutzim were fanatical as well as idealistic—perhaps the two could not be disassociated— and often made a cult of the laborious as well as of labor. The major hardships were unavoidable and had to be endured stoically. Yet in the struggle for moral perfection all lesser graces were needlessly disdained. Women, particularly, had to be chastened.

The young visionaries, male and female, who set the tone for the first pioneer immigration had a fierce ascetic code which made small allowance for human weaknesses or differences. They set themselves the task not only of redeeming a desert land and establishing a Jewish state, but of creating an ideal society in the process. Such a program could not afford to take into account physical or moral frailty. Of course, the Second *Aliyah* which created the mores of the redemption was a spiritual elite. The extraordinary men and women who came in 1905 had in their midst an exceptionally high percentage of sturdy idealists who knew what they wanted. Utopian socialists, students of Marx and Tolstoy, they came with manifestoes and the Bible, eager to transform themselves as well as the land. The second could not take place without the first. Ironically, it was chiefly romantic young intellectuals who left universities and comfortable bourgeois homes who were most ready to undertake the hard labor of draining marshland and irrigating arid soil. In their dedication they gave themselves and others no quarter.

The good society, free of exploitation and discrimination, liberated women of their age-old restrictions. In the struggle for social and national equality, women were to be equal comrades. In the early period, before experience and maturity had softened the youthful dogmatism of the halutzim, equality was interpreted uncritically and mechanically. The high-spirited girls were the first to shriek "discrimination" if the men comrades relegated them to dishwashing, cooking or other domestic tasks in the kibbutz instead of giving them their due share of the more arduous work in the field. Women fought fanatically for the dubious privilege of hewing roads and breaking rock. The annals of the Second *Aliyah* are full of such instances. With time this artificial concept of equality developed into a more realistic and intelligent view of women's function in the rebuilding of Palestine. Feminine insistence on adequate participation in all branches of activity was never to lessen, but frail girls in their teens no longer felt called upon to demonstrate that they were as good as men by lifting pails of lime hour after hour or by hammering away at a pile of rock with "equal" speed.

In the twenties, much of the Second *Aliyah's* unrelenting self-flagellation was still in vogue. The newcomers of the Third *Aliyah* accepted the rigid standard set for them and felt guilty if they proved inadequate. Only years later were they to question the wisdom of the treatment they received. One such woman, recalling her experience in 1920, spoke bitterly of the harshness and lack of understanding shown the new wave of halutzim. A delicate, fair-skinned girl completely unaccustomed to physical labor, she had arrived in Palestine from a German university and had gone straight to a kibbutz. No opportunity was given her for acclimatization. She was at once put on a twelve-hour shift of work in the broiling sun. The food consisted of beans three times a day. She developed dysentery, and when, because of illness, she asked for oatmeal instead of beans, the *havera* in charge of the kitchen told her: "You cannot expect us to bother with chronic invalids." She showed more indignation in telling me this story decades later than she would have ventured to display in those early years. She added, with a wry smile: "That *havera* had come over with the Second *Aliyah*. Since then I've never worked anywhere where one of the heroines of the Second *Aliyah* was in charge." The stern *havera*, however, would probably have protested that she had eaten raw cabbage instead of cooked beans under similar circumstances in 1905.

Golda wanted to leave for Merhavia immediately upon her arrival in Palestine, but she found unexpected reservations among the members of the kibbutz. Most of the settlers in Merhavia were young bachelors and they would have preferred the admission of an unmarried woman. Furthermore, they feared that Golda might be a typical American girl, spoiled by comfort and incapable of hard physical work. The application of the Myerson couple required consideration. While waiting to be passed on, Golda gave English lessons in Tel Aviv, an activity which aroused further doubts among the comrades, for teaching was a soft intellectual oc-

cupation. They believed that Golda should have chosen
housework to prove her ideological fitness. But Golda, while
full of the correct enthusiasm for physical labor in a kibbutz,
saw no sense in washing floors in Tel Aviv instead of teaching. It took a number of months for the skeptics of Merhavia
to gamble on Golda.

When Golda arrived in Merhavia with Morris, she was
one of 8 women among 32 men. As a married couple, she and
her husband enjoyed the privilege of a room to themselves,
an unusual luxury for a still struggling kibbutz. On the whole
the physical conditions of Merhavia were considerably
better than those in other kibbutzim in the Emek. Comrades
of Ein Harod, which had been established that year, used to
call Merhavia "bourgeois" because it had a few sound cottages and some large trees planted by the 1909 pioneers.

Nevertheless quinine was still being served with the meals
and malaria was routine. In due time Golda contracted the
disease and recovered. There were other dangers. She was
warned not to walk in the fields in a white dress after nightfall, since white made too easy a target for snipers from the
neighboring Arab village. This also was routine, but it did
not lessen Golda's delight in her new life. The lovely unfamiliar landscape enchanted her—the bursts of green to
mark a settlement along the wide bare plain, and the low
mountains with their ancient names. There was Mount
Tabor, rounded like a woman's breast, and there the cave
where Saul met the witch. And each blade of grass now
growing in Merhavia was a testament to the future.

Her first job was picking almonds in a grove situated near
the spot where the large central hospital of the Emek now
stands. Her back hurt and her hands turned yellow, but she

had plenty of stamina. Of that there could be no question, despite her American background.

However, when the trial period of several months ended and the question of formal admission to the kibbutz came up for a vote, a few doubters still remained. Golda was a hard, conscientious worker but she still betrayed too many American refinements: she sometimes wore silk stockings after the day's work; she insisted on ironing her dress if it was rumpled; she wasted time on carefully skinning the herring—a kibbutz staple—instead of merely washing and cutting it. When she worked in the kitchen, she demanded oilcloth for the tables. After a *cumsitz* (get-together) in the common dining room in the evening, she made a fuss if the male comrades did not wipe off the long planks of the tables. These were potential bourgeois deviations perhaps symptomatic of graver weaknesses to come.

Despite these objections, the majority welcomed Golda and her husband into the fold. And Golda gave no quarter to her detractors. Cleanliness, she declared, should not be confined to the cattle. "I don't see why human beings must be treated worse than our cows. . . ." In this area she was relentless. When it became her task to care for the five babies of the kibbutz, she extravagantly sterilized the bathtub with alcohol during an infectious illness. Golda's "brandy babies" became a wry kibbutz joke. American sanitation was costly.

And she had curious notions about diet. Instead of the ubiquitous herring served to the workers in the raw, chill mornings before they went off to the muddy fields, Golda offered hot oatmeal when it was her turn in the kitchen. She had managed to get oatmeal by barter, and was trying to persuade the comrades of its merits. "We are not babies," they protested.

Life in Merhavia was on the whole a happy time for Golda. Had circumstances permitted, she might have found contentment in the kibbutz. She was not spared inevitable frictions and disillusionments, but her adjustment to essential aspects of kibbutz life was immediate. Her natural vigor and capacity for strenuous physical work were a godsend. A girl who joined Merhavia some months after Golda's arrival recalls that when she came to the kibbutz all the girls of Merhavia were ill, with the exception of the buoyant Golda. As a further blessing, Golda had no preconceived notions about desirable and undesirable types of work. She did not consider dishwashing humiliating, and did not become depressed when her turn came for kitchen work. As a matter of fact, she created something of a sensation at a convention of the cooperatives in 1922 when she arose and eloquently asked why women considered kitchen work a disgrace. The speech, one of her earliest public utterances in Palestine, was viewed as heresy by the female comrades and enjoyed something of a *succès de scandale*.

Another great asset was her sociability. She did not seclude herself in her room during free hours, and was always the last to leave the long, bare table of the common dining room at night. A readiness to talk late into the night, no matter how hard the day had been, was to remain. Comrades who were on solitary nightwatch remember how she occasionally appeared and offered to share the watch. "She cheered us when we were in the dumps, and raised our spirits," a comrade recalled.

These recollections are probably uncolored. The girl's enormous vitality was not exhausted by the day's work.

At the simple kibbutz parties, usually on a Friday night when the boys would put on clean blue shirts and the girls fresh cotton blouses taken from the communal store of clothing, she danced the *horah* longer than anyone else. Stamping in the circle which moved rhythmically to the right and then to the left, she often was the only girl remaining while the boys dropped out to be replaced by others.

She soon made her mark in the kibbutz. Within six months she was sent to take a special course in poultry culture. Some of the other girls who had been in the kibbutz longer were envious. But since the majority of the kibbutz were young men who found her—to quote one of them—"charming and inspiring," the few sour notes of feminine envy were easily disregarded.

She devoted herself to poultry raising with her usual thoroughness and competence. Soon the kibbutz, which had been buying eggs from Arabs, was hatching its own eggs. Not that everything was smooth sailing. Once Golda came into the hencoop to find all the chicks dead: a jackal had gotten in during the night. Another time, when Golda fell ill with *papatesche*, a local fever, her substitute forgot to water the chicks, and brought word that many had died. In her delirium, Golda saw endless rows of dead chicks. This was no sentimental sorrow. Poultry represented a large investment for a poor kibbutz.

The tensions generated by the dogmas of kibbutz society were illustrated by the drama of the "egg." One of the girls married to one of the younger comrades had become pregnant. The older bachelors, men in their thirties, were indignant. They had deliberately deprived themselves of marriage and children in order to put no tax on the resources of the new kibbutz. Now a situation had been created through which their sacrifices were nullified by the "selfish" pregnancy of a careless girl. Since food was scarce, not enough special food was allotted to the young woman. The eggs that were being hatched under Golda's care were supposed to be sold and the proceeds used for the improvement of the kibbutz. Only a few eggs were kept for the sick on special diets and for the modest allotment permitted the kibbutz. But the husband, anxious that his wife have adequate rations, secretly took some eggs from the incubator. The loss was discovered and traced. Religious horror shook the kibbutz when this dishonorable and uncomradely conduct was discovered. Spiritual worlds crashed because a *haver* had proved fallible, individualistic, and egoist enough to abscond with a private egg for a private wife who was producing a private baby who would be unable to do productive work for some years.

By the twenties such an attitude toward babies was fairly unusual. Strong emphasis was already being placed on the importance of having children and of supporting the children's house comfortably, no matter what sacrifices adults endured. The Merhavia incident was a hangover from an earlier period and could perhaps be explained less theoretically by the fact that there were so few women. The bachelors did not want to assume the burden of other people's pleasures.

The aging men and women who had been with Golda in Merhavia remember her today as a good comrade. No greater compliment can be paid to a kibbutznik. She had been a real *havera*. This means that the person so complimented had proved equal to the exigencies of communal life: had not shirked hard or unpleasant tasks; had not moped about the constant need to subordinate personal

moods and desires to the interests of the commune; and
above all had done all this naturally, without too oppressive
a sense of sacrifice. Golda, a gregarious extrovert, readily
took to life in a kibbutz. Youth, abundant physical energy, a
delight in people as well as in the common task, were an
almost certain guarantee of a satisfactory adjustment, and
Golda had these requisites in full measure.

When I asked Golda's former associates in Merhavia for
specific incidents to illustrate her merits as a comrade, they
recalled trifles whose significance was elusive.

A woman who had devoted many superlatives to Golda's
invigorating influence on the kibbutz smiled reminiscently
and said: "One day it had been raining hard; we could not
work outside and felt low and dull. We were shelling almonds
in the kitchen because nothing else could be done. Golda
sat looking a bit regal, like always, telling us things. . . ."
What had registered on that rainy day in the kibbutz was
a natural dignity of manner that would serve the future ambassador and minister in good stead.

Another woman remembered Golda's active sympathy
because she knew no Yiddish, only Hebrew. The nucleus of
the kibbutz was still in the Yiddish-speaking phase, and the
newcomer's excellent Hebrew—shortly to become the most
treasured asset from the national point of view—was not
considered adequate compensation for her ignorance. But
Golda was compassionate. *"Hot rachmones auf a Yiddish
kind wos kent kein Yiddish"* ("Pity a Jewish girl who knows
no Yiddish"), she had said, and the transition had been eased.

Perhaps the best evidence for the kind of role she played
in the kibbutz is in the record of her progress. Within a year
she was the kibbutz delegate to the newly formed council
of the Histadrut, the trade union of Jewish workers in Pales-

tine. Her name appeared at conferences and on committees. At this stage her oratorical powers had no opportunity for exercise or display, but her gift for clear, persuasive exposition was being noted.

Despite Golda's apparent talent for kibbutz life, she and her husband left Merhavia in 1923. No conscientious person left a kibbutz easily; it was a kind of desertion of the group and the idea. The departure from the kibbutz represented a crisis in Golda's life. The very features of communal existence which were immediately attractive to a girl of her temperament were deeply repellent to Morris. He did not have the physique for back-breaking work. He had caught malaria, like most of the others at Merhavia, and the illness depressed his melancholy spirit still more. And he developed a rupture which required an operation if he were to do the heavy physical work expected of him. Above all, he found intolerable both the lack of privacy and the sociability, which struck him as gross rather than idealistic. No doubt his young wife's joyous popularity did not help.

A letter of his from Merhavia (1923) indicated his complete discouragement and disillusionment: "Ah, Palestine, Palestine, you beggarly little land, what will become of you? How ironic sound the fine words at Poale Zion meetings about a free workers' Palestine." His mother, who naturally blamed Golda for her son's sufferings, offered to send Morris money for the return journey. But Morris could not bring himself to leave Golda, and Golda would not leave Palestine. Of that there was no question. She did, however, make a partial compromise and left the kibbutz.

The relationship between the two was doomed. The conflict in character and in views was too intense for genuine harmony. There were valiant attempts at reconciliation, but the battle had been lost at the outset. Perhaps life would have been kinder to both if either had possessed the strength to sever a relationship whose stresses were increased by each capitulation, but neither of the young people had the strength for a clean break. The psychologically puzzling figure was Golda. The tormented and clinging love of Morris was self-explanatory, but why the strong-willed, vigorous girl lacked the courage to face the truth in her most vital personal relationship was less clear. To her affection for Morris was added a sense of guilt. On her account he had become deracinated and emotionally dependent. She was bound by his bondage, and the decision to leave Merhavia seemed inevitable under the circumstances. Besides, she wanted a child, and Morris was determined to have no children in a kibbutz.

After leaving Merhavia in 1923, Golda found work as a cashier in the Office of Public Works (later to develop into *Solel Boneh*) in Tel Aviv. She made no particular impression on one of her supervisors with whom I talked. He noticed her because she was young and pretty, and was refreshingly candid in admitting that he had had no suspicion that of all the interesting young girls active in the office in those days Golda was the one who would reach greatest distinction.

Her work as a cashier was interrupted by pregnancy. The family moved to Jerusalem, where her first child Menachem was born on November 23, 1924. The next few years were devoted almost exclusively to home and family. In the spring of 1925, Golda went back to Merhavia with the baby, but returned after six months. The kibbutz was in a period of disintegration, and in any case she still hoped to salvage her marriage. A second child, Sara, was born in May 1926.

The family lived in a shabby quarter of Jerusalem, near

[83]

Mea Shearim, on the outskirts of the city. Their two-room flat lacked both gas and electricity; an oil stove served for cooking and lighting. Other conveniences were equally minimal. Even the kitchen was in the yard in a tin shack with an oil primus as its chief equipment. Before the second child's birth a roomer occupied one of the two rooms. After Sara's birth this additional income had to be forfeited.

Morris had a job as a bookkeeper with *Solel Boneh*. His small salary, not a living wage by the most modest standards, was further reduced because *Solel Boneh*, also in financial straits, paid in credit slips, not cash. The credit chits were accepted by the local grocer at a discount of 8 percent of their value; the landlord of the wretched Myerson apartment declined to take them on any terms.

In exchange for Menachem's tuition at a nursery school, Golda did the washing for all of the children of the school, without benefit of a washing machine. The water had to be heated pail by pail, and the wash scrubbed by hand with the help of a rough board. Golda's role as washerwoman lasted half a year. Then she got a job teaching English in Miss Kallen's private school; the baby had to be brought along, since Golda's earnings did not permit a baby-sitter.

Whenever she had three piastres in cash, she walked to Spinney's, an English shop, to purchase half-a-pound of bones and a quarter-of-a-pound of meat for soup. The children were given the meat, a rare luxury. Usually it was a matter of getting milk and bread. This was penury the like of which Golda had never known. Her parents had been poor and she had experienced privation. But it was more bitter to worry about food for her own children born in Jerusalem.

Not that her spirit was in danger of being broken. When a husky young neighbor warned the milkman that he was taking a chance in extending credit to the Myerson menage, Golda caned the meddler in outraged fury. "No one will take milk from my children."

Petty debts kept piling up. No matter how artfully and capably she stretched the piastres, there were never enough pounds at the end of the month to pay the rent and grocery bill. Kibbutz austerity had been a way of life gallantly welcomed. This day-by-day struggle for elementary necessities was misery without dedication.

Golda remembers the years between 1924 and 1928 as among the most wretched of her life. The letters between Shana and Golda dealt with unpaid grocery bills, lack of heat, and the need of medicines for ailing children, frequently sick in the unheated Jerusalem apartment during the harsh winter winds and rains.

In one letter Golda described how she had been refused bread and margarine on credit because the grocer had lost faith in the Myerson solvency. In another, Shana promised to send a box of fruit and vegetables, acquired cheaply at a local market, as soon as she could raise the necessary piastres for shipping the food from Tel Aviv to Jerusalem. These details are interspersed with accounts of the children's temperatures, coughs, sore throats or other complaints, yet Golda's unhappiness had additional and more fundamental causes.

At the same time, Golda met this situation with her characteristic energy and competence. With no vocation for domesticity, she was an admirable housewife and cook. Her impatience of the slipshod extended to carelessly rinsed dishes, an untidily set table, or an improperly pressed blouse.

What she could not bear was being swallowed up by her home to the exclusion of every other interest. Her sense of isolation was intolerable.

For four years Golda had withdrawn from all political activity to devote herself wholly to her family. It had been a conscious experiment undertaken at her husband's urging, and it had failed. Neither childbearing nor the tough round of daily tasks had stilled her restlessness. Though she loved her children deeply, maternity had not changed her as Morris had hoped. Besides, even if there had been no inner compulsion, economic conditions made it imperative for Golda to find meaningful work. It was inevitable that she would resume party activities, just as it was inevitable that the movement would not let her gifts rest unused. Palestine was not rich enough in human material for such extravagance.

As soon as her comrades learned that Golda was prepared to end her self-imposed exile, the summons to party work was not long in coming.

In 1928, the Histadrut called her to become the secretary of the *Moatzot Poalot* (the Women's Labor Council) and her public career was launched. During the next few years, she was either representing the *Moatzot Poalot* at international conferences or alternating between Palestine and the United States, where she served for several years as the delegate to the Pioneer Women, the American counterpart of the *Moatzot Poalot.*

Her travels necessitated frequent separations from her home and children. Her domestic problems had not become less complicated with time; in a sense they were insoluble. Writing anonymously some years later for *The Plough Woman,* a group of memoirs by women pioneers, Golda posed the problem starkly:

[86]

Taken as a whole, the inner struggles and the despairs of the mother who goes to work are without parallel in human experience. But within that whole there are many shades and variations. There are some mothers who work only when they are forced to, when the husband is sick or unemployed, or else when the family has in some other way gone off the track of a normal life. In such cases the mother feels her course of action justified by compulsion—her children would not be fed otherwise. But there is a type of woman who cannot remain at home for other reasons. In spite of the place which the children and the family as a whole take up in her life, her nature and being demand something more; she cannot divorce herself from the larger social life. She cannot let her children narrow her horizon. And for such a woman, there is no rest.

Theoretically it looks straightforward enough. The woman who replaces her with the children is devoted, loves the children, is reliable and suited to the work; the children are fully looked after. And there are even pedagogic theorists who say that it is actually better for the children not to have the mother constantly near them. As for the mother who is occupied outside the house—she of course has the great advantage of being able to develop. In any case, the ancient danger of retrogression is lessened; and therefore she can bring more to her children than if she were to remain at home. Everything looks all right. But one look of reproach from the little one when the mother goes away and leaves it with the stranger is enough to throw down the whole structure of vindication. That look, that plea to the mother to stay, can be withstood only by an almost superhuman effort of the will.

I am not speaking now of the constant worry that haunts the mother's mind that something may have happened. And I need not bring in the feelings of the mother when her child falls sick—the flood of self-reproach and self-accusation. At the best of times, in the best circumstances, there is the perpetual consciousness at the back of the mind that the child lacks the mother's tenderness, misses during the day the mother's kiss. We believe, above all, in education by example; and therefore we must ask ourselves: Whose is the example which is molding the child of the working mother? A "borrowed" mother becomes the model. The clever things the child says reach the mother at secondhand. Such a child does not know the magic healing power of a mother's kiss, which takes away the pain of a bruise. And there are times, after a wearying, care-filled day, when the mother looks at her child almost as if she did not recognize it; a feeling of alienation from her nearest and dearest steals into her heart.

And having admitted all this, we ask: Can the mother of today remain with her children? Can she compel herself to be other than she is because she has become a mother? That feeling of alienation between mother and child can occur, and does often occur in an even more serious form when the mother always remains at home and cannot grow with her children. And the modern woman asks herself: Is there something wrong with me if my children don't fill up my life? Am I at fault if, after giving them, and the one other person nearest to me a place in my heart, there is something left over which has to be filled by things outside the family and the home? Can we today measure devotion to husband and children by our indifference to everything else? Is it not often true that the woman who has given up all the external world for her husband and her children has done it not out of a sense of duty, out of devotion and love, but out of incapacity, because her soul is not able to take into itself the many-sidedness of life, with its sufferings but also with its joys? And if a woman does remain with her children and gives herself to nothing else, does that really prove that she is more devoted than the other kind of mother? And if a wife has no intimate friends, does that prove that she has a greater love for her husband?

But the mother also suffers in the very work she has taken up. Always she has the feeling that her work is not as pro-

ductive as that of a man or even of an unmarried woman.
The children, too, always demand her, in health and even
more in sickness. And this eternal inner division, this double
pull, this alternating feeling of unfulfilled duty—today toward her family, the next day toward her work—this is the
burden of the working mother.

The conflict in its full anguish and nakedness was best revealed in her correspondence with Shana and in the letters
of Shana to Sam, who in the meantime had come to Palestine and then returned temporarily to the United States to
mend the family fortunes. In this intimate three-cornered
correspondence, free of the kindly or malicious distortions of
memory, doubt and resentments are voiced. Then, Golda
was not yet a famous woman whose right to public activity
was unquestioned. In 1928, Shana complained about Golda's
absorption in the work of the party and the Histadrut: "She
is a public person, not a home-body. Should we rejoice in
this? She forgets about *tate-mame* [father-mother] and herself."

During Golda's absences the care of the children often
devolved upon Shana, so that her protests merited consideration. By then Shana had a third child; additional duties,
naturally assumed by her, lay heavy. And Shana, too, was
not content to be merely a household drudge. The dream of
her interrupted education was never forgotten.

An apparently trivial incident brought the long simmering
to a boil. During the Arab riots of 1929, Shana was called to
Jerusalem to assist in a home for refugee children from
Hebron, which had suffered great losses in the Arab attacks.
When she objected to giving the children herring for lunch
on a hot summer day, the nurse in charge remarked con-

temptuously: "What do you know about dietetics?" "I decided that no one would be able to say to me, 'You don't know.' I wrote to Sam that I must study. He wrote, 'Come.'"

Shana made preparations to leave her two older children in Palestine and go with her youngest child to Sam and Battle Creek to become a dietitian. Not surprisingly, Golda wrote to her: "Perhaps you understand me now." Shana answered unsparingly: "Sam understands and helps me because he is all my life."

In a letter written on the way to London to an international labor conference, Golda pleaded for understanding. It read in part:

> I ask only one thing, that I be understood and believed. My social activities are not an accidental thing; they are an absolute necessity for me. I am hurt when Morris and others say that this is all superficial, that I am trying to be modern. It is silly. Do I have to justify myself?
>
> Before I left, the doctor assured me that Sarele's health permits of my going, and I have made adequate arrangements for Menachem. And yet you can understand how hard it is for me to leave. But in our present situation I could not refuse to do what was asked of me. Believe me, I know I will not bring the Messiah, but I think that we must miss no opportunity to explain what we want and what we are to influential people.
>
> One thing is clear. I have only two alternatives: one, to cut off my connections with all outside interests as I once did at Morris' insistence, or to go to Ein Harod. I have no further strength for my present life. My sole problem is what is better for the children . . . Perhaps you will not believe me but I tell you if I were sure that the first way would be more wholesome for the children I would not hesitate a bit, but I am doubtful. . . . perhaps you will be able to value what it

means that your and Sam's interests are one and that he understands and respects your plans.

The alternatives which Golda posed in a moment of despair were hardly feasible. There was no real question of returning to the role of housewife with an occasional afternoon off for good works as the children grew older. The second alternative she suggested in her anguish—retreat to Ein Harod—was no longer possible. She had been discovered. The movement needed her eloquence and energy. Her knowledge of English and Yiddish made her invaluable as a delegate to Anglo-Saxon countries. And she was as yet emotionally unprepared for an obvious third alternative—a complete break with her husband. The "present life" had to continue.

Her activities, which seemed impressively courageous and self-denying to the outsider, met with little encouragement in the family circle. This made the inner struggle all the harder for a woman who all her life had to reconcile two powerful impulses—the instincts of a warm, loving woman and the need for action. In later years, public acclaim and the obvious significance of the tasks undertaken would provide justification to a troubled self. But at this stage, reproaches of intimates were added to self-reproaches and questionings.

In a kibbutz Golda would have been relieved of domestic cares as a matter of course, the philosophy of the kibbutz requiring the participation of women in all activities, but she had left Merhavia. The framework of the kibbutz, which enabled many capable and idealistic women to take part in the rebuilding of Palestine at less personal cost, could not be utilized by her.

There was no going back. At an Imperial labor conference in London, she first attracted wide attention. Ben-Gurion heard her appeal in behalf of the workers of Palestine and recognized a new force. More than once in the years to come he was to make sure that it would be employed fittingly.

WITH THE HISTADRUT

In 1932, Golda arrived in New York with her children to spend two years with the Pioneer Women's Organization. The young woman who was returning after a decade seemed more than ten years older to the comrades who met her. She was still beautiful, but although she was only in her early thirties, her face was already assuming an expression which might vary from strength to severity but whose firm cast was becoming increasingly characteristic.

The Pioneer Women's Organization of America shared the Palestinian conviction about women's capacities and responsibilities. Started by a handful of women in 1924, the organization set itself the task of raising funds for such projects as the founding of agricultural training farms for girls or the establishment of nurseries for the children of working mothers. These women differed from other Zionist groups in their primary concern for activities which increased the scope of feminine participation in the building of Palestine. In addition, they were a part of the labor wing of Zionism

—which meant identification with the Poale Zion and the Histadrut.

When Golda arrived for two years of service, the organization was eight years old. Because of its emphasis on Yiddish and on the labor movement, its appeal was at first chiefly to first-generation immigrants, women with a socialist-Zionist tradition. Later the terms halutz and kibbutz were to become the stock in trade of the entire Zionist movement and the mainstay of Zionist orators of whatever political affiliation. But in the early thirties American Jewry knew little of the socialist pioneers "who made the desert bloom." Palestine's cooperative way of life required apostles, and Golda's purpose was to broaden the membership of the Pioneer Women, bringing the message of pioneer Palestine to Americanized women and enlisting their enthusiasm.

In Golda, the ideal formula for this mission had presumably been found: youth, American background, ten years in Palestine, extraordinary eloquence in English, Hebrew and Yiddish. The small groups of Pioneer Women in towns and cities throughout the United States who raised the money were, for the most part, in the lower income groups. The dues and quotas had to be amassed dollar by dollar through a variety of activities from raffles to cake sales. The original founders of the Pioneer Women had longed to be heroines of the Second or Third *Aliyah*. If they were in New York instead of in the Emek, that was because of some failure of fortune. The dream still beckoned. They needed its spiritual sustenance. This meant that meetings had to be many, earnest and impassioned. Suspicious of frivolity, it was a long time before the women tolerated purely social gatherings where the ladies might play bridge instead of listening to a lecture about A. D. Gordon, Borochov, or other socialist-

Zionist theoreticians. When they succumbed, out of regard for the desires of the younger members who had American ideas as to how to spend a profitable afternoon, the capitulation was halfhearted. The passion for theory to motivate practice was never really lost.

Much of Golda's time had to be spent on tour addressing these various groups. Sometimes there was a handful of plainly dressed middle-aged women who spoke English with an accent; sometimes there were more fashionable gatherings of women and girls born in the United States and products of American schools. Both listened raptly to Golda.

An enthusiastic tribute to her from a lady clearly belonging to the first contingent appeared in a 1934 issue of the *Pioneer Women's Journal:* "Goldie brought us a waft of fragrant orange blossoms, sprouting vegetables, budding trees, well-cared-for cows and chickens, stubborn territory conquered, dangerous natural elements vanquished, all the result of work, work, work. Work not under pressure or for personal gain, but sweat and blood, field and plow, road and cement, barrenness and endurance, swamps and disease, dangers, deprivations, obstacles, tribulations, inspiration and work, just for work's sake, just for the ecstasy of creation."

As an editor of the *Pioneer Women's Journal,* she had to write, an art which never came readily to her and which she never acquired. Her directness and simplicity—her outstanding oratorical virtues enriched by her voice and the force of her personality—became matter of fact and undistinguished when she had to write rather than speak. But if her written exposition was tame, her oral eloquence was unforgettable. She was not only engaged in bringing wafts of orange blossoms and honest sweat. Plunged in the political struggle, she

[95]

also had to defend the socialist concepts of her movement against the attacks of Zionist parties which opposed the dominant role of labor in Palestine. To the proponents of untrammeled initiative and free competition, unhindered by the romantic notions of cooperative colonization or the labor standards of the great trade union of the Histadrut, she could point out with a wealth of illustrations and irony that there had been no competition when the Emek had been drained and settled in 1922. Where were the entrepreneurs on this and that hazardous occasion?

Golda had been quite right in declaring that there had been precious little competition for the privilege of draining marshes and irrigating malaria-ridden wasteland among any save ideological zealots. Halutz accomplishments of the Second *Aliyah* and Third *Aliyah* had received emotional and vocal recognition from all sectors of Jewry with a sentimental interest in Zionism. By the thirties, there were substantial achievements in Palestine. The Emek was flourishing. Tel Aviv had arisen and was a bustling city. Inevitably, a small group of petty Palestinian capitalists with economic stakes to defend became active enlisting the aid of bourgeois Zionists throughout the world against the dogmas and practices of Labor. The rise of Hitler, too, had an unexpected effect. After 1933, middle-class German Jews of exceptional foresight and energy began to migrate to the Jewish homeland in which they had previously displayed little interest.

They found not only the climate alien; much of the social and political atmosphere was, from their point of view, either oppressively utopian or dangerously radical. These blue-shirted intellectuals who made a cult of manual labor might be permitted their social daydreams in a remote kibbutz where no civilized person would want to live anyway, but it was carrying a phantasy too far if they actually wielded the controlling power in the Jewish community.

American Jewry, which Zionism was just beginning to affect, had barely learned to gasp enthusiastically at the exploits of the noble halutzim, when they were informed that these heroes were all right in their historic moment, but now the pioneer stage was over. Instead of being true blue-and-white, Labor would have to be viewed as unwholesomely tinged with pink, if not red. A socialist-Zionist was hyphenated. You could not even trust his Zionism, because he was probably worrying more about the social revolution than the Jewish homeland. It was Golda's job to point out that if the halutzim were more socialist than Zionist they could have spared themselves a long sea journey and promulgated the social revolution among all the comforts of home.

The long American visit was frustrating and not too happy. Golda was already too much a part of the reality of Palestine to be content with so long a period of unremitting propaganda within a fairly narrow circle. The love and admiration she received were no substitute for the sense of direct activity whose results depended on what she did rather than on what she persuaded others to do.

At more than one meeting she was asked: "Why do you talk about the Histadrut in general instead of the work of the women?" For Golda a narrow insistence on woman's role as distinct from the other sectors of the Palestine Labor movement never came easily. It was natural that she should first attract attention in the *Moatzot Poalot*, but she was never a feminist in the sense that other notable women Palestinian leaders such as Bebe Idelson or Ada Fishman were. She did not make a cult of women's rights but took feminine equality for granted. From the outset she was a leader who was a woman rather than a woman leader. At the same time she was realistic enough to appreciate the fact that women's organizations, with their feminist inspiration, had won the initial victories which made possible the free functioning of a woman like herself. She also understood that their significance was not merely historic. Women had special needs and special capacities which could most economically be channeled through women's organizations. In Palestine, the training of immigrant girls, the assurance of adequate provision for working mothers and their children were the logical province of the Working Women's Council. The enlistment of women to support such programs could more readily be achieved through women's organizations which adapted their appeal, their educational techniques and their times of meeting to the special needs of women.

The Pioneer Women had undertaken an ambitious program. In addition to the maintenance of training farms for girls in Palestine and the support of other projects of the *Moatzot Poalot* the members were concerned with preserving the values of Yiddish culture in which many of them had been raised and keeping pace with the developing Hebrew culture of Palestine. At the same time they wanted to take their stand beside other liberals on the American scene. No aspect of this threefold program could be ignored. The *Pioneer Women's Journal* came out month after month, partially in Yiddish to maintain the bond with a language and literature precious to much of Jewry, and partially in English at first for the younger members and gradually for the older ones, too, as the immigrants took root in America.

Golda fully appreciated the value of the organization as well as the idealism of the individual women. But despite the warmth with which she was surrounded and her complete intellectual realization of the importance of a women's organization for the majority of women, she found the atmosphere personally constricting. There was a greater challenge in working with men.

In 1934, the American stint ended. When Golda returned to Palestine, her training days were over. She did not go back to the Working Women's Council. Instead she was invited to join the *Vaad Ha-Poel*, the executive committee of the Histadrut.

The Histadrut, the General Federation of Jewish Labor in Palestine, was no ordinary trade union primarily concerned with the living conditions of its members. Before the establishment of the state, the Histadrut was a labor commonwealth in the making. From the beginning, the Histadrut viewed itself as a practical colonizing agency concerned with stimulating pioneer immigration and in assisting in its settlement. Nothing necessary for the country's growth was outside its province. If private enterprise was fearful of risky or unprofitable ventures, the Histadrut, through its credit institutions and building companies, provided capital as well as labor. *Solel Boneh*, the building cooperative, constructed roads in the desert which no private contractor would undertake. Inevitably, hostile critics cried out against this labor union which assumed so many of the entrepreneur's prerogatives. But, for the Histadrut such distinctions were semantic. Within its framework, the dynamic pioneering elements in the country were channeled. It served as a rallying point for all labor trends from the orthodox Mizrachi Labor Youth to the leftist Hashomer Hatzair. The members with their families constituted not only 30 to 40 percent of the population but were its most vital segment.

During the thirties or forties the *Vaad Ha-Poel* occupied

[99]

a modest building on Allenby Avenue very unlike its imposing structure which is now one of the show places of Tel
Aviv. There was nothing to distinguish the building or its
small, plain offices as the center of the Palestine Labor
movement except perhaps the deliberately proletarian dress
of the men and women in the courtyard or in the cooperative
kitchen in the basement. The official-looking gentlemen with
briefcases wore the khaki shorts and open blouses of the
pioneer. The women used no powder or lipstick. If a girl with
make-up was seen in one of the corridors, she was either a
tourist or employed in a very minor capacity. No one of significance in the movement would violate the canons of austerity of dress. But whatever the lack in elegance, nowhere
in Palestine was there a more glittering array of ability.

In the meeting room reserved for sessions of the executive
committee gathered most of the key figures in the creation
of the Jewish state: blunt Ben-Gurion, always sure of himself
whatever the issue, making his point in clipped, emphatic
sentences; brilliant, sophisticated Moshe Shertok, later to be
known as Sharett, whose polished analysis of a complex question was no less painstaking at a Histadrut meeting than it
was to be when he became the chief diplomat of Israel; big,
solid Eliezer Kaplan, who was to die in office as minister
of finance of the struggling state; wise, shrewd David
Remez who was to be minister of communication; handsome
Pinchas Lubianiker (Lavon), whose sardonic wit angered
as many hearers as it amused, and who was to be a figure of
fierce controversy as minister of defense; humorous, capable
Joseph Sprinzak, who managed to be both biting and genial,
and who was to occupy the dignified post of speaker of the
Knesset, the first parliament of Israel; eloquent Zalman
Rubashov (Shazar), the future third president; or Dov

Joseph, a lawyer from Canada who was to have the stern task of rationing food during the siege of Jerusalem.

The list of remarkable figures continued—men like Joseph Baratz of Degania; or quiet, retiring Eliahu Golomb, one of the founders of the Haganah, who like Berl Katznelson—ideological leader of the movement—was to die before the establishment of the state.

The women, too, had their share of striking personalities: tiny, energetic Bebe Idelson, head of the *Moatzot Poalot;* silent, scholarly Rachel Katznelson, able writer and editor; Yehudith Simchonith, most femininely charming of the feminists; rugged, yet unexpectedly gentle, Ada Fishman (Maimon); Rachel Yanait, wife of Ben-Zvi, and like Ada, founder of a children's agricultural farm to be defended through riot and war.

A large number of the other men and women who convened in the big hall would eventually become members of the *Knesset,* a shade more formally dressed, older, and probably with freshly Hebraized names. The Histadrut was the motor of Zionist realization. To be a member of the *Vaad Ha-Poel* in 1934 meant that one was at the forefront of the Zionist struggle, economic and political, throughout the coming fateful years.

Golda speaks of her years in the leadership of the Histadrut as one of the richest and most creative periods of her life. It was a time of the purest hopes and the most generous illusions. The visionaries had not as yet been obliged to starch and black-tie their dreams or to adapt the original pattern to a flimsier material.

Golda began modestly enough as the organizer of a tourist department of the Histadrut for the purpose of welcoming distinguished visitors and explaining such exotic institutions as a kibbutz or *Tnuva,* the consumer's cooperative. More than one member of the British Labour party, then in the role of His Majesty's loyal opposition, came, saw, and was suitably impressed by the new social forms through which the national goal was being realized. When Foreign Secretary Ernest Bevin issued the White Paper restricting Jewish immigration into Palestine, Golda remembered with special bitterness the sympathetic admiration with which British Labour leaders had noted the achievements of the labor movement in Palestine.

Within a year she was elected to the secretariat of the executive committee. In this capacity she was one of the inner circle. She was entrusted with a variety of executive posts that indicated both her energy and the range of her abilities. By 1936, she was put in charge of all the mutual-aid programs of the Histadrut and became chairman of the board of directors of *Kupat Holim,* the Workers' Sick Fund, which, as a completely functioning system of socialized medicine for all members of the Histadrut and their families, provided medical services for 40 percent of the population. During the same year, when Arab riots broke out and the British began to build army camps in the country, she supervised labor conditions of workers in these camps. Her department was responsible for all labor negotiations with employers. After the death of Dov Hoz, she became head of the political department of the Histadrut.

Blessed with abundant physical and spiritual energy, she was as effective in an office as on a platform. Her organizational gifts, her grasp of detail, and her ability to carry out a concrete project were exceptional, and she enjoyed a capacity for plain, unspectacular hard work day in, day out.

In the midst of these activities she periodically left Palestine to represent the Histadrut at an international conference or to attend the sessions of the Actions Committee of the World Zionist Organization.

In 1937, she was again sent to the United States, this time in behalf of *Nachshon,* a new maritime enterprise of the Histadrut, named after the Nachshon of legend who was the first to leap into the Red Sea and so lead his people toward the Promised Land. After the 1936 Arab disturbances when the British authorities closed the Jaffa port, the Jewish community in Palestine determined to build its own harbor in Tel Aviv and to learn the arts of the sea as it had learned anew the arts of agriculture. "We must train our people for work on the sea as we have trained them, these many years, for work on the soil—one more step toward the independence of our people," Golda declared. She expounded the need to invest in the Tel Aviv port and to buy ships, train sailors, develop fisheries and make of the sea an important factor in the upbuilding of the country.

Her far-flung eloquence was accompanied by a painstaking attention to detail. She conducted a voluminous correspondence with shipping companies in England and other countries, discussing questions of tonnage, shipment facilities for citrus fruits, guaranteed space for the conveyance "at economical rates" of colonists and child refugees to Palestine, employment of Palestinian personnel, as well as technical shipping problems. With the aid of a few advisers, she had to be in a position to evaluate highly specialized analyses and make binding decisions accordingly. The sense that she was always a key person in the execution of any project she advocated gave sinews to her oratory.

Golda Meir: Woman with a Cause

Her rise as a leader in the Histadrut was by no means a triumphal progress. Idealism and abnegation are more impressive at a banquet in Miami than in a community where such qualities are matter-of-course staples of the national diet. And the granite strength, so admirable at a distance, can seem uncomfortably hard close at hand. Eloquence which becomes sharply polemical on the home scene when dealing with close associates and immediate issues is likely to win as many enemies as friends.

One of her great assets as a labor leader was that she had no fear of unpopularity. She did not court her public. On more than one occasion she was entrusted with the delicate task of putting through a measure opposed by the workers and of winning their support for a policy which entailed further sacrifices on their part. It was she who assumed the highly unpopular mission of persuading the Histadrut workers to accept a fresh unemployment tax in addition to their already heavy dues and taxes. Between 1935 and 1939, unemployment increased to a level that was beyond the capacity of the available funds of the Histadrut to relieve. Employed workers who were earning little resented further burdens and demanded that the Jewish Agency and the national institutions assume the responsibility for additional relief. But the *Yishuv*, the Jewish community, was slow in recognizing its obligation to the unemployed worker. In the meantime hunger and destitution were a reality. Still another unemployment tax had to be levied by the one body with an adequate sense of social responsibility.

Golda went from factory to factory, addressing workers' meetings, arguing, expostulating. The thesis was simple: since the *Yishuv* as a whole was remiss in its obligations, the Histadrut had to shoulder the load rather than appeal

[104]

for help to the Jews of the Diaspora. In one address (1939) she said:

> We shall not go to the Jews of the Diaspora to seek relief. Our topic of discussion with them cannot be the matter of unemployment, the matter of hunger. Not that is our subject. When we went to the Jews of the Diaspora, we always asked them to do their utmost to enable us to build, to create new things. We placed before them a great demand to dedicate their efforts to those who must come here. Only for this we sought their help. Even this demand was not always heard, or heard by few. And today when we turn to those fortunate Jews who still have the chance to act and who live in peace, we must be able to proclaim the nature of their special mission: to aid in the building of the country rather than in sending doles to the poor. How precious are the moments still left us for this great task. Who knows how hard it may be tomorrow?

It took tremendous courage and moral authority to present the case in these terms, to insist that American Jewry be reserved for larger purposes and to demand that the workers tighten their belts still further. Such counsel was no more welcome from a union representative than from an employer. She was denounced from the Left as unfair to labor. The Right had a natural abhorrence of the Histadrut, whatever its policies, and had little relish for her request that the entire *Yishuv* proceed more wholeheartedly with its emergency taxation.

In such a discussion the crux of Golda's success inevitably had to rest on her ability to rally the workers to an acceptance of the justice of the concept she presented. But even allowing for the high proportion of idealists to be found in the Histadrut membership of those years—the years when the immigrants had come out of conviction rather than out of necessity—the appeal had to be supplemented by the blunt warning that a failure to vote the tax would result in the curtailment of the medical services provided by the *Kupat Holim*. Golda's sharpness in debate, her ability to puncture self-interest masquerading as self-righteousness, her fearlessness in the face of attack, were her tactical weapons. In the tumult of a heated assembly, she acted as a kind of battering-ram bearing down with a frightening directness on sham or subtlety. The tax was voted.

On more than one occasion she was obliged to defend the pay scale within the Histadrut by which a Histadrut worker was paid according to years of service and the number of family dependents rather than by the type of work performed. A charwoman cleaning the building of the *Vaad Ha-Poel* might earn more than Golda, its newly instituted executive secretary. The principle that pay should be determined by need and a refusal to distinguish between superior and inferior types of work was part of the Histadrut's ideology and was applied rigorously to all who served within its various institutions. As might be expected, there were periodic rebellions. On one occasion the nurses of the *Kupat Holim* demanded that they be paid on the professional scale of the Hadassah hospital rather than on a family scale. Although Golda as usual fought the demand vigorously, when she lay ill in the Beilinson hospital of the Histadrut, one of the nurses remarked: "She is our enemy but we want her to get well."

A hostile critic of Golda went so far as to accuse her of perversely opposing the workers: "In the Histadrut, she was always against the workers. She enjoys being in the opposition. There is a sadistic streak in her." This represented a

[106]

minority view. The general viewpoint was voiced in different terms by a longstanding associate in the *Vaad Ha-Poel*. "When people say that Golda opposes the workers in such questions as wage increases because she is an organization person, they are wrong. She is the leader of a movement, a cause, rather than of a trade union. In her eyes the Histadrut is not primarily an organization for the workers, but an instrument for creating the Jewish state through the workers."

This difference in conception eventually proved one of the fundamental causes for division between the two factions of the Labor movement, the middle-of-the-road Mapai and the leftist Mapam. The latter stressed conditions of labor, while the Mapai and Golda viewed such vital questions as pay increases within the larger framework of the national interest which called for the creation of optimum conditions for continued colonization. If this meant hardship for the individual worker, it had to be accepted as part of the ascetic tradition of the pioneer.

The higher she rose in Palestine's hierarchy of Labor, the more vocal became the voices of her detractors. Inevitably the shabby *argumentum ad feminam* was dragged out in an attempt to explain her achievements in terms of the backing of powerful male friends. Of course she had devoted and influential friends whom she charmed as a woman as well as a comrade. In the course of close association in a common struggle, bonds were formed which remained unbroken for years, but to attempt to explain Golda's success on such a basis was the resource of malice or stupidity.

A Histadrut leader who belonged neither to the perfervid pro-Golda zealots nor to her opponents said: "Was she helped by powerful friends? Of course, but she had the stuff. She was a rough diamond who needed polishing, but the diamond was there. You can't put over a phony. The public can scent the difference between a piece of glass and a jewel. Being a woman was not in her way. In a sense it helped her because she brought to her work much womanly feeling and emotional fervor. Some of the women leaders in Israel, even though engaged in exclusively women's work, are really men in women's garb. Golda was always a woman."

Still other charges were: "She has no ideas of her own. She is merely the brilliant expositor of some man's ideas," or "She is merely the popularizer of the party viewpoint as formulated by Ben-Gurion and company." The question at issue—had Golda independence of judgment and the courage to defend her viewpoint?—was best answered by her fights at party conferences and *Vaad Ha-Poel* meetings against positions assumed by her closest friends and acknowledged teachers, notably Remez.

One point on which both friends and foes (masculine) brought in an adverse report was an unexpected weakness—Golda cried when personally offended. As one man put it with unconcealed irritation: "In social questions she has a genius for belligerent opposition. In regard to a political or ideological issue, she is strong as iron. But if in the course of the debate someone offends her personally, she can begin to cry like a high school girl or a spoiled child." And another man added: "It's not fair." But here the women were kinder: "Golda is very sensitive under her Spartan exterior, and she feels deeply."

But although Golda cried disconcertingly when hurt as an individual and although she weakly permitted herself to be exploited by friends or intimates in purely personal matters, no one denied her striking moral and physical courage on any ideological or national question. Nor did she belong to the type who is brave only in a familiar environment. The girl from Milwaukee would face the high commissioner so forcefully in presenting the demands of the Histadrut that she impressed the British long before they had to deal with her as the acting political head of a country in rebellion.

THE STRUGGLE STARTS

AFTER 1936, when a fresh wave of Arab disturbances broke out, the mandatory reacted to the pressure of Arab terrorism by steadily whittling down the seriousness of its commitment to the Balfour Declaration. The White Paper of 1939, which ended the hopes for a Jewish national home and envisaged a minority status for the Jews in the midst of an Arab state, disillusioned even the most stubborn believers in British good faith. At the same time the mounting tragedy of European Jewry made large-scale immigration into Palestine a matter of life or death for Hitler's victims. At the Zionist congress held in Geneva in the fateful weeks of August 1939, the policy debate reached a furious climax. The alignments were indications of character, as well as political perspicacity, and cut sharply across party lines.

The various viewpoints crystallized into two main lines of thought. The wise, tired voice of Chaim Weizmann, the Zionist statesman who had persuaded Britain to issue the Balfour Declaration, could be heard counseling prudence: "We have been betrayed but we must continue constructive work in

Palestine despite restrictions and setbacks. Not the policy of the Zionist Executive is bankrupt but the world. Ours is the sorrow but not shame. We oppose the use of arms except in self-defense. Jews must follow a Jewish course. They must not howl with the wolves or resort to violence. Instead, we should exploit whatever possibilities remain within the framework of the White Paper."

The leaders of American Zionism in the main agreed with Weizmann. The president of the American Zionist organization, Rabbi Solomon Goldman, decried any manifestation of force. As a religious teacher he reminded his hearers that Johanan ben Zakkai, the apostle of peace, had been held in greater reverence by Jews than the military hero Bar Kochba. Rabbi Abba Hillel Silver, too, opposed extremist measures on the ground that they could not be successful. Even illegal immigration should be abandoned. And he voiced the misgivings of a large sector of World Zionism when he warned the *Yishuv* against pretending to a might it did not possess.

But against these voices of reason and good sense the Palestinians raised a more strident cry. Ben-Gurion, not yet world famous, a short, stocky, white-haired man with an *idée fixe,* tenaciously declared to his followers that: "Jews should act as though we were the state in Palestine, and should so act until there will be a Jewish state." Everybody knew what that meant. Illegal immigration should go on whether the result would be armed clashes with the British authorities or not. Settlements in remote outposts should be started with or without government sanction.

Throughout the entire discussion, timidity increased in direct proportion to the distance from Palestine. The Americans were the most wary. The Palestinians were psychologically better prepared for an active fight against the

White Paper, no matter what forms the struggle might assume. The Labor faction—overwhelmingly Palestinian and numerically nearly half of the congress—declared with a terrible simplicity: "If the refugee ships are turned back, we will not stand with our hands folded."

Not only American General Zionists were startled by the bravura of the Palestinians. Many of the American Labor Zionists, including me, shared the alarm. Even among the Palestinians there was no intellectual unanimity. Many had grave doubts about the feasibility of Ben-Gurion's course. The whole vocabulary of resistance was as yet unfamiliar to a movement which had evolved a doctrine of defense but had opposed counterterror during the Arab riots. A minority in Palestinian Labor urged that Weizmann be heeded; the more sophisticated and politically experienced the individual, the more likely he was to belong to the moderates.

Golda was with Ben-Gurion, not because she was a loyal disciple who always devoutly followed the master, but for obvious reasons of character and outlook. She had none of the intellectual's paralyzing hesitations and timidities. In one of her rare moments of self-analysis she once told me: "I can honestly say that I was never affected by the question of the success of an undertaking. If I felt it was the right thing to do, I was for it regardless of the possible outcome." From the point of view of national dignity and human justice, the correctness of Ben-Gurion's position was axiomatic. For Golda and men and women like her that was enough.

The rumble of World War II began in the last days of the congress. The Britain of the execrated White Paper had become the enemy of the still more execrated Hitler. Ben-Gurion launched the inspired slogan: "We will fight the White Paper as though there were no war, and we will fight

the common enemy as though there were no White Paper."
In the meantime, the delegates, rushing back to "safe" countries, were bidding farewell to comrades determined to return to Poland and Eastern Europe.

The Americans leaving for the remote safety of the United
States felt both guilty and relieved. We were fleeing from the
doomed continent as fast as the boats would take us, but it
was hard to part from the Palestinians who were going back
to their uneasy home in the Middle East. None of us knew
when, if ever, we should meet them again. None of us fore-
saw the course that history would take and that the European Jews would be those to perish.

In those last hours it was the Palestinians who, as usual,
assumed direction. The Labor faction sat all night making
plans to maintain contact between the various segments of
the movement throughout the war. When I said good-bye to
Golda, she was conferring with members of the World
Hechalutz, the pioneer youth organization, and planning
how the links should be kept unsevered. The next morning
she was to leave with the other Palestinians for Italy to wait
for a boat to Haifa. I remember wondering impatiently why
the Palestinians did not rush away at once, like the Americans. They might be interned in Europe for the duration.
But Golda asked quietly: "Who is going to make the plans?"

Upon their return, the Palestinians had a paradoxical
task: they had to arouse the *Yishuv* to full cooperation with
England in the war effort and to resistance to the British
authorities on the question of illegal immigration. Every
young man in Palestine had to be made to understand that
bringing in a ship of refugees at night, despite British arms,
and enlisting in the British Army were part of the same struggle. In the period before the British agreed to a Jewish bri-

[113]

gade, it was not simple to effect a reconciliation between the love for Britain, the ally, and the hate for perfidious Albion. The fury against the Nazis overrode every other consideration, but the irony of fighting to help destroy Hitler while being forbidden to rescue Hitler's victims was not lost on the population.

Golda was actively involved on both fronts. As a member of the Histadrut executive she had to negotiate with the British Government on such questions as rationing, wages and health services. She was invited by the government to become a member of the War Economic Advisory Council whose functions were to maintain contact between the government and the public in all matters relating to the war economy of Palestine, to secure the fullest public cooperation in economic measures, and to consider questions of production and distribution. In the midst of these daily activities she was also one of the most passionate campaigners for the recruitment of Jewish volunteers. Immediately after the outbreak of the war, the Jewish Agency (a body officially set up to represent Jews in Palestine and abroad in all negotiations with the British administration) and other representative bodies of the Jewish community in Palestine issued a proclamation urging enlistment in the war effort, whether in the army, the navy or industry. The Histadrut made a similar appeal to its members. Since there was no conscription in the country, a decision was adopted to exclude from the Histadrut anyone not abiding by the ruling of the authoritative institutions.

This wholehearted commitment did not prevent the government from questioning the motives of the tens of thousands of Jewish volunteers. At the Sirkin-Richlin Arms trial (September, 1943) during which two young Palestinians were accused of stealing arms from the British Army in order to turn them over to the Haganah, the prosecutor did not hesitate to suggest that one of the reasons for Jewish volunteering was the desire to obtain arms.

The records of the Sirkin-Richlin trial are of particular interest. It provided one of the first large-scale public opportunities to see Golda in one of her most effective aspects—that of facing the government with courage and candor, and yet remaining intellectually in command of the situation so as to prevent any blundering admission.

Q. *You are a nice, peaceful, law-abiding lady, are you not?*
A. *I think I am.*
Q. *And you have always been so?*
A. *I have never been accused of anything.*
MAJOR BAXTER: *Well, listen to this from a speech of yours on May 2, 1940 (reading out of a file): "We, the workers, will combat any appearances of Fascism. The whole Yishuv will join hands in fighting the White Paper. If the Revisionists interfere, we will fight them too. For 20 years we were led to trust the British Government but we have been betrayed. The Ben Shemen case is an example of this." Ben Shemen is where much arms were found, isn't it?*
A. *I do not know how many arms were found in Ben Shemen.*
Q. *Now listen to what you said on May 2, 1940: "We never taught our youth the use of firearms for offence but for defensive purpose only."*
A. *That is right.*
Q. *"And if they are criminals, then all the Jews in Palestine are criminals." What about that?*
A. *If a Jew who is armed in self-defense is a criminal, then all the Jews in Palestine are criminals.*
Q. *Were you yourself trained in the use of arms?*

A. *I do not know whether I am required to answer to that question. In any case I have never used firearms.*

Q. *Have you trained the Jewish youth in the use of firearms?*

A. *Jewish youth will defend Jewish life and property in the event of riots and the necessity to defend life and property. I, as well as other Jews, would defend myself.*

PRESIDENT OF THE COURT: *Please reply only to the questions.*

Q. *Do you remember what quantity of firearms was found in Ben Shemen?*

A. *I don't know.*

Q. *And if you had been asked in the middle of your speech how much arms were found in Ben Shemen, what would you have replied?*

A. *What I answered you.*

MAJOR BAXTER (*reading again from the C.I.D. file*): "*Macdonald and his friends are mistaken if they think they can do as they like with us. There are not enough prisons and concentration camps in Palestine to hold all the Jews who are ready to defend their lives and property.*" *Right?*

A. *If a Jew or Jewess who uses firearms to defend himself against firearms is a criminal, then many new prisons will be needed.*

Q. *Do you mean to say that there are many firearms?*

A. *There are many who are ready to defend themselves.*

Q. *Is the accused, Sirkin, known to you?*

A. *He is known to me. He is a member of the Histadrut.*

MAJOR BAXTER (*continuing to read from the C.I.D. file*): "*We must do all in our power to help the illegal immigrants. Britain is trying to prevent the growth and expansion of the Jewish community in Palestine, but it should remember that Jews were here 2,000 years before the British came.*"

Despite the heavy irony of Major Baxter's, "You are a nice, peaceful, law-abiding lady, are you not?" Golda's affirmative answer was not wide of the mark. In 1943, the Histadrut and

[116]

Mapai still opposed violence, except in immediate self-defense. The practice of *havlaga* (self-restraint) in the face of Arab terrorism had been a principle, as well as a tactic, during the bitter years of 1935 to 1940 when the youth of the land had been sternly trained not to reply to arson or bombs with counterterror. The notion of indiscriminate punishment, of mass retaliation which might strike the innocent rather than the guilty, had been completely alien to the moral pacesetters of the *Yishuv*. A questioning of these values was to take place, set into motion by the crematoria and accelerated by the battle for independence, but at the time that Golda appeared before the Jerusalem military court she was as honestly concerned with justifying the means as the end.

Her proud declaration in regard to the members of the Haganah, "If they are criminals, then all the Jews in Palestine are criminals," stirred the community. This was what they liked about Golda—her ability to face the British authorities unabashed and yet without histrionics. The British respected her. The most snobbish among them were impressed by her natural dignity, and if they ever failed in the civility due a representative of the *Yishuv*, she calmly insisted on a retraction.

Encounters with the British were soon to change in character. Since 1942, Palestine had known of the Nazi extermination program. The reaction of this small community of 600,000 was unique and immediate. While the rest of the world contented itself with diplomatically couched remonstrances or mournful protest meetings, the Jews of Palestine were obsessed with the notion that they had a direct responsibility for the fate of the doomed 6,000,000. The minutes of the *Vaad Ha-Poel* and of the various party conferences record debates in which proposals for rescue were discussed, proposals which entailed the participation of Palestinians. At a meeting of the executive committee of Mapai (November 1943), Golda declared: "There is no Zionism save the rescue of Jews." This dynamic conception, by which Zionism became not only the means of securing a shelter for the rescued but the major instrument of rescue, became a popular slogan repeated in the Diaspora, acted upon by the *Yishuv*.

One of the meetings of the *Vaad Ha-Poel* was particularly affecting. One afternoon in April 1943, while the executive council was in session, a message came through from the Warsaw ghetto. The ghetto fighters wanted to know if the leaders of the Labor movement in Palestine advised them to make a last stand. Golda remembers the meeting as one of the most difficult days of her life. The members of the *Vaad Ha-Poel* harbored few illusions about the chances of the ghetto's success against the Nazi tanks and planes. At the same time, they could not repress the desire that somewhere in the Nazi hell Jews should die fighting instead of letting themselves be herded to the gas chambers. The men and women sitting around the long tables believed in resistance whatever the price, but how could they tell others to go to immediate death? As Golda put it: "How could we in Tel Aviv tell them to die?" But as the heavy-hearted debate dragged on, the radio gave the news: the Warsaw ghetto had risen.

Three years later Zivia Lubetkin, one of the heroines of the ghetto and one of the few survivors of its last stand, was welcomed by the *Vaad Ha-Poel* in the same room where its members had helplessly debated possible courses of action. Golda was one of those who addressed the slim dark girl whose name had become legendary in the annals of Jewish

[118]

martyrdom. She tried to convey what she and her comrades had felt on that day in April when the Warsaw ghetto was going down in flames:

> Zivia, friends say that you don't like speeches and receptions. I understand this but don't be angry with us. You cannot take it ill if a family feels the need to express the emotion which wells up in the presence of the one member that has been saved. We feel the need to tell you somehow, in some fashion, how we lived during these six years cut off from you. Word came from you now and then that you did not understand your isolation, our failure to reach you. Perhaps a suspicion that we were living at ease, that we were making inadequate efforts to bore our way to you, stole into some of your hearts.
>
> I don't know how to tell you how often we sat in this room throughout these terrible years consumed with only one thought and desire—to make a bridge from us to you, to give you a sign that we were one, to reach you with some act of salvation. To ease our hearts in those years we sought comfort in the idea that your last stand was the outcome of a road we had traveled together; we linked it in spirit to the stands we had made in Palestine at various times. We knew that we were the disciples of one movement, we, the parents, and you, the children, but on that day we felt that the parents were unworthy of the children.

Her words to Zivia were recorded in the minutes of the *Vaad Ha-Poel*, reflecting the *Yishuv's* unceasing search to find a means of help, but no substantial action for Hitler's survivors could be taken till the close of the war. The refusal of Bevin's Labour Government to let Jews enter the national home even after Germany's defeat, set into motion the rebellion against Britain's rule.

I arrived in Palestine in the fall of 1945. Six years had elapsed since I had seen Golda in Geneva. Now I found her at the center of the resistance movement which was beginning to take shape. I also saw the inner revolution that was accompanying the outer. The transformation from Palestinian to Israeli was psychological as well as political.

When Ben-Gurion first announced that Zionism, in view of Britain's White Paper policy, had to concentrate on the withdrawal of the mandatory power and the immediate establishment of a Jewish state, most of his listeners applauded a good speech. When, however, he outlined the steps for the immediate implementation of this program, many thought that the line between vision and lunacy had been crossed. All the clever people pointed out with varying degrees of irony and consternation that the mighty Jewry of Palestine was hardly in a position to challenge the British Empire, the Anglo-American oil interests, and all the Arab states of the Middle East. The thesis was not difficult to demonstrate.

Ben-Gurion shaped Palestine's struggle. The small, stubborn man with the powerful head set the objectives and planned their execution. Logically, the Ben-Gurion "line" extended back to the beginning of the century when a handful of zealots, Ben-Gurion among them, first settled in the marshes of the Emek with the intention of transforming them into a homeland. In this vision he had not been unique. From that point the line evolved, with no startling leaps, for nearly forty years. There had been debatable issues throughout the period, but the basic departure in the point of view represented by Ben-Gurion did not make itself felt sharply till much later. The difference between him and such men as Weizmann lay not in eventual goals but rather in the ways of achieving them. But Ben-Gurion insisted that a nebulous desire for a Jewish state in some convenient decade was not the same thing as a plan to achieve a Jewish state within a specific calendar year, and that the difference involved objectives as well as means.

The first sharp break in questions of policy came in 1945 in regard to the *ma'avak* (the fight). Not only the community as a whole but the entire Labor movement, including the Mapai of which Ben-Gurion was the head, was split by the question of "activism," the use of force to oppose the British. The notion of an open physical conflict was alien to the psychology of the *Yishuv*, as well as frightening. There was little enthusiasm when the decision, duly voted on by party councils, was taken. Speaking at the funeral of the first victims, Golda sternly declared: "We have no alternative," and those words became the slogan under which the struggle advanced from the first bringing in of illegal ships amid the fire of British cruisers to the declaration of a Jewish state.

Ma'avak assumed fresh forms month by month. In its first stages, conflict with the British was limited to the bringing in of immigrants. Palestine rejoiced in passive resistance and bloodless engagements. When refugees detained by the British at the camp of Athlit were freed by the Haganah without loss of life, the *Yishuv* sang the glory of such a victory. Not only the appalling odds alarmed the *Yishuv*. The tradition of a people's army, devoted to defense and averse to bloodshed save for defense, was deeply ingrained. This frame of mind was to change, but the change did not come easily. The ramifications of the struggle increased till *ma'avak* became war. And every development which intensified or altered the nature of the conflict was attended with the same arguments as the first apprehensive step.

The struggle in Palestine had its counterpart in a phenomenon in Europe which had been given the name of *bricha* (flight). The surge of the Jewish survivors in Europe to the

DP camps, there to wait for the final flight to Palestine, was as much a part of the battle for the Jewish state as events in Palestine. Their anguished drive toward Palestine was instinctive, requiring no stimulation. But the harnessing of this force by Palestinian emissaries to the DP camps was conscious strategy. The despair of the survivors was not permitted to decline into a blank acceptance of any fate or to dissipate itself in futile searches for any haven. The DP's emotional fixation on Palestine became an explosive force which finally sprang the gates open; this energy had to be channeled and directed. The risk of *bricha* was in its way as great as that of *ma'avak*.

The flight to the DP camps began before the passage of the United Nations resolution calling for the establishment of a Jewish state. There was no assurance that the international atmosphere would improve. On the contrary, the reports of postwar commissions sent to study the Palestine problem were increasingly discouraging. The terrible prospect that Jewish survivors would rot indefinitely on German soil appeared not unlikely. It took a fierce faith to continue to feed the flame of Zion as the third winter in the bleak barracks dragged on.

The "We have no alternative" psychology sprang from an overwhelming sense of international betrayal. Jews were alone. Even as late as 1945, Jewish Palestine still nurtured the illusion that justice would follow upon knowledge. People in responsible positions naively believed that if the world press, instead of a few Zionist journals, informed the huge reading public of the wonders of Jewish achievement in Palestine and of the tragedy of the Jewish survivors, then the end of World War II would see the fulfillment of the pledge made at the end of World War I. Even the astonish-

ing calm with which the world had accepted the murder of
6,000,000 Jews failed to dissipate this conviction. Perhaps
mankind had not adequately been shaken by the murder
factories because these were too monstrous for credence. But
the realities of Palestine had beauty and nobility.

Inevitably there followed a deep disillusionment with a
world to whose conscience so many passionate and vain
pleas had been addressed. The Nuremberg trials gave plenty
of publicity to Nazi abominations but Jews continued to
languish in DP camps. The British Labour party had plenty
of knowledge about the rights of the Zionist case, as their
spokesmen had eloquently attested, but it was under their
aegis that the doors of Palestine were closed to Jewish survivors. And finally the United Nations was amply informed
of the full-scale Arab invasion in defiance of its decisions, but
the threat of sanctions was never raised till the Jews were
getting the upper hand. The deduction from such reflections
was clear: neither the plaudits nor the blame of the outsider
matter. On the basis of its experience, Israel developed a
somber self-sufficiency.

In 1947, the Jews of Palestine still followed the deliberations at the United Nations with a religious hope. They
greeted the passage of the partition resolution with a rapture
unique in modern Jewish history. But after months of lonely
battle, they took only a casual interest in the discussions at
Paris or Lake Success, convinced that in the last analysis
they would be left with only as much as they could defend
with their blood and that the only decision likely to be observed would be that of arms.

Israel became more than a continuation of Jewish Palestine. It evolved into something new. The dreamy goose of
socialist visions, international hopes and Zionist idealism had

hatched an eagle. A few years earlier I had understood the men and women whose vocabulary teemed with abstract nouns and who kept obstinately calling on mankind in the name of righteousness and humanity. Those were the kind of Jews I had always known, except that in Palestine they were arduously engaged in practicing their preaching.

The visionaries lost some of their dreams. They learned that to build a city on a sand dune, like Tel Aviv, or to plant a rose garden by the salty shores of the Dead Sea, or to terrace the stony mountains of Jerusalem, was not enough. Thirty years of pioneer heroism proved to be less convincing than six months of soldiery. No people had clung so stubbornly to the faith that a cause would prevail by the force of merit as the people of the Bible in the land of the prophets. But the process of illumination begun in the crematoria was completed by the debates in the United Nations. The cynicism of the proceedings was not lost on a single housewife or adolescent in Israel. If the tiny state could demonstrate that it could repulse six Arab armies abetted by the British Empire, then it was eligible for membership in the gang.

The *Yishuv* learned to say bitterly: "Our future depends on our strength." In any other land, among any other people, the sentiment would have been banal. One has to appreciate in what spirit the youth of Palestine had been reared to appreciate the significance of the change.

I remember a Passover ceremony at the large collective settlement of Ein Harod in 1933. The Seder did not strictly follow the traditional pattern. One of the innovations was the addition of unfamiliar questions to the usual four *kashes* (questions). One child asked why there were rich and poor in the world, and was informed that the trouble lay in an unjust economic system which the cooperative society of

[124]

Ein Harod strove to rectify. There were other questions in a similar vein. A child asked: "Why do the Arabs live on hills and we in a valley?" (Ein Harod is in the Valley of Esdraelon.) The answer given was characteristic. "Since we think only of peace and of reclaiming the soil, we are not afraid of settling in a valley."

The children who heard this answer grew up to be the youths who had to storm the heights of Kastel along the road to besieged Jerusalem, and the elders who had taught them marveled at their exploits and rejoiced in their victories.

In the mass of the people there grew the conviction that since the fate of Palestine—which included the fate of DP's in Europe and Cyprus—primarily depended on their single-handed achievements rather than on any international instruments of justice, many so-called reasonable considerations no longer made sense. There was no point in meditating on the fact that 600,000 Jews were fewer than 40,000,000 Arabs and no match for the British Empire. Rational misgivings based on the astronomic disparity of the opposing forces could only be indulged in if common sense offered any program save certain suicide. To the majority of the *Yishuv,* no such program appeared feasible. Surrender to British and Arab terms meant writing *finis* to the Jewish national home. Since there was no choice, calculation—whether in regard to arms or men—became a luxury that the Jews of Palestine could not afford. Once they started to employ the terminology of size and numbers, they would be paralyzed into inactivity. Many a good Zionist in the United States went around panic-stricken as he meditated on 600,000 versus millions. By no stretch of the imagination did it appear to be a fighting chance. But the *Yishuv* instinctively chose the course of salvation.

Of necessity, the formula was grotesquely simple: act as would any people whose life was threatened. The important thing was not that the group was small but that it was a nation. The assumption of nationhood could offer no resistance against defeat, but could release the necessary spiritual energy. The essence of Zionism had always been that Jews in their torment should act, not like helpless people but like *a* people. Every pioneer settlement in Palestine testified to this faith. Now the act of faith, the *auto-da-fé*, had come.

Once the formula had been accepted, the line became clear. A nation did not permit a foreign power to close its borders. A nation fought back invaders as best it could. A nation went to the rescue of its persecuted members. Above all, a nation which had before it no alternative save extinction could not permit itself to reckon whether tanks could be repulsed with hand grenades or tramp boats be intercepted by cruisers.

Suddenly a subtle and hyperintellectual people, given to endless ratiocination even in its phantasies, dropped all the if's, however's and therefore's with which its vocabulary Talmudically abounded, and with insane directness dashed forward toward an apparently impossible goal. True, the Jews of Palestine had by choice been men of action devoted to the practical realization of their dreams from the outset. But even the famous cult of Labor had been bolstered by essays of Gordon and echoes of Tolstoyanism. Now the people was behaving as if it had less than its share of high I.Q.'s.

MA'AVAK

IN 1945, this psychological transformation was just beginning. At a Mapai caucus, at a Histadrut conference, or informally over a cup of tea in Golda's apartment overlooking the Mediterranean, arguments were waged pro and con physical resistance to the British. Astonishingly many of the misgivings were ethical as well as tactical. There were quite as many discussions as to whether it was morally right to use violence against the mandatory power in order to bring in refugees as there were about the feasibility of the course. The Labor movement was particularly concerned that its policies should be neither confounded with nor contaminated by terrorism. The problem was how to be effective without resorting to the excesses of the terrorist Irgun or the Stern Gang, dissident paramilitary groups which had broken away from the Haganah. In the *Yishuv* there was practically unanimous agreement about the propriety of using force to bring in immigrants or to establish new settlements on empty land belonging to the Jewish National Fund. When Kfar Giladi or another kibbutz opposed the entry of British soldiers come to search for illegal immigrants, mass demonstrations in Palestine declared: "The whole *Yishuv* is Kfar Giladi." When the police attempted to search a quarter of Tel Aviv where immigrants without certificates were supposed to be hiding, residents stopped buses going through the section and asked for the assistance of all able-bodied men to protect the immigrants from seizure. Any illegal ship that managed to evade the British would be sure of the help of almost all of the *Yishuv*. "Almost," because inevitably there were groups who discovered ideological reasons to mask a normal desire for a quiet life undisturbed by active intervention in behalf of the survivors of German death camps.

For the majority, real heart searchings began as the struggle developed, culminating in acts of resistance less obviously connected with the preservation of human rights— such acts of sabotage designed to interfere with British troop movements as the mining of railroads or the burning of boats used to intercept illegal ships. The fear that any act of resistance not directly allied to immigration or the settlement of new points might degenerate into vandalism or indiscriminate reprisal was repeatedly voiced. More than once there were warnings that the line of demarcation between various kinds of violence could not be kept. For many sensitive spirits, the fear that the Haganah, the secret defense force of the *Yishuv*, might become like the Irgun was more oppressive than the likelihood that it was no match for the British. Golda was in the midst of this moral conflict.

Her apartment in a workers' cooperative house in Tel Aviv faced the sea. Three flights up, it was a delightful refuge in the hot months despite the long bus ride to reach it from the center of the city. In 1945, Histadrut executives had no automobiles, and even a taxi was an occasional luxury. During the rainy season in winter, the unheated apartment was often bitterly cold, but Golda, like most Palestinians, was adamant if not persuasive on the subject of the comfort wrought by small electrical heaters and warm clothing.

By now Golda and Morris were separated with no further attempts at reconciliation. She lived in a four-room apartment with her children and a friend, Leah Biskin. Although the front room in which Menachem industriously practiced on the cello was a bedroom at night, and although Golda slept on a couch in the living room, the apartment was always neat and uncluttered. Because of frequent bouts of ill health in the past years, she now had a Yemenite cleaning woman who came once a week to do the heavy scrubbing and washing, but the daily chores fell to Golda.

On Friday when the *Vaad Ha-Poel* closed early in preparation for the Sabbath, Golda baked and cooked like any good Tel Aviv housewife. Exhausted by a harrowing week of crucial decisions, conferences and public meetings, she still stirred the batter, seasoned the carp or carefully ironed a white blouse which she had washed the night before. The egalitarian concepts of the Histadrut allowed for no such luxuries as adequate domestic help for its chief executives. Golda knew that when her masculine colleagues came home after a strenuous day and evening they were not expected to shop, cook and clean the house. Nor did they mend and iron for a family. A wife, sister or mother presided over these activities. To that extent, feminine equality was proving a one-sided affair with double the responsibility and half the perquisites. But in fairness, none of her distinguished male comrades was tempted to bake a cake or stuff a carp. Golda, on the other hand, found it relaxing to stand in the kitchen pre-

paring a meal for the family after a turbulent day. On Friday
night and all day Saturday unannounced guests kept dropping in, and Golda was busy most of the Sabbath, clearing
away dishes and serving more tea and cake as new guests
arrived.

Each weekend Golda's intimates remonstrated. It seemed
reasonable that she should cook for them, but why all the
company? Let Golda indicate that she was not running a
hotel; she was entitled to a few hours of peace and quiet. She
listened to the remonstrances as though in agreement and
then pointed out that friends from America could not be
turned away nor could a *haver* who had just come from Ein
Harod, nor the several solitary women who lived alone and
had no family with whom to spend the Sabbath, and if in the
midst of the sociability an unexpected consultation had to be
held with some members of the party who had arrived for
the purpose, should she show them the door?

The days when the British declared a curfew were among
the most restful. No one could leave the house and no one
could come in. There would be a few quiet hours of catching
up with mending and ironing. On such days of home-arrest
Golda might carefully turn a skirt, resewing it so that the
shiny surface would be on the inside. But the tranquility was
illusory. She was either receiving or giving directives by
telephone, and her apartment, with its view of the sea and
beach, was ideally located for the observation of incoming
ships and consequently was one of the centers for directing
illegal immigration.

Though the general character of the illegal activities and
the identity of their presumed leaders were known both to
the authorities and to the Jewish community, the strictest
precautions had to be taken about specific operations. Even

parents and children were careful to keep their assignments secret from each other, despite the harmony of their purposes. One day Golda was secretly engaged in composing an English leaflet about the ill-fated, illegal ship *Struma,* for the benefit of the British soldiers who might be won to compassion for the unfortunates they were driving back. A day later Sara, her thirteen-year-old daughter, a member of the youth group of the Haganah, left the house at dawn without offering any explanations. Subsequently Golda discovered that her daughter had left so mysteriously in order to paste on walls and billboards the leaflets Golda had written. This kind of discretion was practiced in many a Palestinian household. The *sabras* (native-born youths) refused to be impressed by the fact that their parents might be the chief figures in the resistance. If the eighteen-year-old head of a group commanded silence, Ben-Gurion himself might inquire in vain.

The country was in a state of creative tension. Every time a handful of Haganah boys scored a "victory" against the British Empire, and every time a funeral was held for two or three settlers fallen in defense of their kibbutz, it was a major event. Glory or calamity could be found in the fate of one man as well as in that of a thousand. In the anonymous world of mass destruction, this pinpoint in Palestine was stubbornly behaving as though an individual mattered. It was an extraordinarily moral affirmation for a small Jewish community to make among the ashes of the crematoria.

The spirit was contagious. A few years later the Arab invasion aroused a new martial spirit. However, this first stage in the transformation of the *Yishuv* was marked by a moral fervor, a scrupulous examination of means as well as ends that was to remain singular in the postwar world. Probably no rebellion in history had been accompanied by so many proclamations, speeches and theoretical expositions. The *Yishuv* had to understand, the British Tommy had to understand, and the various countries of the Diaspora had to be enlightened about every particular act. If the Haganah blew up a British installation, a warning was sent to enemy headquarters half an hour earlier so that there would be no needless loss of life. In contrast, Irgun terrorism had to be denounced at home and abroad. Nothing could just happen without exegesis.

As an exponent of the struggle and as a practical organizer of some of its facets, Golda was in the forefront. No one except those directly involved ever knew the details of a proposed action, whether it was bringing in a refugee ship or blowing up a British military installation. Although intimates were sufficiently well disciplined not to inquire, her role of leader and tribune was public enough.

I had known Golda on and off for years. I had always considered her strong, capable, and an excellent speaker. But till that winter when I went to Palestine to collect material for a book about Jewish resistance to the Nazis, I had no conception of the moral force which she represented. I permit myself to write personally because it seems the most direct way of communicating the impression she made. She became the spokesman of Palestine's struggle, not because of superior eloquence—Palestine teemed with orators as any party conclave could demonstrate—but because of temperament and character, a union of intellectual directness and moral elevation which so desperate a cause required.

At party conferences the fight raged between the activists and their opponents. The antiactivists included some of the best brains in the Labor movement, men whose personal devotion to Palestine had been thoroughly tested by years of sacrifice. Their warnings against a suicidal *Masada* psychology had the ring of reason. *Masada*, the heroic last stand of the Jews against Rome, had meant final obliteration. Better to preserve what had been achieved, even on ignominious British terms, than to court complete destruction. Perhaps another turning point in history would allow further advance. In the meantime, cherish the gains. Such arguments made sense. Their origin was not ignoble. The antiactivists were as deeply motivated by the love of Palestine, as deeply concerned for the Jewish future, as the activists. Nor were their views lightly dismissed, for they voiced doubts which the most passionate of the activists shared. Before the majority was won to a resolution proclaiming *ma'avak* as the policy of the Labor movement, there was the most rigorous heart searching. At a great gathering of the Histadrut in Haifa, representatives of the several constituent parties, delegates of the small and large kibbutzim, discussed the certain hazards and possible successes. Was there not the danger of being intoxicated by one's own slogans: "We will open the gates" or "Down with Britain"?

The leader of the activists was of course Ben-Gurion. He had conceived the policy, and he was its theoretician and promulgator. No matter how fundamentally romantic his vision, he used the terminology both of the philosopher of history and of the astute diplomat. Such and such were the historical forces. The time had come for England to withdraw and for Jewish independence to be proclaimed. The only way to secure the Jewish state was to act as though you were the state—this meant assuming control of immigration and brooking no interference from authorities false to their trust. These general theses were developed by Ben-

Gurion with an apparent cold logic and precision that, for the unwary, obscured the fiery imagination from which they sprang. He had taken the temperature of history and had estimated that his program was not delirium. The prognosis was good when taken in the context of his world view, and the examination was made bearing in mind the past and future as well as the present. He persuaded his hearers of the practical wisdom of the course while calmly admitting the chance of failure.

Golda's power welled from another source. She lacked the scholarly equipment for the kind of semipolitical, semi-philosophic analysis on which Ben-Gurion embarked. Her argument was addressed to the moral sense of her hearers. When she declared: *"Ain lanu derech acheret,"* ("We have no other way"), she really meant *people such as we* have no other way. For of course there were other ways. At the same time, she did not belong to those who tended to minimize the risks. As she listened to some of the heedless proponents of *ma'avak*—speakers who apparently had no sense of the enormous dangers of such a policy—Golda arose and said: "I think that the Biblical injunction which bade soldiers with fear in their hearts to fall back should now be reversed. Only those with fear in their hearts should be for *ma'avak.*"

What were the other ways? Accept the crystallization of the Jewish national home at its present figure? Accede to the curtailment of immigration and the possibilities of land purchase and development? This meant that the *Yishuv*, instead of being the seed of the Jewish state, would shrivel into an impotent Jewish community lost among the multitudes of Asia. This was not Zionism. Just as to be a Zionist twenty-five years earlier had meant getting aboard the *Pocahontas*, so now to be a Zionist meant a refusal to accept the spiritual destruction of the homeland, which would in any case be followed by its physical destruction. The whittling away of the promise had to be resisted. Above all, could the *Yishuv* accept any compromise which betrayed the hopes of the survivors in the DP camps?

Given a certain moral atmosphere, the questions answered themselves. It was Golda's unique genius as a speaker to create a climate in which simple moral truths assumed the force of the self-evident. She was of course not alone in this attitude. She expressed the dominant mood of the *Yishuv*. In every kibbutz, village and town of Palestine, men and women were engaged in similar discussions, persuading the timid or the clever.

In these early months of the struggle there was a solemnity, a sense of final decisions and commitments, which was never to come again as purely. The people knew that whether they failed or prospered the days of the utopian community which dreamed of eternal peace and a new world order were over. The visionaries, who had dropped pens for plows, would now have to beat plowshares into swords. Such had not been the dream. At the funeral of a settler killed during a British search of the kibbutz Givat Hayim, Golda looked out for a moment at the rows of rustling trees, the new white buildings of Ain Shemer where the corpse lay, and voiced what everyone felt: "We have hated death, we are for life . . . but we have no choice. . . ."

Throughout this period Golda was ill frequently. The magnificent constitution which had been her birthright had taken its fill of punishment. Acute gall-bladder attacks, sudden nervous collapses and other alarming symptoms were frequent. When the doctors of the *Kupat Holim* warned her that a continuance of her pace might be fatal, she answered cheerfully, "A lot of us die at around fifty." It was true. The tempo of life in Palestine was not conducive to longevity, but then, as Golda remarked, the halutzim had not come for a rest cure.

During these bouts, if they were not severe enough for hospitalization, she lay completely prostrated on the living-room couch which served as a bed at night. The problem was to get her to agree to stay in bed the next day if the pain subsided. But "tomorrow" might hold a meeting with the high commissioner in Jerusalem or some other mission whose nature she did not disclose. I would say weakly, "But, Golda, you'll lose more time in the end." Her son Menachem would remonstrate furiously: "She's killing herself"; her friend Leah Biskin would come in and mutter something derogatory about her general intelligence. But we all knew that if she were capable of motion, she would get up for tomorrow's business.

One of Golda's friends, deploring her recklessness, appealed to Freud: "Perhaps she is motivated by an unconscious suicidal impulse. Her personal life is complicated and troubled; this may be her way out." Such hypotheses had best be left to the psychoanalyst. So many of the figures of the Second and Third *Aliyah* displayed a similar disdain of the body and its needs that one must view the trait as common to the breed. Not that these men and women were ascetics; the body was to be used abundantly in joy or labor, but one could not be its slave via regimens, pills or prolonged rests.

I have often wondered whether the British had any inkling as to how young, how ill-prepared and ill-armed were their antagonists. My occasional glimpses of the "soldiers," boys and girls of the Haganah, would give me the uneasy feeling

[136]

that I had wandered into the junior class of the local high school. The contingent of adolescents became in time a skilled and effective fighting force, but in the early formative stage—the period when the Haganah went from defensive to offensive action—the mixture of valor, improvisation and juvenility sometimes had an *opéra-bouffe,* as well as a tragic, quality. A brief contact with the "underground" gave me a notion of how casually important enterprises sprang into being.

One evening Golda mentioned the fact that a secret radio station was to be started. It would be called *Kol Israel* (the Voice of Israel). Its purpose would be to keep the *Yishuv* informed despite British censorship and to present the Jewish side of the struggle to the British soldiers and the Arabs. For this reason the broadcasts would be given in Hebrew, English and Arabic. The number of English-speaking people in Tel Aviv who could be entrusted with such a broadcast was limited at that time, so I offered to do the English broadcast. Now conspiracy began. I was told that someone would contact me in my room the next day. Sure enough, the next day an old acquaintance, Katriel Katz, turned up. It seemed he was in charge of the proposed radio. The broadcasts would be made from various apartments in the heart of the city. The place would be shifted from day to day to confuse the British. The broadcast had to be completed, the set dismantled and the participants out of the house, within a given number of minutes. A longer period would give the British a chance to pinpoint the place of origin and surround the house. If our precautions should fail and British police arrived, I need not worry. The entire block of the apartment house would be patrolled by Haganah boys who would sound a warning whistle in good time. The boys would at once hide the set and run to the roof. "Don't worry about them," said my adviser, "they are limber." I didn't quite see myself leaping over roofs, so I ventured to ask, "What about me?" My friend assured me that this, too, had been arranged. It was taken for granted that a middle-aged American lady would not be able to scamper along the rooftops. Should we be caught, I was to go into the living room of the apartment from which the broadcast would originate. The family would be sitting, drinking tea, and I would explain to the British that I was a visitor—an aunt or a cousin. No, I suggested, just a visitor who knows nothing of the goings on in the next room.

The text had to be composed on the morning of the broadcast so that fresh news could receive immediate comment and evaluation. It had to be meaty yet passionate, because our purpose was to sway as well as to inform. I found myself holding out for a little more sobriety in the appeals to the moral sense of the Tommies. Finally, we would hammer out something that pleased all tastes.

The day of the first broadcast was—I can think of no brighter word—memorable. This was my first, belated taste of conspiracy, and the preliminary preparations were surrounded by a suitable aura of mystery. I was to be called for by a young man I knew. He was to go with me by taxi to a central part of the city. There I was to go with still another lad to the house from where the broadcast would originate.

I did not share the general conviction that we would not be caught. I understood precious little about the techniques involved, but I had a notion that the great British Army, equipped with radar and what not, would certainly be able to detect the handful of youthful amateurs with whom I was involved. In any case, I would be prepared for the horrors of an unsanitary Middle Eastern jail. My Palestinian heroes never knew that their American sympathizer went to each broadcast armed with a cake of soap and a wad of toilet tissue brought from the United States.

On the night of the first broadcast we went through the various stages outlined. I was dropped and picked up a number of times before we reached the "large" five-story apartment house in the heart of Tel Aviv. Later I was told that an apartment house was better than a private house for our purpose because the number of apartments was more confusing to the detector. So far everything had gone according to plan. But at the apartment itself, what seemed to me a serious deviation was taking place. The tenants, a nice couple with a child, got ready to leave as soon as we came. Apparently they had not taken kindly to the notion of drinking tea to cover up my presence in case of a British raid. Anyhow, they left unconcernedly. My young friends, three boys and a girl, looked even younger than any such young friends should look. In my agitation I judged them to be about sixteen years old, but they probably ranged all the way up to twenty. Moshe, who became my special friend, was definitely nineteen. I noticed, not without alarm, that no one in the group made a move to stop the hastily departing family, so I said, "Aren't they supposed to stay?" The leader assured me that it did not matter and that in any case I could go to the living room and sit there pretending to be a family friend if need be. The scheme did not sound fool-proof but it was hardly my place to argue. I could not afford to look more concerned than these children. Anyhow, there was no time. The boys rigged up the set in the bedroom, and in a few minutes Moshe was announcing, in his magnificent Hebrew: "This is the Voice of Israel, the voice of Jewish

resistance," words which would be heard regularly floating
through the streets of Tel Aviv and reaching remote kibbutzim in the months to come. Moshe also read the Arabic text.
Then came my English stint. The first broadcast was over.
We still had not changed our places when we heard a
knock at the front door. One of the boys quickly dismantled
the set and hid it in the room. There was another knock.
I clutched my soap and offered to depart to the living room.
But the boys, apparently forgetting the scheme, whispered:
"Don't move." There was another knock; I was waiting for
the boys to leap to the rooftops as I had been promised. Instead, one of them went to the door while we sat tensely in
the bedroom. It was one of our patrol with a message. There
were no British.

On subsequent occasions there was less ceremony. Moshe
and I would go directly to whatever apartment had been
chosen; there would be only one other person to assist in the
broadcast. The apartment tenants had one thing in common—they did not hang around for the proceedings. The
whole thing went with skill and celerity. The important thing
was to leave the premises as quickly as possible after the
broadcast. The blond Moshe seemed completely at ease
and sure of himself, but at the end of the broadcast he would
be covered with sweat. That was the only sign of nervousness
that I ever noticed. My contact with *Kol Israel* was short-
lived. After a few broadcasts a number of people recognized
my voice. That made me too dangerous an associate, but
Moshe carried on until the establishment of a powerful
station. The broadcasters were never caught.

Golda never mentioned the *Kol Israel* activities to me after
the first time. It was taken for granted that no one chattered

or confided. The population showed amazing discipline.
My landlady, a simple-minded woman, was indiscreet
enough to ask me who the boys were who came to see me.
(I continued assisting in the preparation of the texts for
the broadcast.) Her husband silenced her at once. "One
does not ask silly questions." My brief experience enabled
me to see how complete was the involvement of the community. The good citizens who loaned the use of their apartments were jeopardizing their welfare despite their calculated departure during the broadcasts. Almost every family in the country was somehow involved in the rebellion.
For the first time in my life I was in a situation where
political activity was not confined to a vocal minority but
was the direct concern of every citizen. No doubt the small,
homogeneous character of the *Yishuv* made this possible.
(Years later I met Katriel Katz again. He was Consul General of Israel in New York City.)

As *ma'avak* developed, the Anglo-American Committee of
Inquiry—another one of those commissions that were perennially examining the vexing Palestine problem—arrived to
hold hearings in Jerusalem. Golda was the representative
of the Histadrut. Of her appearance at the hearings on March
25, 1946, the Palestine *Post* wrote:

> With her direct approach to the essence of the Jewish prob-
> lem, her assumption that it was understandable and human,
> and in her clear and unevasive replies, Mrs. Golda Myerson,
> the only woman to testify before the Inquiry Committee in
> Jerusalem yesterday morning dispelled the uncomfortable
> court-room atmosphere, the irritation and the boredom that
> had latterly prevailed. The Committee and audience listened
> with keen attention to the witness who represented the His-
> tadrut.

As usual, Golda spoke extemporaneously. She told the commission:

Gentlemen, I am authorized on behalf of the close to 160,000 members of our federation to say here in the clearest terms, there is nothing that Jewish labor is not prepared to do in this country in order to meet and accept large masses of Jewish immigration. Otherwise our life here, too, becomes senseless. What it meant to us to be only a short distance away from the *Struma,* to see hundreds of Jews who fled from a place where they could not live go down to the depths of the sea and we were helpless to save them!

We have many grievances against the Government. . . . But the chief accusation that we have against Government is that the policy of the White Paper forced us to sit here helpless at a time when we were convinced we could have saved hundreds of thousands, and if only tens of thousands, if only one Jew! We are convinced that Jews went to their deaths because they were not allowed to come into the country where they could have been saved. . . .

I don't know, gentlemen, whether you who are fortunate enough to belong to the two great democratic nations, the British and the American, can, with the best of your desire to understand our problems, realize what it means to be a member of a people that is forever being questioned, not on problems that have to be solved from time to time, but in regard to its very existence, its very right to be what it is. . . . Together with the young and old in the DP camps, the mass of Jewish laborers in this country have decided, because they have no other way out, *within our generation,* to do away with this helplessness and lack of security and dependence upon others. We only want that which is given naturally to all peoples of the world, to be masters of our own fate, only of *our* fate, not of others and in cooperation and friendship with others. . . .

The commissioners were particularly interested in Arab wage standards and labor conditions, and Golda had to give a detailed account of these relevant matters. But the questioning in regard to basic political issues continued. Dr. Aydelotte, an American member of the commission, asked: "If the Jews could have the same privileges as a minority that you promised the Arabs as a minority, would they be content?"

Golda answered: "No, sir, because there must be one place where Jews are not a minority. I believe that the Jews have come to this situation of helplessness and persecution and lack of dignity in their lives as Jews, not as individuals but as Jews, because of this curse of being a minority all over the world. There must be one place where their status is different."

On the question of immigration the dialogue was equally explicit:

Q. Your organization is in favour of large-scale immigration?
A. Unlimited.
Q. At once and unlimited?
A. Unlimited immigration.
Q. And at once?
A. Yes.
Q. Where would they be housed?
A. We have 600,000 Jews in Palestine. There is not a Jew alive in Palestine, I think I can say that with full authority, there is not a Jew in the city, there is not a settlement in agriculture, that would not throw its doors open and fill their houses and their settlements to capacity. Be it tents, be it barracks! We have housing plans and we are building.
Q. Do you think it would be possible to bring 100,000 Jews into Palestine this year?
A. There is no doubt in my mind.

Toward the end of the long hearing, the question of language came up:

Q. It is necessary to break down every kind of factor which tends to divide people. Now would you say Hebrew was helpful as a means of uniting workpeople in different countries? Take your experience at an International Labour Conference, for example.

A. If you will pardon me, probably this is an example of something I tried to make clear in my remarks. Hebrew is our language. May I say, for instance, if we come to an International Labour Conference the fact that somebody speaks another language besides Hebrew makes it difficult for us. Hebrew is our language, just as English is your language, just as French is the language of the French and Chinese the language of China. None of these probably would be questioned as to why they spoke their language.

Q. I am speaking of the poor Chairman of the Governing Body. Would you not think it a desirable thing that every child should be taught at least one language which has a chance of being international?

A. All our children are taught at least one language; in the higher schools they are taught at least two more languages, English and Arabic.

Q. So that in the future there may be a considerable increase in the use of an international language?

A. For international purposes, yes.

In conclusion, Judge Hutcheson asked where she had gotten her fluency in English. Golda answered: "I came from Milwaukee, Wisconsin."

The report of the Anglo-American Committee was not to be made public till May. In the meantime, illegal immigration was assuming a more desperate character. Great Britain was no longer content with trying to intercept ships when they reached the shore of Palestine. In April, because of British pressure, the old cargo boat *Fede,* carrying some hundreds of refugees, had been intercepted and held at the Italian port of La Spezia. The refugees had begun a hunger strike. At this point Palestine reacted with a characteristic and imaginative demonstration. Golda suggested that the leaders of the *Yishuv* engage in a hunger strike as a token of solidarity and protest. A session of the *Vaad Leumi,* the National Council of all Palestinian Jewry, under the chairmanship of David Remez, considered the suggestion and voted to declare a hunger strike. The participants were strictly limited to representatives of the various groups in the *Yishuv.* The fast was to have the solemnity of a religious rite, and only a chosen few could take part. The fasters had to be leading figures, not only because of the greater publicity value in terms of arousing world and British opinion, but also because the right to participate was a privilege earned by service. There was still another condition. The fasters had to be in good physical shape at the outset, so that they should not collapse too quickly. Each participant had to pass a medical examination.

Since Golda had just come out of the hospital after one of her sieges of illness, her physician refused the necessary permission. She was in no condition to undertake the fast. As the hunger strike had been her idea, she declared that she would fast privately at home. The doctor, thoroughly familiar with her stubbornness, decided it would be safer to have her under medical supervision with the rest of the group, and gave the certificate.

Another would-be faster of shaky constitution, Zalman Shazar, circumvented the medical examination by rushing to a gynecologist in Rehovoth, a close friend who interpreted well-being not only in physiological terms. Zalman, too, was able to present a medical certificate in time for the beginning of the fast. Two women besides Golda took part, Rachel Kagan, a representative of Wizo (the Women's International Zionist Organization), and Yehudith Simchonit of Mapai.

The fast was staged at the Jewish Agency building of Jerusalem, to insure its maximum impact on British officialdom. The fasters had separate rooms but during the first two days they met frequently for discussions. By the third day they grew weaker and took to reclining in their chambers for longer intervals.

A complication arose because Passover came on the third day of the fast. Chief Rabbis Herzog and Uziel came to the strikers with the demand that the fast be stopped lest the festival be desecrated since there was an injunction bidding every Jew to eat at the Seder. The group, most of them unorthodox, held another meeting and came up with a solution. According to the Law, the injunction could be met by eating a piece of matzoth the size of an olive. The strikers decided that they could hold a symbolic Seder, and yet not break the fast.

The Seder held that night had no dishes save the pieces of matzoth the size of an olive. Among the guests were Rabbis Herzog and Uziel. Ben-Zvi and his wife Rachel also came. Zalman, though hardly able to speak, read from a haggadah printed before the Jewish expulsion from Spain. The courtyard of the Jewish Agency was filled with throngs come to join in the Passover chants and to pray for the success of the fasters. The next day pious Jews wrapped in their prayer shawls came to recite the liturgy in the courtyard instead of

going to the Wailing Wall. The Passover had not been desecrated.

The fasters went out periodically to address the crowds in
the courtyard. None of them was young or physically fit
and their strength was failing. But Golda spoke of endurance,
and Zalman recited poetic passages from the Talmud.

On the night of the fourth day a telegram came from Har-
old Laski, who was conducting negotiations in Rome con-
cerning the release of the *Fede*. He urged the strikers to stop
fasting. Another meeting was held. Golda objected that informal promises were not enough. One had to wait for an
official government statement. Ben-Zvi dispatched a telegram to Laski asking for a government guarantee. In a few
hours the statement came. The fast, broken only by a glass
of tea without sugar twice a day, had lasted 104 hours. Zalman went to the hospital for three weeks in a state of collapse. The other strikers came off in better shape. The *Fede*
was released.

A curious echo of the fast was sounded in New York. On
the third day, members of the Zionist groups in the city decided that perhaps they, too, should join in the protest.
Despite many qualms, a decision was taken that representatives of the General Zionists, the Labor Zionists, Hadassah
and other groups, should emulate the Palestinians. Stephen
Wise volunteered at once. A committee went to make arrangements at the HIAS building, where the fasters would
repose in public lest the skeptical New York press accuse the
starving Zionist luminaries of snatching a secret sandwich.
It was a grandiose scheme; unfortunately, by the time all
the arrangements had been completed, the fast in Jerusalem had ended and New York lost the opportunity of see-

ing eminent American Zionists of all groups coming together at a fast instead of a banquet. When Golda heard of the abortive hunger strike, she voiced the sentiments of most Palestinians: "We thought there would be an instantaneous reaction. What efficiency!"

HEAD OF THE
POLITICAL DEPARTMENT

EVENTS were conspiring to force Golda into an unexpected role. On May 1, 1946, the Anglo-American Commission of Inquiry before which she had testified issued its report. It recommended the immediate entry into Palestine of 100,000 refugees, a recommendation accepted by the United States Government. A month and a half later, Ernest Bevin, who had pledged Britain's readiness to abide by the commission's recommendations, recanted on his promise. Britain's Foreign Minister issued a statement rejecting the proposal on the grounds that the entry of 100,000 Jews would require the dispatch of a British division to quell Arab disorders. This turnabout shattered the few remaining illusions of the *Yishuv* about the possibility of a peaceable settlement. Apparently the only way to convince Britain was to demonstrate that more divisions would be required to keep Jews out of Palestine than would be needed to let them in. To drive home the point, Haganah carried out a major military operation not directly connected with illegal immigration. At midnight on June 16, all frontier bridges throughout Palestine were blown up in a simultaneous operation. The land links between Palestine and neighboring countries were cut, and the British administration was paralyzed and isolated. It was a daring and effective coup.

The British were properly impressed and infuriated. At 10 Downing Street, the Cabinet, spurred on by Bevin, decided to crush Haganah and Jewish resistance. On Saturday, June 29, 1946, the British Army instituted mass raids throughout the country. The leaders of the *Yishuv* were imprisoned; the venerable Rabbi Maimon was forced to ride in a truck despite his pleas to be permitted to walk to the camp in order not to violate the Sabbath. The men and women of the settlements were penned in barbed-wire cages, to be searched and examined. Suspected activists were clapped into jail. The result was to strengthen the *Yishuv's* will to resist.

The male leaders of the *Yishuv*, including Moshe Sharett, the head of the political department of the Jewish Agency, were behind barbed wire in the detention camp of Latrun; Ben-Gurion had escaped arrest because he happened to be attending a conference in Paris. Friends of Golda went to her apartment in Tel Aviv as soon as the roundup began and implored her to go into hiding. It was assumed that she, too, would be arrested. But Golda declined to hide. "If they want me, they know where I am." However, the British did not arrest her. To Golda, this deference to her sex was a compliment more irritating than pleasing. Despite her objections to such discrimination, chivalry presumably prevented her arrest, though no such chivalry had been observed in the treatment of female settlers or refugees.

Latrun would probably have been easier for Golda than the situation in which she now found herself. She was chosen to be the acting head of the political department of the Jewish Agency during the period of Sharett's detention. This meant that for all practical purposes Golda served as the head of the political department in Jerusalem till the establishment of the state, because Sharett, upon his release from Latrun, went at once to the United States to take charge of the fight for the partition resolution in the United Nations.

Golda had not received the post by default. Though the top echelon of the *Yishuv's* leaders sat in Latrun, many able and experienced men were at large, not to mention many able women. That Golda was chosen for this awesomely responsible task, in preference to a number of brilliant and energetic men available, indicated what a commanding figure she had become. Now she was to be the representative not only of the Histadrut but of Jewish Palestine in all political negotiations with the mandatory power. Two men, now officials of the Israeli Government, who had been her close associates in her nearly two years of service as acting head, gave me an account of the doubts they had when she was appointed—misgivings shared by many of Golda's friends.

They worried about the fact that, unlike Ben-Gurion and Sharett, men of great and cosmopolitan learning, she was not a scholar. How would she be able to cope with complex and subtle political problems requiring a close knowledge of their historical background as well as of various contemporary ramifications? And there was something else. She was considered to be most effective as a spokesman to Jews, people who as friends or adversaries were passionately involved in the issue she presented. How would she react to an atmosphere of cold hostility conducted according to protocol? She was supposed to be emotional rather than logical; how would she take to the polite chill of diplomacy? Some of these questions prejudged the case. Those who had worked with her intimately in the previous departments which had been in her charge knew that the "emotional" woman had a gift for steady, precise work and clear thought which few could better.

The British never underrated Golda as an antagonist. In one of her first conversations with High Commissioner Cunningham about illegal immigration, she expressed her regret that she was the one to discuss the matter instead of one of the elected representatives now in Latrun. Cunningham assured her: "You are doing very well, Mrs. Myerson." In her relations with the British, her simple, proud Jewishness, stood out. The feminine excitability which had sometimes appeared at an intimate Histadrut meeting was never in evidence in the tense meetings with the British. There, pride kept her restrained. The decorum of the struggle was never stained by tears, even when she pleaded for the Jewish children interned on Cyprus.

In a conversation with Cunningham, the high commissioner stated that Sharett had been accused of grave derelictions. She replied, "If he is guilty, then I am equally guilty." Cunningham then suggested: "Perhaps you should be arrested, too?" to which Golda replied, "Perhaps."

This was an unequivocal exchange, but dealings with the British required tact as well as courage. As long as the power of imperial Britain ruled the land, it was the objective of political negotiation to minimize its weight. The less trouble with the mandatory the better. Less trouble meant fewer searches, curfews and arrests. Whenever the chief secretary summoned Golda for an unpleasant session of threats and remonstrances, she had to be both firm and diplomatic. The line between dignity and provocation had to be carefully watched so as not to invite needless reprisals. Golda unexpectedly showed an amazing skill in walking this tight-rope.

She instinctively knew when to disdain acrobatics. When Chief Secretary Gurney remarked amiably, "You know, Mrs. Myerson, if Hitler persecuted Jews, there must be some reason for it," Golda did not bother about exposition or persuasion. She arose and said brusquely, "That is how all anti-Semites talk," and walked out of the room. She refused to negotiate further with Gurney. Another member of the Agency, sent to continue the discussions, reported that Gurney had asked innocently: "Why is Mrs. Myerson so angry? I think very highly of her."

Her political work entailed close collaboration with the military leaders of the resistance. No military action of political significance could be taken without consulting Golda. Her post gave her considerable authority over Haganah, and local military commanders were expected to consult with her about all operations which involved policy. In the early stages, Haganah ordered its men not to resist arrest by the British, in order to avoid bloodshed. When in one instance the British threw boys who did not resist in front of the Damascus Gate to be murdered by Arabs, a change of instructions was indicated. The change of policy had to be referred to Golda.

There were also immensely delicate and explosive internal problems. It was essential to forestall, insofar as possible, some of the disastrous consequences of Irgun terrorism. To the British request that the *Yishuv* aid in the tracking down of terrorists, Golda had replied: "We will not become a nation of informers. We cannot make informers of six hundred thousand Jews, each watching his neighbor and friend and reporting what he thinks may be wrong with the person he

[153]

suspects." But whenever Haganah learned of some contemplated irresponsible act which would entail wanton loss
of life and serve no purpose except to inflame world public
opinion against the Jewish struggle, swift steps were taken
to prevent the mischief. Golda was involved in the plans to
thwart the proposed outrage without violating secrecy.

Still later, when the fighting with the Arabs started, she
had to share responsibility for grave military acts such as
the holding of Gush Etzion. Though besieged by the Arab
Legion and in a hopeless position, this bloc of settlements in
the mountains outside Jerusalem held out for several months
in order to engage part of the legion and give the capital time
to prepare. The stand of Gush Etzion helped save Jerusalem.

Her associates were surprised at the rapidity with which
she got her bearings in the specialized, often completely unfamiliar, tasks before her. One quality that stood her in good
stead was a complete lack of pretense. She was aware of the
limitations of her knowledge, and she knew how to ask for
advice and take it. It was one thing to declare: "We will resist," and another to weigh the political implications and
strategic feasibility of individual acts. She often had to assist
in determining which group of Haganah boys would go to
their probable deaths in a given action. She was sustained by
her native courage and capacity for decision. One of the men
who worked closely with her gave her independence of judgment a blanket endorsement: "She consults naturally. On the
whole she has the right measure of independence and the
ability to listen to people."

At the same time there was no letup in the public speeches
at mass meetings or demonstrations. The files of The Palestine *Post* and the Hebrew press for that period recorded
her amazing energy, doctor's orders notwithstanding.

Though she was now the head of the political department, she did not stop being the heart of the *Yishuv*. One day she was defending the Jewish right to arms after a British raid of a settlement: "To take away these arms actually means an invitation to destroy Ruhama for the third time. Ruhama was burnt down in 1929; the settlers were forced to leave again in 1936. We cannot give up these arms, because experience in the past gives us no assurance that in a time of trouble anyone else will guarantee our defense. . . . Jewish settlements have had arms since 1906 and none have ever been misused."

On another day she was at the fishing village of S'dot Yam, a settlement that had built invasion craft for the British Navy in 1942. Settlers arrested by the British had been released in time for the celebration of the village's tenth anniversary. Golda greeted them with the words: "If those who arrested you had come in friendship instead of with dogs, they would have seen what you have created from a stretch of waste sand. . . . the settlers of S'dot Yam understood that the sea could be a link as well as a barrier between the Jews of the Diaspora and the *Yishuv*."

Her inexhaustible power to feel, to be quickened instead of deadened by the multiplicity of outrages, was a gift she shared with many of the Palestinians whose increasing responsiveness to the Jewish tragedy was in inverse ratio to the heavy passivity with which it was met elsewhere. The men and women who listened to Golda never admired the speech as a "speech." But when she finished speaking, her listeners knew what they must do and they had the will to do it. The addresses of Ben-Gurion or Sharett made much richer reading, but there were moments of pain and resolution which no one could voice as vibrantly as Golda.

Golda Meir: Woman with a Cause

On August 12, 1946, the British Government announced that henceforth illegal immigrants caught in the waters of Palestine would be deported to Cyprus or "elsewhere." Two ships carrying a total of 1,300 refugees had just entered Haifa. The government, to forestall demonstrations, ordered a curfew, but 1,000 unarmed Palestinians converged on the port and tried to break through the barriers to prevent the deportation. Three lives were lost.

That week Golda was in Paris attending a meeting of the Jewish Agency executive, held there because Ben-Gurion was in danger of arrest if he returned to Palestine. The executive was considering a new British proposal. After declining to honor the recommendations of the Anglo-American commission, the British, with the cooperation of America, had come up with the Morrison-Grady plan, a federalization scheme to set up provinces or cantons in Palestine, one of them Jewish. The Agency executive in Paris rejected the plan on the grounds that it failed to provide independence and denied Jewish rights in 85 percent of the country. The executive took a still more significant step. It passed a secret resolution favoring the establishment of a Jewish state in a part of Palestine; in other words, partition. Ben-Gurion declared: "We must demand only one thing, and that is a Jewish state in Palestine or in a part of Palestine."

Nine years earlier, at the 1937 World Zionist congress which had considered a proposal of partition put forward by the royal commission, Golda had belonged to the fiery "nay-sayers" to whom the notion that Jews should accede to another truncation of Palestine (the original homeland of the Balfour Declaration had already lost two thirds of its territory through the lopping off of Trans-Jordan in 1923) was inconceivable. Both Weizmann and Ben-Gurion belonged to

the "yea-sayers" who favored partition, though for different
reasons: one out of weariness; the other out of a militant optimism. But in the changed world situation of 1946, it was
bold policy to demand a viable Jewish state in a part of Palestine; it was defeatism to consider further collaboration with
England, which was unmistakably committed to liquidating
the Balfour Declaration. Golda had learned a good deal
about *Realpolitik* in the past decade. Now she was for partition.

Questions of major policy were to be determined by the
twenty-second Zionist congress which met in December
1946, in Basel. It was the first congress since the end of the
war. The delegates had met last in August 1939, in Geneva.
Basel was frosty. The female delegates scurried around for
warm woolen underwear, but the congress had a chill which
no woolens could lighten. The great Jewries of Poland were
missing, represented only by a few DP's who had managed
to reach Switzerland from their camps.

There was an additional cause for gloom. The political
prospects of Palestine seemed to have reached their nadir.
The likelihood that the survivors penned in the DP camps
would reach Palestine or receive visas for other countries
seemed equally illusory. The only hopeful note was injected
by the activism of the Palestinians, but many of the sensible
American delegates who voted with them out of sympathy
guiltily feared that perhaps they were encouraging suicide.

I had not seen Golda since the winter before in Palestine.
She was addressing a Mapai caucus when I arrived with a
group of American Labor Zionists. We were late. I knew that
she noticed our entrance—late while Zion burned. That was
one of the difficulties of Golda for people like me. One's
trivial weaknesses no longer seemed trivial, and one's major

imperfections no longer appeared reasonably explicable. Almost every contact with her stimulated one's inferiority complex, not for the differences in achievement but for human failure on the levels where equality was possible. My embarrassment because I had needlessly come late to a meeting where urgent questions were being considered reminded me of an encounter with Henrietta Szold in my youth. In the course of the conversation I happened to say lightly, "I wish I were thinner." An innocuous remark, but Miss Szold's unexpectedly stern rejoinder was: "Wish for better things." These implacable women!

At the congress, I had occasion to observe Golda in the role of astute and resourceful party whip engaged in securing the passage of the resolutions which the activists of Mapai favored. The Zionist movement had reached the crossroads. It had to follow the path of Ben-Gurion or that of the moderates at whose head stood Weizmann. At the political committee of the congress, at the party caucuses, at the general debate, the Mapai leaders, Golda among them, battled over the phrasing of the political resolutions, fighting off the attacks of the moderates, the extremist revisionists and the leftist Hashomer Hatzair. She sat there hour after hour, unflagging, ready to pounce on some apparently trivial point, giving no quarter, hammering away at the opposition. The sources of this energy in her, in Remez, who held the chairmanship of the congress for a whole day and night without relief, in Sharett, now released from Latrun, in Ben-Gurion and others of the Palestinians, were unfailing.

The victory went to the activists, though the vote was close, 171 to 154. The congress voted not to participate in the London conference on Palestine called by the British, and it did not reelect Weizmann as president, because he was considered the chief proponent of compromise and collaboration with the British. Ben-Gurion remained the chairman of the executive, and the congress reaffirmed the demand for a Jewish state, which meant rejection of the Morrison-Grady plan.

It was a bleak, disheartening congress, one which saw the fall of the great figure of Weizmann. Its ambitious political objectives echoed hollowly in the large auditorium of Basel. How could they be realized? But in the press conference which Golda gave immediately after the congress, she declared: "Zionism and pessimism are not compatible." That seemed to be the answer.

From the congress I went directly to visit the DP camps in the American zone of Germany. There the resolutions of the congress had been accorded a terrifying reality. In every camp, I saw the Star of Zion with the somber figure 6,000,000 in its midst; sometimes there would be just the number 6. On every wall were the slogans of a militant Zionism: ON THE WAY or THE GATES WILL OPEN. Most poignant of all were the cold classrooms of the barracks where little children of all ages studied the geography of Palestine, which they called *"Arzenu,"* the Hebrew for "Our Land." They lived in *Arzenu's* air, they sang its songs, they spoke of their arrival in "Our Land" with a matter-of-fact assurance which tugged at the heart of a listener who had no absolute confidence. The wretched barracks on the blood-soaked soil of Germany were a phantom exorcised by the sun and orange blossoms of *Arzenu.* When I asked the teachers of the children, themselves DP's, if they were wise in feeding a hope which might fail, they answered me with words I had so often heard in Palestine: "We have no other way; without this map [of Palestine] the children would despair." And of course emissaries of Palestine worked in the midst of the DP's, organizing the convoys of the illegal immigrants who would march over the mountains till they reached a port in Italy or France where a ship waited.

One gathering of DP's at which I was present broke into applause at the announcement that a group of illegals was "already in Cyprus." The whole situation was coming to a boil. On February 14, 1947, it was announced that "His Majesty's Government had decided to refer the whole problem to the United Nations." There would be another commission of inquiry, this time by the United Nations.

In Palestine, clashes with the British grew increasingly violent. At the same time the senseless outrages of the terrorist groups—such as the bombing of the British embassy in Rome—were complicating the problems of those in charge of transporting the illegals. Golda declared in condemnation of terrorism: "These groups take it upon themselves to decide what is best for the Jewish people. They do not bring their views before any democratic forum. They decide and act, but the consequences of their acts must fall on the entire *Yishuv*. A small minority cannot impose the methods and consequences of the struggle on an entire people."

But British tactics continued to inflame extremist sentiment. The climax came on July 18, 1947, when the *Exodus*, carrying 4,500 refugees, entered the port of Haifa. In the course of a clash with the British, three Jews were killed, including a young American member of the crew. Over 100, including women, were badly injured. Bevin decided that the ship would not be sent on to the detention camps of Cyprus but would be returned to France. The deportees vowed that they would not disembark in Marseilles nor would the French Government take them off by force. For three

Golda, 1930

1935

1956

1962

Golda (right) and a friend, New York, 1919

A family photo taken in Denver in 1915, with her sister Shana (seated), her brother-in-law Sam Korngold and her niece Judith.

Working on the kibbutz at Merhavia, 1922

Golda with Mrs. Roosevelt, 1956

Presenting her credentials to the Deputy President in Moscow
when she arrived as Israeli ambassador in 1948

A historic photo and a historic moment. Approximately 40,000 Russian Jews miraculously appeared outside the Moscow synagogue to hail Golda and the state of Israel as she attended Rosh Hashanah services in 1948. Normal attendance was 2,000. Golda's head is visible in the foreground of the picture.

Conferring with President Kennedy, 1962

Addressing a United Nations committee on
the refugee problem, 1962

Outside the Israeli consulate in New York, 1962

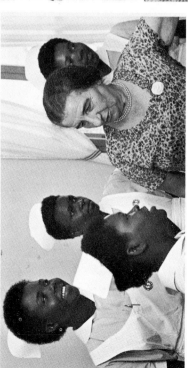

Her work with and help to the emergent nations of Africa have won Israel new friends and political allies. (*Top left*) With nursing trainees at an Israeli hospital. (*Lower left*) Meeting with Miss Margaret Kenyatta at the Israeli-staffed Institute for Social Workers in Kenya. (*Above*) At the International Training Center for Community Service in Haifa.

weeks men, women and children lay crowded in the swelter-
ing hold of the ship, without adequate provisions. The danger of disease was constant. Again many a conscientious
Zionist in the Diaspora felt qualms he could not down, despite the magnificence of the demonstration. The British
were threatening to send the refugees back to Germany.
Dared one make political ammunition of tragic women and
children? Would it not be wiser to let them debark in France?
But the Jewish Agency rejected the British Government's
request that it persuade the deportees to land in France.
Golda informed the chief secretary in Jerusalem that it was
the Agency's duty to facilitate Jewish immigration into Palestine: "It would never lend itself, even under cruel menace,
to any attempt to prevent Jews from reaching their national
home." The *Yishuv* sent a message to the *Exodus* promising:
"All of you will yet come to us," and quoted Deuteronomy:
"If any of thine be driven out unto the outmost parts of
heaven, from thence will the Lord, thy God, gather thee, and
from thence will fetch thee." Of the 4,500, only 130 disembarked in France. The British Government then sent the
refuges to DP camps in the British zone of Germany. The
threat had been fulfilled. Nobody except a band of hardy
believers and many simplehearted children was sure that
the promise, too, would be fulfilled.

On September 9, 1947, the *Yishuv* held a day of mourning,
"Hamburg Day," for the refugees landing in Germany. At a
protest meeting in Tel Aviv, Golda declared that "the black
drapes on the Zionist flags were not in mourning for the
4,500 Jews being landed in Hamburg but for the vanished
justice and morality of Great Britain."

In another connection, she remarked wryly: "Those responsible for British Government policy cannot forgive us

[161]

for being a nation without the British Government's approval. They cannot understand that the problem of the Jews of Europe has not been created for the sole purpose of embarrassing the British Government."

The organizers of illegal immigration kept special watch over the *Exodus* refugees. Escaping from the British Zone in small groups, they were led to Mediterranean ports. Each *Exodus* refugee had a Haganah certificate granting him priority in boarding the illegal ships. By May 15, 1948, almost all the *Exodus* DP's were in Israel.

The boon of being sent to Cyprus, which had been denied the *Exodus,* was a mixed blessing. For the refugees, the sole virtue of this Mediterranean island was its closeness to Palestine. In other respects they were in worse straits than those in the DP camps of Germany. There the American authorities had made an honest effort to provide for the minimum basic needs of the survivors in their zone. The British on Cyprus, on the other hand, showed less regard for the well-being of the refugees they captured than would the warden of any modern penal institution for hardened criminals. During the first year that the British sent passengers of captured ships to Cyprus, more than 23,000 people, including many children, had been imprisoned. Of these, 7,000 had been admitted to Palestine as part of the legal monthly immigration quota. At that rate the latest arrivals would have to wait at least two years before their turn came to reach Palestine.

Only the most primitive hygienic facilities were provided for the 16,000 people crowded into tents and Nissen huts. Such elementary necessities as tables or chairs were never supplied, though the inhabitants were compelled to live there for a year or two. Family groups herded together in tents had no opportunity for normal privacy by day or night.

Worst of all was the water shortage. In the hot camps, pitched on bare sand without grass or shade, suffering from the heat was intense. Yet water for drinking was at a premium, and water for washing almost unavailable. Though the camps were situated on the shore, the precious relief of bathing in the sea was denied the inmates as a punitive measure. They could fester in filth behind barbed wire. Adults, inured to suffering, could endure even this though morale was low, but children were in serious danger. Epidemics of dysentery had broken out. Medical authorities sent by the Joint Distribution Committee, which as in Germany was doing its utmost to alleviate the misery of the refugees, feared that infants and young children would not survive.

The British allowed a monthly quota of 750 to Palestine. The prisoners were released in a strictly chronological order, according to the date of their capture; first in, first out. The refugees themselves demanded rigid adherence to the schedule for release. But the physical threat to the children introduced a new element.

In Palestine, Golda and other members of the Agency undertook to persuade the British to permit the immediate release of young children. The negotiations with the British were successful. As long as the monthly quota was not exceeded, the British agreed to grant priority to families with babies, regardless of the date of their arrival, provided the individuals affected agreed to waive their turns. This meant that men and women who had been in the barbed enclosures for over a year might be asked to wait another year.

Someone had to go to Cyprus to persuade the refugees to waive their rightful turn in favor of families with children. It was not a popular mission. As a rule the various parties in the *Yishuv* jealously insisted on adequate representation in any delegation, but in this instance no one insisted on being included. When Golda volunteered for the job, even some comrades of Mapai tried to dissuade her, assuring her that she was bound to fail and that the party would be blamed.

There was good reason to be afraid of the outcome. The men and women herded on Cyprus were not saints. With nerves and bodies at the breaking point, these shattered survivors of the death camps and the DP camps were to be urged to suffer more. Golda had no illusions about the delicacy of her task. She went knowing that she might not succeed, but she followed her formula: "If it was right, it had to be tried whatever the result."

Her arrival at Cyprus was one of the most poignant moments in her life. As soon as she was within the barbed-wire pen she was met by a welcoming group of children who gave her a bouquet of paper flowers. Familiarity with the Palestinian love of flowers was necessary to understand the effect of this offering on Golda. Perhaps because in Israel flowers are a symbol of victory over the desert, they are bought and given constantly and lavishly. On the Sabbath table there may be candles; there are surely flowers. In the Cyprus camp, where not a blade of grass grew, the children had painstakingly contrived a dusty posy made of faded paper, for even paper was a luxury. The paper flowers of the children of Cyprus affected Golda profoundly. Not that she was unacquainted with barrenness. Her own daughter was in Revivim, a kibbutz in the desert of the Negev, but her daughter's sacrifice was fruitful; some day the sands would bear. The paper flowers were the ultimate of sterile suffering. That was the horror of Cyprus.

After the emotional welcome the business had to begin.

In the several Cyprus camps, each ship was represented by a committee; the shiploads, in the order of capture, formed the basis of camp organization. Golda had to go to the various camps and their local committees to persuade them of the justice of the Jewish Agency's request. She went from tent to tent, from committee to committee, to plead the case. It was not an easy task nor did it go smoothly. Despite Golda's conviction that the sacrifice was essential, it was no simple matter to face tormented, embittered and enfeebled men and women and ask them to surrender their chance to escape for a stranger, even if the stranger was a child. The worst of it was that the babies would be accompanied by their families. That was the only feasible way of arranging the transfer. This meant that sometimes a family group of four adults, parents and grandparents, would be enabled to leave because of one child. Those who appreciated the need of saving small children felt no inclination to sacrifice themselves for their fathers and mothers.

Then there were groups of unmarried men who were indifferent to the prior claims of babies. Some of the ships from Italy had come entirely without children. On the other hand, ships from Rumania carried family groups. In such cases there was not even the bond of shipmates to ease the forfeit. In addition, the camps were full of rumors that the British would soon stop sending Cyprus refugees to Palestine, and that therefore deferment might mean not another year of misery but perpetual captivity or exile.

It was in this atmosphere that Golda had to go from group to group. It is to the credit of the human race that the vast majority of the refugees agreed. A center of opposition stemmed from a camp controlled by the rightist Zionist-revisionists, but these were a small minority.

Negotiations also had to be conducted with the British head of the camps, who proceeded to raise difficulties about some of the details. His enthusiasm for the increased tension in his camps was understandably limited. In his first interview with Golda he was curt and uncooperative. At their next meeting the Briton appeared unexpectedly meek. Afterward it was learned that in the interval between the two meetings he had received a telegram from the Palestine Government, urging him to be careful with Mrs. Myerson because "she is a very forceful woman."

In the course of three days—from November 11 to November 14, 1947—Golda had achieved her purpose. Ten days later, the *Ocean Vigor* came to Haifa with 1,420 children and parents. There should have been 1,500, but a last-minute hitch occurred at the troublesome camp and reduced the number. Certain refugees claimed that they had not consented to the arrangement and prevented 80 infants and parents from leaving the camp. Despite the fears of the skeptics, the mission had been successful.

I understood the extent of Golda's achievement when I saw the barbed-wire desolation of Cyprus in February 1949. Bevin had suddenly announced that Cyprus was to be cleared immediately. The nine-month-old Jewish state, war torn and crowded with refugees pouring in daily, could have all the Cyprus DP's at once. The British were already closing most of the camps when our party came to see the finale. We could not enter the infamous Nicosea camp, because, as the British Tommy on guard there put it: "There are no more Jews here"; but in the other camps one could still see the bleak tents and unfurnished huts. One woman was cheerlessly gathering a few belongings. When I asked her if she was not happy at last, she burst out crying: "The years, the lost years!"

She was embarking with the next to the last boatload of Jews to leave Cyprus. The last one, which marked the end of bondage in Cyprus, was received at Haifa with all the ceremony which the historic occasion merited. The suffering of 51,600 Jews in the barbed-wire cages of the British was over.

For three weeks, as soon as Bevin had given his unexpected order to free the Jews of Cyprus, the S.S. *Atzmaut* (*Independence*) had shuttled back and forth bringing the last thousands out of Cyprus. The captain of the ship was "Ike" Aronovitch, the same twenty-five-year-old Palestinian who had been the captain of the *Exodus*.

On this next to the last trip the boat was jammed, tier on tier, with 1,600 men, women and babies—some born in Cyprus—who filled the hold and decks. As on almost every trip, a child was born, to be named *Atzmaa*. The dark hold, crowded with human beings one above the other, was not a pleasant sight according to objective standards. But the smiling faces of the women clutching their babies, seen dimly in the faint light, indicated that they understood.

The night was rough and the February morning when we approached Haifa cold and wet. Everybody had crowded on the deck for a first glimpse of the Promised Land. I was sorry that there was no sunshine and that green Mount Carmel was hidden by the fog. And I knew that there would be no bands, no gala reception, because this boat was not the last.

I wanted to say something comforting to the chilled, drenched people around me. I turned to a young woman near me, and pointing to the coastline which could at last be seen, said not too confidently, "It's beautiful, isn't it?" She did not need my hokum. She answered almost sternly, "It's beautiful because it's ours." Instinctively she had used the Yiddish equivalent for the word which was the motive power of all Israel's striving: *shelanu.*

The pathos of those final hours in Cyprus—the woman crying "the lost years"—and the exaltation of the arrival— *unser,* "ours" *shelanu*—made clear how much those who surrendered their turn had given, as well as the moral authority of the woman who had dared to appeal to human goodness.

THE ARABS ATTACK

THE fact that the partition resolution was being favorably discussed at the United Nations no doubt lightened Golda's task in Cyprus. Her promise of a Jewish state to which all in Cyprus would soon come had a ring of comforting political realism as well as messianic hope. Only two weeks after her return from Cyprus, the resolution in favor of a Jewish state in a part of Palestine passed the General Assembly. The partition resolution provided for the establishment of an independent Jewish state, an independent Arab state, and the internationalization of Jerusalem. The rapture of the *Yishuv* reached out to all the Jewries of the world. Atheist and orthodox used the language of the Psalms in thanksgiving. In New York, even non-Jews, touched by the historic significance of the moment and dimly aware of what the victory meant to those whose lives had been given to make the fable true, crowded eagerly around Moshe Sharett.

While the Jews of Jerusalem danced in the streets on the night of November 29, 1947, an Arab woman watching the celebrants from a balcony remarked scornfully to an American correspondent, "Let them dance now; they will all soon be dead anyhow."

Exactly a year later, in November 1948, David Ben-Gurion, War Minister of Israel, revealed how nearly this threat might have been prophecy. On the day the partition resolution was passed, the total stock of ammunition in the possession of Haganah consisted of 10,000 rifles, 1,900 Sten guns, and 66 mortars. Even this scant stock was constantly subject to British search and confiscation. The secret defense force had no tanks, no airplanes and practically no heavy artillery. Though reputed to be a citizens' army of 60,000, Haganah actually had available for immediate military action a striking force of 3,000, mainly members of *Palmach*, its specially trained shock troops.

The men and women chanting thanksgiving prayers in the synagogues, the boys and girls stamping the *horah* till dawn on the sidewalks of Tel Aviv and in the fields of the Emek, knew that they were not equally matched against enemies whose intentions had been vociferously publicized at Cairo and Damascus, Ramalla and Lake Success. But only David Ben-Gurion and those closest to him understood the full disparity. Perhaps it was just as well that the dancers did not know. They were soon to learn. But by then the decision had been taken.

Attacks by local Arab bands began the very next morning. On November 30, eight Jews were killed on the Haifa-Jerusalem road and on the boundary between Jaffa and Tel Aviv. The disturbances rapidly spread throughout the country. The familiar pattern of ambushed roads and sporadic attacks on Jewish quarters and settlements, still painfully remembered from the riots of 1936–1939, began to unfold. But with this difference: the Palestinian Arabs had not forgotten their economic and physical losses of ten years before. Despite the prodding of the Arab higher executive and the Arab League, Palestinian Arab villagers showed little enthusiasm for becoming involved in renewed violence. Their hesitance was quickly overcome by local extremists, mainly disciples of the Grand Mufti, chief moslem religious dignitary and head of the Arab higher committee, and by the pressure of the "infiltrees," Arab guerilla forces who openly crossed the Syrian and Lebanese borders and came from across the Jordan.

Invasion by Arab irregulars—volunteers and mercenaries, not members of regular Arab armies—began as early as January 9, 1948 when a well-equipped Arab force led by Syrian officers crossed into northern Palestine from Syria and attacked two Jewish settlements. Irregulars were consistently making less public entries into Palestine and encamping in Arab villages and towns in preparation for the formal invasion by the Arab states. Kaukaji's men crossed the Jordan and entrenched themselves in the Nablus-Jenin-Tulkarem triangle, the Arab mountain stronghold, and occupied Arab villages dominating the highways.

Fawzi El Kaukaji, commander of the Arab Liberation Army and distinguished by a pro-German record going back to World War I, had spent World War II in Berlin with the Mufti, also then enjoying Hitler's hospitality as a Nazi collaborator. Kaukaji's main job consisted of recruiting Moslems to serve with the Nazis. At the end of the war he reached Syria, having been permitted to land at the Lydda airport without interference by the British authorities.

As a leader of a fascist Black International, he gathered recruits for the liberation army not only among Syrians, Iraqis and Lebanese but among assorted European pro-fascists and professional anti-Semites who had made their way to the Middle East. British Mosleyites, German prisoners of war released from camps in the Middle East, and Moslems from Yugoslavia, rallied to the anti-Jewish standard.

By February, some 15,000 irregulars equipped and armed by the Arab states were entrenched in the heart of Palestine, busily involving the country in open warfare. The mandatory, true to its promise not to assist in the implementation of the United Nations partition resolution, made no attempt to control the local bands or to check the invaders. Though still committed to the maintenance of law and order within the territory under its jurisdiction and pledged to its protection against aggression, the mandatory power contented itself with energetically disarming the Jews. Despite a few exceptions to the general rule, British policy in the final phase of the mandatory regime could best be described as one of "malevolent neutrality," with the malevolence increasing in inverse ratio to the neutrality.

The Arab states, meanwhile, massed their armies on the borders of Palestine, deferring actual invasion till May 15, the end of the mandate, to avoid embarrassing Great Britain. No secret was made of this Arab design. A council of the Arab League held in Cairo shortly after the passage of the partition resolution undertook to provide financial aid to Arab bands in Palestine and to train volunteers from the Arab countries. A training camp was set up in Damascus, where some 20,000 volunteers received instruction. The Arab League assumed that after three months of harrying and depredation by irregulars, Jewish Palestine would fall an easy prey to its regular armies. The Arab states would enjoy a swift triumphal march.

Golda was in Jerusalem, continuing the work entrusted to her while Sharett remained at the UN. As Ben-Gurion's headquarters were in Tel Aviv, she had to make the dangerous journey between the two cities several times a week. Contrary to expectation, Jerusalem was fast becoming one of the most dangerous spots in Palestine.

The terms of the partition resolution had provided that the entire area of Jerusalem, including the almost wholly Jewish New City, was to be separated from the Jewish state and placed under an international trusteeship. This had been a heavy blow to Jewish hopes. Even more bitter than the physical loss in terms of population, land and institutions had been the taking away of the age-old center of Jewry's deepest religious and national feelings from the new Jewish state, the divorce of Zion from Israel. The decision had been accepted by the Jews of Palestine out of obedience to the United Nations and regard for the peace of the Holy City. Naively, they had assumed that the powers who advocated internationalization would safeguard Jerusalem.

Though Arab spokesmen at Lake Success and in various Arab capitals made no secret of their aggressive designs, Jews did not abandon the hope of peace to the last. At a great public gathering in Jerusalem on November 30, 1947, Golda Myerson, in a direct appeal to the Arabs, declared: "Our hand is offered to you in peace and friendship. Take our proffered hand!"

The appeal went unheeded. Arab riots broke out at once, and from December 1, 1947, Jerusalem became the target of unremitting pillage, arson and violence, culminating in full-scale assault. On December 2, Arab mobs began to surge through the commercial center of Jerusalem, smash-

[173]

ing windows, looting shops and stabbing civilians in full view of the British police. By the end of the day the toll of Jewish dead and injured indicated what was in store for Jerusalem.

As elsewhere, local Arab gangs were rapidly reinforced by the arrival of Iraqi and Syrian volunteers whose infiltration the British authorities professed themselves powerless to check, while the Trans-Jordan Arab Legion, British-officered and equipped with all the instruments of modern warfare, stood by poised to strike.

The Jewish community of Jerusalem was even less prepared for the onslaught than were other sections of Palestine. The outlying agricultural settlements, because of their exposed position, were fortified by a long pioneer tradition of self-defense. Jerusalem, the religious, cultural and administrative center of Palestine Jewry, the site of the Hebrew university, the Hadassah hospital and ancient religious institutions, had a high proportion of academicians, civil servants and orthodox Jews engaged in the study of their holy books. Such a population inevitably had little or no military training. Besides, the consciousness that they were the inhabitants of a city sacred to three faiths engendered a mistaken sense of security.

Strategically, Jerusalem was virtually an island set in an Arab sea of some 200,000 and torn away economically from Tel Aviv, Haifa and Galilee. Its Jewish population was a conglomerate in which Oriental Jews predominated. Delicate Yemenites, fur-hatted Afghans, husky Kurds, picturesquely garbed Jews from Bokhara, flashing-eyed Moroccans, together with Jews from Spain and Turkey, constituted the Sephardic community. And in the orthodox quarter of Mea

Shearim, Ashkenazi Jews with long earlocks still wore the traditional garments of eighteenth-century Poland.

The motley character of Jewish Jerusalem was bound to present special problems during the siege, when unity of purpose was essential. The Jewish officers to whom the city was entrusted made no secret of the doubts and fears with which they undertook their task. How could this conglomerate of religious zealots, tradition-bound clerics and their followers, thirteenth-century primitives from the ancient Jewries of the East, and twentieth-century sophisticates from Europe and the United States, be welded into a fighting force?

Ultraorthodox fanatics, intent only on the study of the Holy Scrolls, had demonstrated with white flags, preferring surrender to worldly interference with their prayers for the Messiah. Oriental Jews had fled from the unknown sound of artillery. "Officials," with no understanding for military exigencies, had kept prating about the liberties of the population. And above all there was the paralysis produced by the maddening conviction that the world would hold Jerusalem inviolable.

As a result, the Jews of Jerusalem found themselves unarmed, untrained, and except for a small Haganah unit, virtually helpless in the face of mounting Arab outrages whose force the mandatory power did nothing to check. On the contrary, the British kept dismembering Jewish Jerusalem by the creation of so-called "security zones" through which Jews could not pass and which cut off various sectors of the city, diminishing the Jewish area and increasing the difficulty of contact between the separated sections. These security zones, bristling with barbed wire and concrete dragons' teeth, made the strategic position of the Jews still more vulnerable. In addition, the British police kept arresting any members of the Haganah they could discover and disarming any Jew lucky enough to have some means of self-defense. While the Arabs continued to accumulate huge stocks of arms in the Mosque of Omar—safe from British search as a sanctuary—British police went so far as to measure the length of the pocket knives that Jews might carry. A knife longer than four inches was confiscated.

By December 1947, it was already clear that the policy of the mandatory power wished for the surrender of Jerusalem to King Abdullah of Jordan rather than its transfer to an international authority. Though the Jewish community still assumed that an international force would intervene in the event of a formal Arab invasion, steps for defense had to be taken.

The role of the Jewish military was not an enviable one. The Haganah had to act in secret for fear of British detection. Not only was its authority perforce underground and conspiratorial, but it constantly had to gain its support in Jerusalem from unexpected circles. Old men and women, children, middle-aged civilians, had to accept of their own volition the rigorous discipline of a phantom military regime which had no public power to conscript or to command. Even the Jewish civil authorities were at first reluctant to grant the military staff complete control over the life of the community. Though Arab outrages mounted and the toll of civilians grew, the Jewish city council balked at establishing a military government. Only the imminence of invasion finally brought this necessity home. In the meantime, the Haganah staff tried to fashion an army, recruiting its soldiers among the motley tribes of Israel, each stubbornly cherishing its costumes and customs. To the last, some fanatical *Yeshivas* (orthodox religious schools) refused to let their students enlist. Boys whose patriotism exceeded this brand of piety had to steal away secretly to join the defense units.

Nevertheless, in the midst of the chaos, abetted by the confusion among the Jews themselves, a pattern of defense for Jerusalem began to take shape. Middle-aged gentlemen past their limber prime conscientiously drilled in backyards and cellars. Younger men appeared at the designated "barracks" which lacked beds, uniforms, arms and instructors. Each recruit had been ordered to bring his own mattress and blankets, but in many instances that meant depriving the home of its sole bedding.

The attack on the civilian population was to assume an even more ruthless form. The Arabs had a cheap formula for victory: the reduction of the city through famine and thirst. Surrounded by thickly populated Arab villages, the 100,000 Jews of Jerusalem were completely isolated from the rest of Jewish Palestine. Their sole link to the coast ran almost entirely through Arab-held territory. Arab strategy concentrated on breaking this link. Water, food, arms and men could not reach Jerusalem if the road to Tel Aviv were cut and the pipeline from Ras-El Rain severed.

The Battle of the Roads began early in December, though the mandatory power had promised to maintain freedom of traffic on the Tel Aviv-Jerusalem highway. The British gave their customary interpretation to this undertaking. Jewish buses would be painstakingly searched for arms while Arab attackers enjoyed a minimum of interference. The disarmed Jews then had the privilege of fighting it out.

This concept of "neutrality" resulted in the repeated massacre of unarmed civilians forced to ride the gauntlet of Arab bands crouching in the hills. The skeletons of overturned buses which can still be seen all along the winding Jerusalem highway testify to the ambushed convoys whose passengers were murdered by Arabs.

Nevertheless, the contact with Jerusalem had to be maintained. The inadequately protected convoys of Egged buses set out regularly on their perilous journeys, accompanied by Palmach girls with Sten guns hidden under their skirts. British soldiers did not search women as a rule.

Primitive devices to reinforce the buses came into being. Since Jews had no armor plate, they used metal sheets so thin that the buses were derisively called "sardine tins." To make matters worse, the thin sheets would be wedged between layers of wood to save precious metal. This economy made the buses cumbersome as well as readily penetrable.

During these months when Golda was intimately involved in problems of political strategy and military defense, she was singularly lucky. Though constantly exposed to danger in Jerusalem and on the road to Tel Aviv, she escaped injury. Once a shot fired through her office window missed her. On another occasion, bullets whistled through her car: a fellow passenger was wounded; she was not touched.

On December 3, 1947, she had a hair-raising adventure. On this occasion she had been provided with special guards for a stretch of the journey to Jerusalem. The guards were to meet her car at the British police station outside the Arab village of Abu Kabir. The chauffeur misunderstood her directions and drove her alone into the hostile village. By the time she noticed the mistake she was already in the heart of the village, wondering whether she would be murdered on the spot. Whatever the reason—whether she was not recognized or whether the Arabs were as flabbergasted as she—nothing happened. She ordered the driver to turn back to the police station where the startled guards took over.

She had no lack of opportunity to display her presence of mind. On December 31, she was in a convoy from Jerusalem to Tel Aviv which was stopped by British soldiers, despite the fact that the day before the chief secretary had promised Golda that searches for arms would be discontinued in view of constant Arab ambushes. Golda at once stepped out of her car, went up to the captain with an air of authority, and proceeded to tell him that the search was illegal. She asked the captain for his name, which he meekly gave while the soldiers stood around smiling. When the captain demanded her identity papers and saw her name, she heard him say to one of the soldiers: "I think we have bitten off more than we can swallow."

Two Sten guns were found on a girl traveling in Golda's car. The girl was arrested, and when Golda wanted to know where the prisoner would be taken, she was told "Faluja," an Arab village. There was no telling what might happen to the girl at night in an Arab village. Golda refused to leave and insisted on accompanying her. This was more than the British had bargained for. Finally both women were taken to a police station in Jewish Hedera. On seeing Golda, the police chief served drinks in honor of New Year's Eve, compliments were exchanged, and Golda was urged to spend the night in Hedera, since at nightfall the trip to Tel Aviv was extremely dangerous. But Golda was not going to miss her meeting. The girl was released, and with a big escort the chief of police personally accompanied Golda to Tel Aviv.

The deference shown Golda by the British did not stem

from a gentlemanly regard for women. It has been said by those supposedly well informed that His Majesty's Government hated Ben-Gurion but respected Golda. Sometimes the favorable opinion of an adversary may be a dubious recommendation. No one, however, could have been more uncompromising in her dealings with the British than Golda. She impressed them by her quiet strength, never by weakness.

In Tel Aviv, the worsening situation had to be assessed. It was only a matter of time before the lumbering convoys, doggedly crawling through the deep gorges and up the steep hills, would be completely blocked. Jerusalem would be isolated. And the reports reaching Ben-Gurion from the various settlements indicated how heavy a toll was being taken.

The first brunt of battle had been borne by the frontier settlements. The role of the collective farms in defending the country was so decisive that the war has been described as "the Battle of the Soil." Up north, in the uplands of Galilee and on the borders of Lebanon and Syria; in the east, along the vulnerable Jordan Valley separated from Trans-Jordan by the easily forded Jordan River; in the green valleys of Esdraelon and the Sharon; in the southern blaze of the Negev, these outposts formed the first line of defense, shielding the urban centers and checking the enemy. Ben-Gurion, in appraising the victory, credited the outcome of the struggle to two factors: "The heroic stand of the Jewish settlements and the military achievements of the young Defense Army of Israel which developed from the Haganah."

As the struggle developed, the element of tactical improvisation steadily diminished until a phase was reached when the brilliance of a plan became as impressive as the daring of its execution. But in the first months the strategy, if such it might be called, was shaped by necessity. The commanders, like the people, had no alternatives—no choice of weapons or trained troops to be deployed in this or that formation. Before May 15, the struggle reduced itself to a sloganlike simplicity. Defend each settlement, whatever its size or position, as though a major strategic point were involved.

In a sense, this estimate of the importance of the various collective farms that bore the first impact of invasion was by no means exaggerated. The cottages might be few, the able-bodied adults capable of fighting anywhere from 20 to 100, yet in view of the smallness of the Jewish area of Palestine and its exposed character, each settlement could truthfully boast that its valor was essential, not only to its own protection but to the country as a whole. Dan, Kfar Szold, and Daphne, in North Galilee, held the border against the Syrians and Lebanese. Mishmar Ha-Emek guarded the approach to the valley of Esdraelon and the strategic road south. Degania defended the Jordan Valley against a Syrian army crossing the Jordan from the east, and scarcely visible pinpoints in the desert engaged in delaying actions against the Egyptians driving north. The farms that stood like fortresses provided the time element which enabled the Haganah to prepare, and above all, to secure arms. Since nowhere in Palestine was there space where the Jews could withdraw, time became the dimension of salvation from Negba to Jerusalem.

The endurance of the agricultural settlements not only preserved the territorial integrity of the Jewish state but barred the way to the urban centers. The resistance of Mishmar Ha-Emek guarded the gate to Haifa as well as to the valley of Esdraelon. But the Haganah had to become an army by May 15. It had to secure weapons, equipment and training before the Arab states struck in unison. The question of securing heavy arms was crucial.

While the United States Government placed an embargo on the sale of arms to the Middle East, on January 14, 1948, Great Britain declared that it would continue to provide arms to the Arab states in accordance with its treaty obligations. This meant in effect that the Jews were barred from securing defensive weapons while their attackers had free access to the arsenal of the British Empire.

MISSION TO AMERICA

THE Jews of Palestine knew that there could be no Jewish
state unless they were able to contain and thrust back the
Arab invaders. So far the sole international result of Arab
aggression had been to cause a change of heart among supposedly staunch supporters of the partition resolution. Instead of rallying to the defense of the victim, the United Nations became the scene of maneuvers and retreats that bore
no correspondence to the realities being created in Palestine.
The American representative at Lake Success, Warren R.
Austin, informed the Security Council on March 19, 1948,
that the United States no longer favored partition. Ambassador Austin explained this reversal on the grounds that the
United States was now convinced that partition could not
be implemented without violence. He coupled this withdrawal of American support with a proposal for a temporary
trusteeship. The American move was naturally interpreted
by the Arabs as evidence that their attacks were bearing fruit
on the diplomatic front, if not on the battlefield, and served
to encourage guerilla violence.

In such an atmosphere, the political and military leaders of the Jewish community were obliged to forge the machinery of modern warfare. They understood that tanks and airplanes could not indefinitely be repelled with Sten guns. If there was to be a Jewish state, there would have to be an air force and motorized units.

Unless the *Yishuv* got arms, no amount of valor would avail. Various emissaries of the Haganah in the United States were attempting to raise the needed funds from a sympathetic American Jewry that was contributing decently, generously—and inadequately. Eliezer Kaplan, treasurer of the Jewish Agency, returned discouraged from the United States in January. In his detailed report to the executive in Tel Aviv, he explained that it was unrealistic to expect more than $5,000,000 to $7,000,000 from American Jewry. His reasons were cogent: American Jews were tired; they had been giving lavishly since the beginning of the Hitler tragedy; wartime prosperity was waning; in short, there was no use in expecting the impossible.

The report was catastrophic. If arms could not be bought and funds for the maintenance of the army secured, the war and the Jewish state were lost. Ben-Gurion sat through the report, boiling with indignation. At its conclusion he arose and made only one comment: "I suggest that Kaplan and I leave at once for the United States."

At this point Golda did something unprecedented: she proposed herself for the mission. She turned to Ben-Gurion and volunteered to go in his stead, saying, "What you can do here, I cannot do, but what you can do in the United States, I can do." Ben-Gurion was unconvinced. Despite Golda's urging that no one could replace him in the overall command of the struggle, he stubbornly insisted on going himself to make American Jews see the light. Then Golda suggested that the executive vote as to who should be the emissary. The executive voted that Golda leave at once.

It was a fortunate decision. It would have been madness to let Ben-Gurion leave Palestine at so crucial a time. No one had his breadth of vision when major decisions had to be made. In addition, Ben-Gurion was not notable for tact or winning ways. He was as likely to antagonize as to convince.

Golda flew to the United States directly from Tel Aviv. She left without adequate clothes or other necessities, because the journey back to Jerusalem, where her belongings were, was too hazardous to undertake for a winter coat. Under normal conditions a good car could travel the distance between Tel Aviv and Jerusalem within an hour, but a convoy had no time schedule. A delay could not be chanced. Golda, lightly clad and with no luggage except a handbag, stepped off the plane in New York on a bitterly cold January day. Rarely had a personage—and she was obviously a personage, in view of the reporters on the scene—arrived so scantily equipped.

When Golda made her bold suggestion that she could succeed as well as Ben-Gurion in America, she spoke a shade more confidently than the facts warranted. She had not been in the United States since 1938. On her previous visits her experience had been limited to the Labor Zionists and the Pioneer Women, her ideological comrades. Now she had to establish contact with broad sectors of American Jewry, including non-Zionists as well as those in the upper financial brackets who were the largest donors to the United Jewish Appeal. Other leading Palestinians, making the same plea and telling the same story, had failed. What assurance could she have that she would succeed?

As soon as she arrived in the United States she learned that two days later, on January 21, a conference of the Council of Jewish Federations would take place at Chicago to discuss the welfare needs of Jewish communities in the United States and abroad. Henry Montor, the director of the United Jewish Appeal, was already in Chicago. If she could address the council, she would at once reach the heart of organized Jewry in the United States. In New York, her advisers tried to dissuade her from the attempt. The council was not Zionist. She would be wasting her energy and at most elicit a little ineffectual sympathy. Furthermore, the council was beset with pleas for funds for local needs; many American-Jewish communities wanted new hospitals, temples and cultural centers. The membership was growing weary of appeals for "overseas." Then there were technical difficulties. Every hour of the conference program had long been prepared. This was not a Zionist convention where an emissary from Palestine could be squeezed in at the last moment.

Despite these counsels, Golda telephoned Montor. Arrangements were made that she speak in Chicago the following afternoon. Even though there were some hectic hours when flights were canceled because of bad weather, she got there in time.

When it was learned that she would actually address the Chicago conference, Golda was given further advice by good American Zionists. She was warned by highly placed gentlemen that she must not tell the stark truth. "You will never succeed," one of them said. "We have been telling American Jews all along that the Haganah can take care of Arab attacks. Jews will not be stirred by a story of desperate trouble and need. They will believe that they will be throwing away good money after bad."

But when Golda stood up in Chicago before a respectful audience of influential American Jews politely getting ready to hear another Zionist appeal for funds, she paid small attention to the warnings she had received. As always, she spoke without a prepared speech. She gave an off-the-record talk in which the catastrophic situation of the *Yishuv* was described in detail. The threat to its existence was not minimized. It was a graphic picture of suffering and courage, but such a picture alone would not have secured the tremendous effect she achieved that afternoon. The story of danger and privation was illuminated by the sense of the greatness of the cause for which all this was endured. Her appeal, no matter how tragic in detail, was to Jewish pride, not to pity.

Her appearance, too, was in its way effective. The stately woman, plainly dressed, with hair severely parted in the middle and tied in a knot, violated all the rules for lady speakers. One of her hearers tried to describe how she had affected him. "We had never seen anyone like her, so plain, so strong, so old fashioned—just like a woman out of the Bible."

She told her audience:

We must ask the Jews the world over merely to see us as the front line and do for us what the United States did for England when England was in the front line in the World War. All we ask of Jews the world over, and mainly of the Jews in the United States, is to give us the possibility to go on with the struggle. . . .

I want you to believe me when I speak before you today, that I came on this special mission to the United States today not to save seven hundred thousand Jews. The Jewish people have lost during the last few years six million Jews, and it would be audacity on our part to worry the Jewish

[187]

people throughout the world because a few hundred thousand more Jews were in danger.

That is not the problem. The problem is that if these seven hundred thousand Jews can remain alive, then the Jewish people as such is alive and Jewish independence is assured. If these seven hundred thousand people are killed off, then at any rate for many, many centuries, we are through with this dream of a Jewish people and a Jewish home. . . .

My friends, we are at war. There is not a Jew in the country that does not believe that in the end we will be victorious. The spirit of the country is such—we have known Arab riots since 1921 and '29 and '36 when for four years we had Arab riots. We know what happened to Jews in Europe during this war. Every Jew in the country knows that within a few months a Jewish state in Palestine will be established. We have to pay for it. We knew that we would pay for it. We knew that the price we would have to pay was the best of our people. There are a little over three hundred killed now. There will be more. There is no doubt that there will be more. But there is no doubt that the spirit of our young people is such that no matter how many Arabs come into the country, the spirit of our young people will not falter.

The spirit is there. This spirit alone cannot face rifles and machine guns. Rifles and machine guns without spirit are not worth very much. But spirit without these in time can be broken with the body.

The problem is time. The time factor is the most important factor now in this issue. Millions that we get within three or four months will mean very little in deciding the issue now. The problem is what we can get immediately. And, my friends, when I say immediately, it does not mean next month. It does not mean two months from now. It means now. . . .

I have come to the United States, and I hope you will understand me if I say that it was not an easy matter for any of us to leave home at present—to my sorrow I am not in the front line. I am not with my daughter in the Negev, nor with other sons and daughters in the trenches. But I have a job to do.

I have come here to try to impress Jews in the United States with this fact, that within a very short period, a couple of weeks, we must have in cash between twenty-five and thirty million dollars. Not that we need this money to use during these weeks, but if we have twenty-five or thirty million dollars in the next two or three weeks we can establish ourselves. Of that we are convinced, and you must have faith; we are convinced that we can carry on. . . .

We are not a better breed; we are not the best Jews of the Jewish people. It so happened that we are there and you are here. I am certain that if you were there and we were here, you would be doing what we are doing there, and you would ask us who are here to do what you will have to do. . . .

You cannot decide whether we should fight or not. We will. No white flag of the Jewish community in Palestine will be raised for the Mufti. That decision is taken. Nobody can change that. You can only decide one thing: whether we shall be victorious in this fight or whether the Mufti will be victorious in this fight. That decision American Jews can take. It has to be taken quickly, within hours, within days. . . .

At the conclusion of her address, the men and women who listened to her rose cheering, stirred as they had never been stirred before. American Jewry had been won.

The "twenty-five or thirty million dollars" which Golda was asking for at once, "not three months later," was five times as large as the grand total that Kaplan and his advisers had viewed as the realistic maximum. Yet her audience responded to the appeal with the immediacy she urged. The community leaders pledged the sum, and before the day was out began negotiating for loans to make cash promptly available. It was an unparalleled success story which left the professional fund raisers dazed.

After the Chicago conference, she began to speak for the United Jewish Appeal, and the miracle was repeated. Particularly striking was the impression she made on rich, upper-class American Jews, both Zionist and non-Zionist. Sophisticated men, suspicious of phonies and impatient of theatrics, believed her and were moved by her. She embodied every phase of the Palestine drama. At the same time, she was tactful enough not to antagonize her hearers with an assumption of righteousness. Her anger was reserved for those of her fellows who professed the faith but refused to practice the teaching.

In describing her personal relations with men of previously unfamiliar social strata, Golda told me: "I was not overawed and I was not condescending." Very few in her position would have been able to avoid one of these pitfalls. She had had considerable experience in meeting British lords on an equal footing. That had been easy for an individual supported by the honor of a cause whose spokesman she was. It was perhaps a little harder to step graciously and naturally into the friendly splendor which now welcomed her.

Golda's task was twofold. In addition to large public meetings, she personally had to talk to individual donors and persuade local leaders in each community to take out loans from banks to provide the sums needed before these had been received from the donors who had pledged future payments. With Henry Morgenthau, former Secretary of the Treasury, Edward M. Warburg, William Rosenwald and others, Golda traveled up and down the United States, raising dollars to buy arms.

The response of American Jewry was magnificent, but

sometimes she found intolerable the circumstances under which she had to arouse the ignorant or indifferent. In February, she flew to a "Big Donor" dinner in Palm Beach. The meeting was held in a luxurious hotel. The superb dinner, the swank surroundings, were too much for Golda. She sat at the head table, thought of the Haganah boys standing guard in the winter rains without overcoats, and the contrast between the world which she had left and the world before her overcame her. She bent her head to hide the tears streaming down her cheeks. Worse, she felt that she could not get up before this glittering gathering and tell her tale of blood and heroism. Henry Morgenthau, sitting next to her, noticed her distress; he understood and symphathized, but he knew that she must speak. By the time the chairman called on her, she had regained her self-control, and that night the gentlemen of Palm Beach pledged $1,500,000.

The pace of the work was terrific. As she traveled, speaking several times a day, the men who accompanied her—big industrialists for the most part—changed off, unable to maintain the tempo. But Golda had to make every hour count. From Paris, a Haganah emissary cabled her that he could buy tanks if he could get $10,000,000 at once. She telephoned: "Buy." Another emissary in Europe, trying to purchase ammunition, sent word that he would return to Palestine. He, too, needed $10,000,000, and there was no use waiting for the impossible. Golda cabled: "Stay." The money arrived.

In the two and a half months that Golda spent in the United States she raised $50,000,000. When she returned to Palestine, Ben-Gurion said to her: "Someday when history will be written, it will be said that there was a Jewish woman who got the money which made the state possible."

TRYST WITH ABDULLAH

B Y the time Golda returned to Palestine in March, the road to Jerusalem had been cut. In February, the Arabs had blown up a mountainside between Bab-el-Wad and Kastel, creating a huge natural roadblock which meant the virtual isolation of the city. The fate of Jerusalem depended on the construction of an alternate road through the hills and on the maintenance of the scant water supply. By May, the "Burma Road"—secretly hewn through the rocks by volunteers working at night to evade the guns of the Arab Legion entrenched in nearby Latrun—re-established a link with Jerusalem and enabled food to reach the starving city. In the meantime, only a tiny moth plane, nicknamed a "primus" (a small stove), maintained contact between Jerusalem and the coastal plain.

Elsewhere the fight against Arab irregulars continued to go well. The Haganah kept driving them back, but one incident in the struggle shocked the country. On April 9, the terrorist Irgun and Stern gang attacked the Arab village of Djer Yassin and massacred the inhabitants, including women and children. The outrage was publicly condemned by the Jewish Agency, and the *Yishuv* drew no comfort from the argument that this atrocity was in reprisal for Arab atrocities.

Before the episode of Djer Yassin, a curious phenomenon, bewildering and at first troubling to the *Yishuv,* was observed. Palestinian Arabs were abandoning their villages, obviously upon orders of the Arab higher command. The first signs of a large-scale exodus of Arabs were noted toward the end of March. In the last week of March and the first week of April, thousands of Arabs started to trek from the Sharon coastal plain to the Arab-controlled hill regions. Many sold their poultry flocks to Jewish friends. The first wave of departure was viewed with genuine regret by Jewish neighbors who urged the Arabs to remain. The Arabs, however, were not to be dissuaded, though they parted from Jewish friends amicably, explaining that they had to leave at the order of their leaders. A number of women and elderly people were transported through Jewish areas by Jewish settlement police and then transferred to Arab vehicles. The Arabs' sudden departure from the coastal plain was believed to have been connected with the completion of the picking of the citrus crop. At the end of the season, instructions to evacuate the Sharon were received from the Arab Higher Committee.

Perhaps the clearest illustration of the Arabs' flight was afforded by the exodus of 70,000 Arabs from Haifa. From the beginning of December, Arab bands in Haifa and neighboring villages had been engaged in constant attacks on Jewish communications and quarters. The fighting reached a climax on April 21st, ending in a complete rout of the Arabs, though only 200 Jewish soldiers were engaged. The British

High Commissioner, who could hardly be suspected of pro-Jewish bias, issued the following statement in connection with the Arab defeat: "The Jewish attack on Haifa was a direct consequence of continuous attacks by Arabs on Jewish Haifa over the previous four days. The attack was carried out by the Haganah, and there was no massacre. Arabs in Haifa were thus themselves responsible for the outbreak in spite of our repeated warnings." On April 22nd, after Arab resistance had broken down, the Haganah offered truce terms which were discussed by seven representatives of the Arab community and by the British Commander of the Northern Palestine District, Major General H. C. Stockwell. Under the terms of the truce, Arabs were to be permitted to go on living in Haifa as equal citizens with full rights under the then existing binational municipal council.

The British indicated that they considered the Jewish truce terms "reasonable." The Arabs tentatively agreed to the terms; later in the day they changed their minds, explaining that they could not accept the terms, for reasons beyond their control. They asked the British and the Jews for assistance in evacuating the Arabs. Jewish leaders assured the Arabs that those choosing to remain would be helped to reintegrate themselves into normal life. However, in obvious obedience to Arab orders, the dramatic spectacle of 70,000 Arabs flocking to the port and seeking to "escape" by any vessel or craft available began. Even the Arab wounded in the Haifa hospital were evacuated, though Jewish authorities urged Arab doctors to remain and tend them.

The startling example of the evacuation of Haifa had a profound psychological effect on the whole Arab population of Palestine. The subsequent flight from Jaffa was a natural corollary of the stampede organized by the Arab leadership in Haifa. A mass psychosis developed which resulted in the abandonment of Arab villages, frequently before these were threatened by the progress of the war. After the full-scale invasion by the Arab states, the process was accelerated.

The Jews watched the departure of the Arabs with mixed feelings. They suspected that Arab flight had been deliberately stimulated by the Arab leaders to inflame Arab resentment and prevent acceptance of a Jewish state by the Palestinian Arabs. Another reason was undoubtedly the desire of the Arab high command to evacuate Arab civilians from territory which the Arab states intended to attack with planes, tanks and mortars. The *Yishuv* knew that the major test was coming—the assault of the Arab states at the close of the mandate.

One avenue that remained to be explored was whether Jordan's King Abdullah could be persuaded not to join the invaders. Abdullah, an astute politician who combined Arab traditionalism with Western rationalism, had had friendly dealings with the Jews on previous occasions. He had expressed himself publicly in favor of Jewish efforts several times in Palestine and had advocated a settlement between Arabs and Jews through peaceful means. In his memoirs, published in 1946, he had expressed admiration for Jewish achievement in Palestine: "I was astonished at what I saw of the Jewish settlements. They have colonized the sand dunes, drawn water from them, and transformed them into a paradise." The rivalry between him and other Arab rulers was an open secret, and he had no interest in strengthening the Mufti.

In November 1947, when the passage of the partition resolution in the United Nations seemed imminent, Golda had a secret meeting with Abdullah in Pinhas Rutenberg's house near the power station at Naharayim, on the Jordan. The conversation was cordial. Abdullah assured Golda that he would not join in any attack on the Jews. If the United Nations decided on partition, he would annex the Arab part of his kingdom. He promised friendship, spoke slightingly of the strength of the neighboring Arab states, mentioned that the Mufti was their common enemy, and assured Golda that he would gladly accept partition. The interview ended with an agreement to hold a second meeting after the resolution had been passed.

Despite these assurances, two points troubled Golda. The king had asked what would be the attitude of the Jews to a proposal to include a Jewish state in Abdullah's kingdom. On receiving a prompt negative answer, he had dropped the subject. Then he had expressed the hope that the Arab state would not be so small that it would embarrass him.

Because of disturbed conditions, no second meeting was held as contemplated, but liaison with Abdullah was maintained. Information was exchanged about Jerusalem, whose internationalization both sides opposed. When rumors that Abdullah was about to join the Arab states became current, Golda sent him a message asking whether their agreement still held good. A messenger from Abdullah brought Golda a soothing answer. Abdullah asked her to remember three things: (1) he was a Bedouin, a man of honor; (2) he was a king; (3) a promise made to a woman is never broken.

Despite this romantic trinity, the Bedouin-royal-masculine promise was shortly broken. Abdullah joined the Arab states. Though little hope remained, it was decided that Golda should try to see him once more. If he were kept out of the war, Jerusalem would be spared attack by the Arab Legion, and the Iraki Army would be unable to march through Jordan against Palestine. British Colonial Secretary Creech-Jones had promised that the legion, a British instrument, would leave the country before May 15, 1948, but these assurances were not viewed as reliable. The Arab Legion was already attacking villages in the Hebron hills, and it was clear that its armored strength would be used to reduce Jerusalem.

Shortly before Golda's second attempt to contact Abdullah personally, an emissary had come from him to inquire whether the Jews were prepared to cede him a part of the territory assigned to them by the partition resolution. Such a concession would raise his prestige in the Arab world for he would then possess more territory than was originally set aside for the Arabs by the United Nations. The emissary was told that the proposal was unacceptable. The Jews would yield no territory of their tiny state. He was also told that the boundaries determined by the United Nations would be valid only if peace was established. In the event of war, the Jews would fight for whatever they could get.

Despite this unpromising exchange, it was thought advisable to make a final effort to prevent hostilities with Jordan. In the first week of May 1948, a second interview between Golda and the king was arranged. This time Abdullah refused to go to Naharayim. It was too dangerous for him to come to the Jewish border, because news of the previous meeting had leaked out and extraordinary security measures had to be taken. He suggested that Golda, dressed as an Arab woman, come to Amman. Golda flew in a primus from Jerusalem to Tel Aviv for the conference with Ben-Gurion in which the decision to contact Abdullah was taken. Only three people in the country knew that the attempt was to be made. Golda's sole companion was to be Ezra Dannin, an Oriental

Jew born in Jaffa, an expert on Arab affairs who was to act as interpreter.

The meeting with Abdullah was set for May 10. Golda and Dannin left for Haifa, where Golda was provided with an Arab costume, veil and all, and practiced moving convincingly in those exotic draperies. From Haifa they drove to Naharayim, Golda as yet uncostumed, changing cars several times to keep their destination secret. The king had sent a car to Naharayim to drive the Jewish emissaries to Amman. At nightfall, Golda put on her robes and veils, and the journey to Amman started. The party hoped to evade the Arab Legion whose guards were already at the border. If they were stopped, Dannin would have no difficulty passing muster as an Arab, because of his excellent command of the language and his close knowledge of Arab customs. Golda, however, was taller and heavier than the average Arab woman; although she could crouch modestly and silently in the dark, they would, if stopped, have to gamble that no questions would be addressed to her and put their faith in the Arab taboo against touching a strange woman.

In the course of the ride, which took several hours, the car was stopped for indentification ten times without incident. Golda was driven, not to the palace but to the house of a rich friend of Abdullah in whom the king had complete confidence. In a little while Abdullah arrived. He appeared cordial but depressed and nervous.

In the course of an hour's interview, Golda recalled the king's promise of November. Abdullah made no attempt to deny his pledge but added that the situation had changed. He had thought then that he was his own master; now circumstances did not allow such freedom. It was clear from his tone that the reference was to British directives. However,

he held out the hope that war could be avoided even at this
late date provided that the Jews did not declare a state and
stopped immigration for several years. He would take over
Palestine unpartitioned, merge it with Jordan after the interval of one year, and give the Jewish community representation in his parliament. He promised the Jews good treatment in the spirit of his liberal views. He concluded by declaring that he earnestly desired peace and regretted the
inevitable ruin of great Jewish achievements in agriculture
and industry if a war should occur. He could not understand
why the Jews should be in such a hurry to declare a state.

Golda courteously answered that a people that had waited
two thousand years could hardly be described as being in a
hurry. Perhaps the Jews had been too patient. She pointed
out that Jewish relations with His Majesty had always been
friendly, reinforced by opposition to their common enemies.
During the last five months the Jews had scored victories.
The Mufti's power was in decline; the invaders had been
pushed back. If Abdullah were to go back to his original
proposal of annexing the territory assigned to the Arabs, an
understanding could be reached. The Jews were much
stronger than a few months ago. If war were forced on them,
they would fight wherever they could and as well as they
could.

Abdullah replied that he realized that the Jews would feel
called upon to repel an attack. True, he had sincerely wanted
to carry out his original proposal, but many things had happened since then. For instance, the Djer Yassin episode
had inflamed Arab feeling. And besides, he added: "Then I
was alone and now I am one of five. I have no choice and I
cannot act otherwise." He again begged Golda to urge her
government to reconsider the matter. If he received a favor-

[199]

able answer by May 15, he would consult with the Arab moderates to preserve peace.

Golda and Dannin tactfully urged that he bear in mind that the Jews were his only friends. He nodded and answered, "I know that very well. I have no illusions. I know you and I believe in your good intentions. I believe with all my heart that Divine Providence has brought you back here, restoring you, a Semitic people who were exiled to Europe and shared in its progress, to the Semitic East which needs your knowledge and initiative. Only with your help and your guidance will the Semites be able to revive their ancient glory. We cannot expect genuine assistance from the Christian world, which looks down upon the Semitic peoples. We will progress only as the result of joint efforts. I know all this and I believe it with all sincerity but conditions are difficult. One dare not take rash steps. Therefore I beg you once more to be patient."

To which Golda replied: "We have no desire to mislead you and we wish to make it perfectly clear that we cannot even consider your proposal. None of our responsible institutions, and not even ten Jews with any influence, would stand for such a plan. We can give you the answer here and now. If Your Majesty has turned his back on our original understanding and wants war instead, there will be war. Despite our handicaps we believe that we will win. Perhaps we shall meet again after the war when there will be a Jewish state."

Abdullah turned to Dannin and in a fatherly tone urged that he, an Oriental, support the king's position. Dannin too offered some counsel. He reminded Abdullah that he had no real friends in the Arab world and that he was relying on the tanks of the Arab Legion as the French had relied on the

Maginot Line. But the Jews would smash the tanks. He also ventured to suggest to the king that perhaps it was time to end the beautiful old custom of allowing his subjects to kiss his hand or the hem of his garment. City people differed from Bedouin tribesmen. The king should be more vigilantly guarded against assassins.

Abdullah accepted the advice as well-meant rather than impertinent but replied: "My friend, I will never depart from the custom of my fathers. I am a Bedouin. I will not become the prisoner of my guards. Let events take their course. I will never prevent my subjects from expressing their affection for me."

The interview ended with more royal expressions of regret for the blood that would be spilled. The impression of Golda and Dannin was that Abdullah was neither happy nor confident, that he did not want to fight but was too involved in Arab and British ties to extricate himself.

After the king left, the Arab friend served a meal; his wife showed Golda her library. Then it was time for the perilous journey back. On the way to Naharayim they could see Camp Mafrak, where the Iraqi forces were already massing. The Arab chauffeur, frightened by the number of check posts they had to pass, decided it would be too dangerous to drive all the way to Naharayim. He let his passengers out in the hills, two miles before the border. It was 3 A.M. and a good half-hour's walk to Naharayim, provided they did not lose their way. Neither Golda nor Dannin was armed, and even Golda later admitted that she was frightened. This time if they were intercepted by a guard, there would be no help. Decent Arab ladies did not go sauntering through the hills in the middle of the night. Fortunately they were met by a Haganah scout from Naharayim who had been on the lookout for them. It was so dark that Golda did not remember his face, but a year later he paid her a visit, introducing himself as the man "who led you over the hills."

Early in 1951, Abdullah told another Jewish emissary that the person chiefly responsible for the war was Golda, who had rejected his offer of peace. Later that year, in July, Abdullah was assassinated. Both Golda and Dannin had been right.

THE STATE

THE meeting with Abdullah had been held on a Monday night. The next day, May 11, Golda was back in Tel Aviv to attend a meeting of the central committee of Mapai, where a last vote as to whether a state should be declared was to be taken. The following morning, May 12, the announcement came from Lake Success that the mandate would end two days later at 12 P.M. At 10 A.M. the *de facto* government of the *Yishuv* met to make its final decision. At the head of the table sat Ben-Gurion. Sharett had just arrived from New York to give his estimate of the international situation. Kaplan and Moshe Shapiro had arrived from besieged Jerusalem. Present too were David Remez, Chairman of the National Council, Zisling of Ein Harod, Ben Tov of Mishmar Ha-Emek, and several others. Golda had come to report on her visit to Abdullah, and two commanders of the Haganah were present to provide a military briefing.

The question about whether a Jewish state should be declared despite the threatened Arab invasion had been fiercely debated by the Jewish Agency and the provisional cabinet since December. The American State Department's current advocacy of a Trusteeship instead of partition complicated the situation further. Zionist policy was again at the crossroads, and as usual the calculation of cleverness and the instinct of wisdom (not to be confused with wisdom of instinct) clashed. It was the same conflict which had separated the "non-activists" from the "activists" in the struggle against the British and later in regard to the degree of resistance to Arab aggression. Till now, the activist line of Ben-Gurion had been successful despite the gloomy prognosis of those who had opposed him, both within and outside the Mapai. Though to their own delight, the prophets of doom had been mistaken, reasons for pessimism seemed sounder than ever.

True, the Haganah had driven out an assortment of Arab "irregulars," and the Palestinian Arabs were in full, if puzzling, flight. It seemed, however, impossible that the Haganah, still lacking heavy arms in any substantial amounts, would be able to repel the invasion of six Arab states. The Arab Legion, under the command of the British Glubb Pasha, was equipped with all the potent instruments of modern warfare. Egypt had a sizable air force. Furthermore, there were reports that Secretary of State Marshall had threatened economic sanctions if a sovereign Jewish state was declared.

Some of the men who were to accept portfolios in the provisional government opposed the proclamation. This is not said to their discredit. Their devotion and their personal sacrifices were no less than those of the "Yea-sayers." One might even argue that their sense of responsibility was more acute than that of the men who voted for what was a desperate gamble.

The people of the *Yishuv* were in overwhelming favor of the state. Though they anticipated a heavy toll in blood and suffering, the majority had no realistic understanding of the unpreparedness of the Haganah and of the odds against the new state. Only the handful in command knew what resources were at hand and were able to judge the significance of the support or antagonism of the several great powers.

The conclusion of the argument was never seriously in doubt. For wise reasons and foolish reasons—out of a historic optimism and a despairing world view, a reckless phantasy and a bitter sobriety to which any hope appeared over-rosy—the decision took form and grew. It was going to happen at last "speedily and in our time," as Jews had prayed for centuries. Now the hour for chants was over. "Our time" was turning into a specific zero hour on a specific day because a small, stocky visionary had for a generation taken his vision literally and had persuaded his people to be equally literal.

There had been a long preparation for the moment of statehood. Within the shell of the dissolving mandate, the structure of a new government had been functioning as a sovereign authority for some months past. Long before the virtual abdication of government by the British, the instrument of self-government was forged by the Jewish community. The *Vaad Leumi*, the Jewish Agency and the executives of the various national funds had always carried a major responsibility for colonization and the organization of the *Yishuv*. The chairman of the executive of the Jewish Agency was David Ben-Gurion; its treasurer was Eliezer Kaplan; its representative before international tribunals was Moshe Sharett. The protection of the *Yishuv* had for years been the responsibility of the secret Haganah, for early in the history of Palestine's colonization, the Jewish settlers had learned that the problem of defense had to be met by them.

The ideological insistence on skilled and unskilled labor had given many Jewish workers training in basic occupations. When the mandatory regime haphazardly abandoned the post office, the railways, the electric supply stations and other essential national services, Jewish authorities were forced to take over. Electricity was supplied; transport was resumed; and the post office reopened.

After November 29, when it became apparent that the British proposed to make their exit demonstratively anarchic, the *Yishuv* had begun to prepare a formal government which could step into the vacuum. Early in April, the World Zionist General Council meeting in Tel Aviv set up a provisional cabinet of 13, headed by Ben-Gurion and a council of 37. For the most part, the cabinet members had already been engaged in carrying out the duties to which they were formally appointed.

While the mandate drew to a chaotic close, the Jews single-handedly had managed to implement the partition resolution. Practically all the territory allotted the Jewish state by the General Assembly of the United Nations had been cleared of foreign bands and was securely under Jewish control.

On May 14, six hours before the official termination of the Palestine mandate, the State of Israel was proclaimed by the provisional state council meeting in the municipal museum of Tel Aviv. Since May 14 fell on Saturday, the assembly was held on Friday afternoon at 4 P.M. to avoid the profanation of the Sabbath. The Scripture reading in the synagogues at the Friday night service was Amos 9:11,14-15:

"I will bring back the captives of my people Israel . . . and I will plant them upon their land, and they shall no more be plucked out of their land which I have given them, says the Lord your God."

The simple ceremony in Tel Aviv at which Ben-Gurion announced "the establishment of the Jewish state in Palestine to be called Israel" had no adequate parallel in history. The declaration of statehood by a small community in a tiny notch of the Middle East was accorded a measure of notice which indicated how the imagination of mankind had been kindled by this stubborn wait for centuries until the promised hour of the "return." Ten minutes after the end of the British mandate, President Truman electrified the world with his *de facto* recognition of Israel. The United States was the first country to recognize the first Jewish state since the fall of the Temple. On the diplomatic front, the "gamble" had proven brilliantly and surprisingly successful.

There were no such happy surprises on the military front. In the dawn of May 15, the regular armies of the Arab states invaded the one-day-old Jewish state on schedule: Lebanon and Syria from the north; Trans-Jordan and Iraq from the east; Egypt from the south. To the western coast-line came the ships full of refugees which had been waiting for the right of free entry.

Arab strategy called for the capture of Jerusalem by the Trans-Jordan Legion within a few days. Then Abdullah advancing southward and Egyptian forces moving north were to encircle Tel Aviv. The Iraqis were to cut Jewish Palestine in two by striking from the center, and the Syrians and Lebanese would advance on Haifa. According to the blitz plan, Haifa would fall on May 20, and Tel Aviv and Jerusalem by May 25.

However, after the initial invasion nothing else went according to schedule. Jerusalem held out, refusing to capitulate. Abdullah, lost in the dream of reducing the martyred citadel, languished in its shadow instead of advancing to Tel Aviv. The settlements in the Negev held up the Egyptian armored columns and turned blitz into a battle of attrition. (Israel was helped by the fact that the Egyptian Army, instead of advancing solidly on Tel Aviv, had split, one column turning east to march on Jerusalem to prevent its exclusive occupation by Abdullah.) And the Haganah swept Syrians and Lebanese back across the borders.

At the same time, one of the first acts of the government was to abolish the White Paper and declare all "illegals" in the country legal residents of Israel. It called on the population for economic as well as military support. By May 24, the first national loan of $20,000,000 had been oversubscribed.

By June 11, the Arab armies were being driven back or contained on every front. A truce arranged by the United Nations mediator, Count Bernadotte, interrupted the fighting for four weeks. The Arabs, still refusing to accept the reality of their defeat, resumed the war on July 10. The ten days that followed proved to be days of spectacular successes for Israel's Army and of continuous rout for the Arabs. The crucial airport of Lydda was taken by the Israeli forces on July 10. Nazareth surrendered to the Israeli Army on July 16. Arab villages either surrendered or were abandoned.

The morale of Tel Aviv had been an uncertain factor. The government could be sure of the settlements and it already knew the fiber of Jerusalem, but flat Tel Aviv, with its aggregate of human beings, posed a question mark. The city had no shelters except the hallways of three- and four-story houses with a few sandbags piled in front of the entrances. How long would the population be able to endure air attack without antiaircraft protection? The terrible days between July 10-18, when Egyptian spitfires attacked, provided the answer. The people of Tel Aviv stood firm like those of Jerusalem.

The Israeli Army appeared to be on the verge of recapturing the Old City of Jerusalem which had fallen to Abdullah and of liberating captured settlements on the Jordan. In the midst of this victorious advance, the Security Council ordered a cease-fire. The second truce started on July 18.

Among the thirty-seven signers of Israel's Declaration of Independence were two women—Rachel Kagan of Wizo and Golda Myerson. Those who signed knew that they had entered Jewish history. But Golda was not given the opportunity of savoring the delight of being a new-born Israeli for more than two days. She was being bombarded with cables from the United States, assuring her that if she would fly to America immediately she would be able to translate the excitement about the emergence of Israel into needed millions. She would duplicate the triumphs of January. Historic rapture had to yield to the necessity of getting more dollars for heavy armor to beat back the well-equipped invaders. As in January, it was impossible to fly back to Jerusalem, which was now being shelled. When she reached New York on May 18, she had even less with her than on the previous trip. The customs officer was particularly puzzled by a curious item in her handbag—a long Arab veil.

The emissary from the new State of Israel was a very different person from the tense, tight-lipped woman I had seen five months earlier when she had come from the embattled *Yishuv*. Despite the fact that, objectively viewed, the situation was even more precarious—the five invading armies had already crossed the borders of the new state—

Golda Meir: Woman with a Cause

Golda was radiant. When I saw her shortly after her arrival, she stopped in the middle of a conversation and said with an almost childish delight, "We have a state; imagine, we have a state." This simple, almost naive pleasure was in its way more touching than the historic solemnity with which the event was formally hailed by her and other spokesmen at public celebrations. The joy was personal, intimate. I realized then, as I realized in other contacts with Israelis, how much longer one lifetime of direct involvement was than 2,000 years of abstract longing.

Golda had always been loyal to old comrades. In the first days after her arrival, the suite of the first-class hotel that she occupied as a government official was filled with old friends, men and women who in their youth had belonged to the "movement" with her, who had never left it, and who now rejoiced in its triumph, with a little embarrassment. They were at ease with Golda because with them she was never the great lady but a "*havera*." They compared her favorably in this respect with the other great of Israel who had become less accessible and less patient of time-consuming sentimental gatherings. Some of these friends had gone to Palestine for a year or two and had returned. All of them had dreamed of a vague day when the children would be grown up, when conditions would be more settled, or when larger savings would be available so that they could emigrate. More than one looking at Golda thought secretly that if he had gone along on the *Pocahontas* he would now perhaps be an important figure in the Jewish state instead of a professional Zionist or a small businessman. A middle-aged woman whom life had not treated kindly said to me with tears, "I should never have gotten off that ship." I had not known until then that she was one of the three who had debarked in Boston in 1921.

Golda planned to spend a month in the United States and then return to Israel. She began work with her usual energy and with the additional glamor of being a representative of Israel. But the radiant mood was to be short-lived. I came to see her one day at the Sulgrave, where she was staying, and I saw that she was preoccupied and disturbed. Then she told her news. She had received a telegram from Sharett asking her to accept an appointment as Minister to Moscow. I remember that all present when she made this disclosure, myself included, shrieked, "How wonderful!" Strangely enough she was not pleased at the offer. She could not be indifferent to the honor paid her, nor could her imagination remain unstirred at the notion of a diplomatic post in Soviet Russia, but her reaction was negative. She said: "At last we have a state. I want to be there. I don't want to go thousands of miles away."

The state was not a metaphysical concept that could be enjoyed at a distance. To be absent the very first year was a kind of exile. To the sense of loss at not being there was added a more personal element. There were close bonds in Israel that she did not wish to sever for long periods, but these reasons could not be voiced. They belonged to the private life which it was a matter of duty to disregard if larger issues were at stake.

The rebellious outcry, "Why do I always have to go away?" had to be stifled. Tremendous pressure was put on Golda to accept, and she capitulated. The appointment was announced on June 7, 1948. She was supposed to leave at once for Israel and then proceed to Russia. The Soviet recognition of Israel had been prompt, and diplomatic courtesy required an equally prompt appreciation of the fact.

Then there took place an accident which cast a cloud on the cordial relations existing between Soviet Russia and the new state. Two days before her scheduled departure, Golda paid a visit to an old friend in Brooklyn. The taxi in which she was riding collided with an automobile, and Golda suffered a fractured leg. She was brought to the Hospital for Joint Diseases. The doctors knew who she was, and the nurses soon learned from the baskets and boxes of flowers that kept arriving from distinguished individuals and from every organization even remotely connected with Jewish interests.

The leg healed but a complication arose in the form of phlebitis. A number of blood clots developed. Ordinarily this would have been viewed as an unpleasant delay in recovery with no repercussions beyond the discomfort of the patient. However, while Golda lay in the hospital, unable to move, rumors began to spread that this was a diplomatic illness. Golda was presumably malingering. The leftist Mapam let it be known that the automobile accident was a "lie," a delaying action to make sure that America's representative would arrive in Israel before the Russian Minister, so that the American would be the dean of the diplomatic corps. To make matters worse, Russia indicated displeasure. Was little Israel presuming to snub the giant?

The innuendos and pointed questions in the Leftist press were especially maddening to those who had occasion to see Golda daily during her stay at the hospital. On the one hand there was a steady stream of telegrams from the harried Israeli foreign office asking her when she could leave. On the other hand, her physicians assured her that it was dan-

gerous to leave before the blood clot was resolved. She wired
to Israel suggesting that someone else be appointed, in view
of her physical condition. The suggestion was rejected. She
would simply have to recover as soon as possible. Golda became restive under the barrage. Her friends knew that as
soon as she could stand she would disregard the doctors' instructions, in her customary fashion. But in the past when
she had gotten up from a sick bed in defiance of medical orders and warnings, she had done so because whatever had to
be done was in her view more important than her health or
her life. Here she had to be sacrificed to appease nonsensical
suspicions. No vital interest would be injured were she to arrive in Moscow a month later. Nevertheless, if her government kept urging that she go as soon as possible, she was in-
terpreting "possible" in her usual style. She did not give expression to any of this, but I felt an unvoiced bitterness in
her at the role of a national figure who received so little human consideration. Except for a small band of intimates, she
had no illusions about the expressions of concern which
surrounded her. When people said, "How do you feel?" they
generally meant, "Do you feel well enough for this or that
task?"

I had planned to fly to Israel at the beginning of July, but
because of the fighting, the air lines canceled their flights.
When the truce came into effect, I decided to fly at once. I
was certain that Golda could not leave for some weeks, despite her avowed intentions, and I was afraid that I would be
unable to reach Israel in case the fighting was resumed.

Although originally I had planned to fly back with Golda,
she did not rebuke me for my skepticism about the date of
her departure. There was always the possibility that an

American citizen might be refused a passport for a troubled area. Besides, she was predisposed to be tolerant of an impatience to reach Israel quickly.

I understood that first rapture with the state better after my arrival in Israel, then six weeks old. From the moment my plane landed at the Haifa airport and we saw the Israeli flag waving over it, the jubilee was on. Though many of the passengers had been in Palestine on previous occasions, it was our first entry into Israel. At every step of the inevitable formalities which are generally endured with a minimum of enthusiasm by the badgered traveler I could hear the admiring comments of my companions: "An Israeli entry permit! An Israeli stamp!"

Even the unlucky passenger whose baggage was scanned with a thoroughness never observed by me on previous trips paid a stiff duty for such items as medicinal cognac and pungent sausage with less bitterness than might have been expected. His companions cheered him up with the reflection that it was all for the *medinah*. How many men in modern times had been blessed with the chance to pay duty to a Jewish state? He finally packed up his costly historic sausage with a smile.

Perhaps the climax of the honeymoon-with-history mood came three days after my arrival, on July 27, the anniversary of Herzl's death, which had been designated as Nation Day. A parade of the victorious Israeli forces marched through Tel Aviv. The people lining the streets, filling every window, were intoxicated, not only by the army's accomplishment but by the fact of the army itself. Israel had a force, no longer underground, but an army with banners—a symbol of strength and renascence. When two tanks captured from the Egyptians rolled past, there was an outcry, but perhaps the

greatest ovation was reserved for the planes that circled over-
head. Tel Aviv remembered the bombings it had endured
day after day.

One old Yemenite, standing on the sidewalk with his son,
whispered to the boy, "I must be a saint; if I were not, I could
not have lived to see this day."

The military punctilio and fanfare worried one of the
older comrades. Such had not been the dream of the early
pioneers. Would the people's militia remain a democratic
force of workers devoted to the goal of a cooperative society,
or would baser values seep in? These were problems sharpened by the success of Israeli arms.

Even the seasoned veterans of the struggle were groping
for words to express their sense of wonder at what had come
to pass. Indeed, the word *ness* (miracle) was the one heard
most frequently. A current joke divided the population into
three classes: pessimists, optimists and *nessimists,* and the
latter seemed to have won the day.

A fellow roomer at the lodgings where I stayed turned out
to be a correspondent of the New York *Daily Worker.* He
lost no time in pointing out Israel's errors, among which the
failure to send a minister to Moscow quickly and gratefully
loomed large. I could see that my hour-by-hour description
of Golda's physical condition made little impression. Not
that he thought me an elaborate liar, but my commonplace
facts did not jibe with his theory of historical determinism
or with the line which had been taken in regard to possible
explanations for the failure of a diplomat to arrive in time.

Eventually Golda left New York for Israel before complete recovery. Her failure to heed medical advice resulted
in chronic suffering and an operation several years later. The
legend of the "diplomatic illness" is revived periodically for

partisan purposes. If Israel inclines to the West, the case becomes that much neater if one can point to evidence of ill will as far back as 1948 when Golda "malingered."

She had to spend a few weeks in Israel to choose those who would accompany her and to prepare for her new post. The mysteries of protocol were unknown to Israel's leaders, most of whom had been homespun kibbutzniks taking pride in their disdain of empty social forms. Ben-Gurion's famous apology to a Mapai conference at which he arrived in a dress suit, "Excuse me, I am wearing my working clothes," was more than a joke. The open blue shirt and khaki pants of the worker were the traditional garb of pioneer Palestine. Even at international conferences or political encounters with top-ranking diplomatic figures, the leaders of the *Yishuv* had refused to compromise on tails. A business suit with collar and tie was submission enough. But the infant state needed special garb. During the first few months after the establishment of Israel, in addition to the major problems, there was a semi-amused, semi-worried preoccupation with correct clothes, bows and handshakes. The wealthy ladies of Tel Aviv, who had always followed Parisian styles, took a malicious delight in announcing that the severely dressed heroines of the Second, or more likely Third, *Aliyah* were scurrying around to fashionable dressmakers for gowns for a gala reception at the Russian Ministry. Perhaps even more surprising than the capitulation to the bourgeois world was the speed with which Labor learned its social forms—and liked them.

Golda, widely traveled and for years familiar with the circles of the great, was the most cosmopolitan member of the Israel mission to Moscow. Some of the people of her party had never been out of Palestine. But even Golda had to steel her-

self to the inevitable wearing of evening dress. She was accustomed to attending gala banquets or receptions dressed
neatly and simply in a plain dress or a suit with a fresh white
blouse. But in Moscow she had to dress in a manner proper
to a minister. Every member of the mission had to be fitted
out. Golda put these problems in the capable hands of Aiga
Shapiro, a woman of charm and taste who was going to accompany her to Russia in the capacity of confidential secretary.

In one respect the "movement," which usually ignored personal feeling, had been unexpectedly perceptive. While in
New York, Golda received a telegram from Israel asking
whether she objected to the appointment of Sarele, her
daughter, who lived in Revivim—the southernmost kibbutz
in the Negev—as radio operator to her staff. Golda was
touched by this consideration. It made departure from Israel
easier.

Blond, blue-eyed Sarele had fallen in love with a comrade
of Revivim—Zacharia, a handsome, bright young Yemenite.
He, too, was to go to Moscow as a code and radio expert.
Golda would not have made these appointments of her own
accord—nepotism—but she was grateful for the thoughtful-
ness shown her.

Before the departure for Moscow, Sarele's wedding took
place in the small cottage of Shana in Holon. Only a few
close friends were invited; otherwise, as Golda put it, she
would have had to invite half of Israel. The ceremony took
place in Shana's garden. Among the few guests was Regina.
Morris, too, was present.

Sarele and Menachem, deeply attached to both parents,
were especially tender to their father; he was the one ag-
grieved. Despite the son's pride in his mother's achievements,

Menachem—echoing the views of Morris a generation earlier—more than once dogmatically declared: "Woman's place is with her husband and children." Sarele, who in childhood had also suffered from her parents' broken marriage and Golda's absences, put it differently. In her quiet, firm way she said, "For such a mother it's worth while."

By now the questions had answered themselves. Only Shana, scurrying about offering cookies and fruit to her guests, sometimes glanced at Golda and—still the worried older sister—shook her head.

The Yemenite in-laws, with dark, sensitive faces, sat decorously together, a little apart from the Westerners whose customs and languages they did not understand. Perhaps they were abashed by the presence of Golda. Those who wondered what would close the gap between them and the animated Western Jews in the garden might have found their answer in the marriage just celebrated under Shana's plum trees.

IN MOSCOW

THE Israeli Legation, consisting of twenty-one people including children, arrived at the airport forty miles from Moscow on September 3, 1948. As soon as the party reached the capital they were received by official representatives. It happened to be the day of the funeral of Zhdanov, a close associate of Stalin, and the long ceremonious procession held up all cars. Out of courtesy to the Israelis, the Russian chief of protocol had the procession stopped for a moment so that the newly arrived representatives might proceed. The deference was impressive to the green diplomats.

For the first few months, the Israeli mission was lodged at the Metropole, a first-class Russian hotel. Later, Israel received an eleven-room house on Glazovsky Perulok, which served both as office and residence. A large amount of household equipment and foodstuffs had been brought from Israel and Europe. The size of the staff was gradually curtailed when it became apparent that the original number was too large for the work to be done.

The mere physical process of establishing a legation in Moscow was difficult, especially with a limited budget.

Hard-pressed Israel, in addition to its other headaches, discovered that diplomacy was costly and that each fresh recognition of the state added to the strain on a scant treasury. In Moscow, almost everything had to be brought from abroad and it was hard to get adequate service. Golda energetically threw herself into the housekeeping problems presented. Various members of her staff, both men and women, recalled apparent trifles: she helped to tack down carpets and faithfully took her turn at washing the dishes if there was no maid. The fact that the minister remained Golda, friendly and informal, instead of turning into an aloof diplomat, was an enormous aid to the morale of the legation. Actually Golda enjoyed some of the housekeeping chores, taking pleasure in shopping and examining the huge government cooperatives, always plentifully stocked with meat, fish, cheese and other foodstuffs.

Golda, in the true tradition of Labor Palestine, organized the legation in the style of a kibbutz. Everybody sat down to dinner together, including the cook. Hotel expenses were paid directly by a central fund. Pocket money was apportioned equally to all, the chauffeur getting as much as Madam Minister. No salaries were paid. It had been Golda's hope that this would remain the established pattern, but the kibbutz arrangement did not last beyond the first year. After her departure, the Israel Treasury decided upon a salary scale which proved to be so much more than the staff members had received under her idealistic aegis that they quite humanly applied for back pay, which was refused.

The modest Israeli legation was warmly welcomed by the foreign journalists and the diplomatic corps. The Israelis were something of a sensation, because they represented the dramatically arisen Jewish state. That the minister was a woman added to the interest. Golda was the second woman in the diplomatic corps, the first one being Mrs. Pandit. The Soviet itself had few women diplomats. Russian women were very active in the life of the country, frequently in highly technical capacities. Women might be directors of factories, agriculturalists or engineers, but only a small number played major parts in politics, so that a woman diplomat was bound to excite curiosity.

Ticklish questions of protocol arose; at the time that Golda arrived, only a few states had as yet recognized Israel. Diplomatic relations could only be enjoyed with the legations of these countries, but there were many occasions when all representatives met at formal receptions. Relations with the British were understandably strained at first. The American Bedell Smith was just as understandably helpful and cordial.

Until a minister presents his letter of credentials, he has no official existence. Before the presentation he receives a briefing from the chief of protocol, giving exact procedural instructions. The question of dress was a problem for Golda. Men wore uniforms or tails. The only other woman, Mrs. Pandit, had worn a sari. Golda's national costume might have been the white cotton dress which the pioneers festively wore on the Sabbath, but this obviously would not do. It was decided that she should wear a long black dress with long sleeves. She would be further adorned with a small black velvet turban and a string of pearls. The hat represented a real sacrifice, since Golda rarely wore one. The pearls, costing all of ten dollars, had been hastily bestowed on her by a friend before her departure from Israel when it was discovered that she had no jewelry except some Israeli pins.

Golda presented her credentials on September 11, a week after her arrival in Moscow. A motion-picture release of her reception by Shvernik, President of the Soviets, was shown in all the cinemas of Israel. The audience in the Tel Aviv movie theatre shouted joyously, *"Golda shelanu"* ("Our Golda") while close friends watched her ceremonial progress on this film silently and a bit awed.

Now the legation could begin to function. Its primary task, like that of every other embassy, was the development of friendly political and economic relations. Some commercial negotiations were started, but by and large its tasks existed within a rigidly circumscribed framework. Every embassy's relations with the Russians were strictly formal, with no social contacts outside the line of duty. Israel was no exception to the familiar pattern. However, friendly terms were established with other members of the diplomatic corps, a process in which Golda's personal popularity was decisive, and even the British eventually were won over.

The Israeli legation kept open house informally every Friday night. The refreshments were coffee, tea and cake. Press correspondents generally dropped in. Foreign Jews, English and American fur merchants or Belgian tobacco dealers who happened to be in Moscow, found the Israeli legation convivial. These Friday nights were merry and crowded, but no Russian Jew ventured to come.

The Israelis had few illusions about the possibility of establishing ties with the some 3,000,000 Russian Jews. It was assumed that Jewish consciousness had become extinct since the revolution and that any Zionist sentiment—in view of merciless government persecution for three decades—was long dead. To the physical destruction of European Jewry had to be added the spiritual loss of Russian Jewry.

As if to drive home this realization, a diatribe against Zionism, by Soviet writer Ilya Ehrenburg, appeared in *Einig-*

keit, the Yiddish Communist daily, a few days after Golda's arrival. Lest Russian Jews misunderstand the recognition of Israel, Ehrenburg—a perennially enthusiastic exponent of the Soviet line whatever that might be—proceeded to expound the familiar thesis: there was no Jewish people. Jews in Soviet Russia and the satellite countries had nothing to do with the Jewish state, which was solely for the oppressed of the imperialist countries. It was ridiculous to speak of a common interest among Jews. One might just as well speak of a common bond among redheaded people; and more of the same.

The day the article appeared, a foreign correspondent came to Golda for comment, which she gave without mincing words. The foreign correspondent, a friend of Ehrenburg, suggested that Golda meet him. Golda agreed but Ehrenburg never came. Some months later the same correspondent pointed out Ehrenburg to her at a Czech diplomatic reception. Golda reminded him of his offer. He went over to Ehrenburg and came back with a message that Ehrenburg was willing to meet Golda but was not prepared to discuss politics. Golda sent back word that she was prepared not to meet him. Nevertheless, later in the evening Ehrenburg came over, obviously in his cups. Correspondents and diplomats immediately surrounded the pair. Ehrenburg asked if Golda spoke Russian or French; Golda said she spoke Hebrew or English. At which Ehrenburg, a Jew himself, announced: "I hate Jews who speak English." Golda replied: "I am accustomed to Jews who speak Hebrew or at least Yiddish." These exchanges went on, Ehrenburg speaking Russian, which Golda understood, and Golda speaking English. The surrounding crowd chuckled at the firmness with which Golda stood her ground in hostile territory.

The conversation with Ehrenburg was dispiriting if not unexpected. During the years of the Hitler massacre, when it had been to Russia's interest to tap each source of anti-German feeling, Ehrenburg had been among the most eloquent and dutifully vocal of the mourners for European Jewry. Then the tie of a common history and a common fate had been apparent to him and other Russian journalists—red blood and not red hair—as Golda had pointed out. But now the pens had to scratch to another tune, and it seemed hardly possible that, except for a few oldsters who still attended synagogue, any sense of Jewish identity had remained among the Jews of Russia. Then something happened which was an eye-opener both to the world and to the Soviet authorities.

Before leaving Israel, Golda had decided that she and her staff would attend synagogue services in Russia. Though neither Golda nor most of the members of her legation were orthodox, they thought it fitting to join whatever small conscious Jewish community existed in Moscow on the first Saturday after the presentation of credentials. Golda asked the men in her party to equip themselves with prayer shawls and prayer books and whatever else might be ritually needful.

On the first Sabbath, the legation went to the only synagogue in Moscow, that of Rabbi Maze (who had received the stamp of official approval). Of the some 500,000 Jews in Moscow, about 300 were in attendance, mostly old men. Here and there a young face might be seen. No one had known that the Israeli delegation would attend except the rabbi. In the course of the service there was a prayer for rulers of the state. The rabbi invoked the blessing of the Almighty on Stalin, and then he offered a prayer for Golda.

After the service, a man came up to the women's section

where Golda had been seated, to ask if she would go down to meet the rabbi. He also wanted to know whether in Israel rabbis shake hands with a woman. This was of course a delicate reminder that an orthodox rabbi could not touch the hand of any female, except that of his wife, and even she had to be ritually clean. Golda was careful not to embarrass the old man and did not extend her hand.

There was tremendous excitement among the male worshipers as she was led through the hall on the way out. They followed her out of the synagogue, and in the crowd she became separated from her party. Since it was Saturday, the delegation had come on foot. An elderly man, noticing that she was alone, walked up to her and said in Yiddish, "Don't talk to me; I'll walk ahead and you follow." When Golda was within reach of her hotel, her guide turned around, recited the Hebrew blessing, *"Shechianu"* ("Blessed are we that we have lived to see this day") and vanished.

The Israelis did not again go to the synagogue till Rosh Hashanah, a few weeks later. Intuitively, Golda felt that too frequent appearances would not be politic. Though no announcement of the legation's intention had been made, it was apparently assumed by the Moscow public that the Israelis would attend the synagogue during the high holidays. The normal attendance on the high holidays was generally about two thousand. On this occasion the crowds overflowing the adjoining streets were estimated at between 30,000 and 50,000 people. Thousands of young men and women could be seen, including Red Army officers and soldiers. The Soviet authorities had expected no such demonstration, and no special police arrangements had been made. When Golda appeared, she was instantly engulfed in the crowd. A remarkable photograph which someone fortunately snapped shows

Golda's head literally among a sea of people of all ages looking excited and joyous. An added touch to the drama was the
presence of some German war prisoners stolidly watching the
Israeli triumph from adjoining buildings.

In the women's gallery, women kept coming up to touch
Golda or to kiss her dress. The service, always solemn, this
time had an added tension. At the conclusion, when Golda
left the synagogue, she was again surrounded. One old man
kept bobbing up in front of her periodically, croaking:
"Goldele, leben sollst du, shana tova" ("Goldele, long life to
you, happy New Year"). The crowd would brush him away
but he would reappear to offer his ecstatic greeting. Finally
the main thoroughfare was reached. The throng had become
so dangerous in its size and emotionalism that Golda's companions thrust her into a taxi despite the holiday, but the
crowd flowed around the taxi. Golda put out her head and
said to them in Yiddish: *"A dank eich wos ihr seit geblieben
Yiden"* ("Thanks that you have remained Jews"). Finally
the taxi was permitted to proceed.

She did not attend the service on the second day of Rosh
Hashanah. The experience had been too moving. As she
put it: "We all went to pieces."

A few days later, on Yom Kippur Eve, the legation went
for Kol Nidre. The streets leading to the synagogue were
again filled with the same enormous crowds. This time,
however, the authorities had been forewarned. Golda had
been instructed not to leave the synagogue till the crowd had
dispersed. But at the end of the service the congregation did
not budge. Neither did the waiting crowd outside. Then po-
licemen appeared, cleared an aisle, and went upstairs to the
women's gallery to escort Golda through a basement to a
back street. But the crowds sensed the trick and rushed to

the side street through which she was supposed to make a
quiet exit. A procession formed spontaneously, headed by
Golda surrounded by police, with the throng following. So
they marched through the streets of Moscow. The Russians
along the way watched this extraordinary spectacle in be-
wilderment. They had seen nothing like it. Golda would
hear an explanatory note to the puzzled bystanders: *"Eto
nasha Golda,"* the Russian for "Golda *Shelanu,*" "Our Golda."

The same demonstration took place on the day of Yom
Kippur. The service was particularly stirring. At Yiskor, the
prayer for the dead, the congregation prayed for the men of
the Haganah who had fallen. When the congregation recited the prayer, *"Lshanah haboh b-Yerushalayim"* ("Next
year in Jerusalem"), the long-suppressed feeling reached its
climax. Of that moment Golda said: "The words shook the
synagogue as they looked up at me. It was the most passionate Zionist speech I had ever heard."

Apparently in crowds people were not afraid to show their
true feelings. One man edged up to a member of the Israeli
legation and whispered: "This is the answer to Ehrenburg's
article." But no individual ventured to establish contact with
the Israelis. Even close relatives of members of the legation
made no attempt to visit or to communicate with their kin.
Any traffic with foreigners was suspect, and it was easier not
to see a brother than to run the risk of being sent to Siberia.

Once, on the street, a man walked up to Sarele, Golda's
daughter, and addressed her in Hebrew. It turned out that
he had been an original member of the kibbutz of Tel Yoseph
in the twenties. He had left Palestine with a disgruntled group
that had decided that social redemption was to be found in
the socialist fatherland rather than in the fields of the Emek.
He was obviously much moved when he spoke to Sarele. He

wanted to know about a sister he had in Tel Aviv. He asked about Berl Katznelson, the teacher and spiritual leader of Palestinian pioneer youth, not knowing that Berl had been dead some years. Sarele invited the former kibbutznik to the legation, but he said, "No, I suppose I have been followed already," and disappeared. For Sarele it was a shattering experience—"That human beings should be so afraid."

On another occasion a member of the legation went to a large office building. A young fellow offered to direct him to the room he wanted. Suddenly, in the corridor with no one around, he slipped the Israeli a note. It read: "Long live the Jewish state." Such readiness to take grave risks to express a moment of innocent feeling was very touching to the members of the legation.

No comment had appeared in the Russian press about the Jewish demonstrations during the high holidays, but undoubtedly notice had been taken. There was no law against attending synagogue, though such attendance would probably have been unhealthy for a person with a responsible post. A few ancient Jews might harmlessly go and mutter their prayers. It was certainly not the thing for Soviet youth.

The spontaneous mass outpouring was evidence of a tremendous surge of sentiment which still remained alive after more than thirty years of ruthless Soviet extirpation of the Zionist movement and the study of Hebrew "as a tool of British imperialism" and "bourgeois nationalism." After the Soviet recognition of Israel, Russian Jews briefly hoped that they could safely show an interest in the Jewish state. At any rate, during September and October, the first two months of the legation's residence in Moscow, many Jews naively sent cables of congratulation and letters of inquiry to the legation. Some even wanted to know if they could go to Israel.

But this open expression stopped abruptly after the synagogue episode. Word had probably gone out that such goings on were inadvisable. After October, few dared raise their heads when the Israelis came to the synagogue, and there were no enthusiastic crowds. Even at the Yiddish theatre, where the Israelis had been enthusiastically surrounded the first time they came, not a soul ventured to approach during the intermissions.

On one occasion, attendance at the Yiddish theatre was a particularly painful experience for the Israelis. The play dealt with the revolt of the Warsaw Ghetto. A stirring theme, but in this play history was being rewritten Soviet style. According to the version presented, the Jews of the ghetto had not revolted of their own accord. They had been aroused by a Polish messenger who arrived to encourage the Jews and lecture them on the need to resist the Nazis. This travesty of the most tragic moment in modern Jewish history had to be watched unprotestingly by the Israelis. That the falsification, offensive to the memory of the Jewish martyrs, was composed in Yiddish, only served to increase the degradation. Golda had to maintain a diplomatic silence, but years later when the infamous "doctors' plot" was staged in Moscow, she could passionately remind the ghetto survivors in Israel —some of whom had joined the pro-Soviet Mapam—of how their story was told in Russia.

On November 7, the anniversary of the Bolshevik Revolution, Foreign Minister Molotov held a large reception at his home in honor of the day. All the legations were invited. Formal dress was required, a circumstance particularly painful to Jael Namir, the fifteen-year-old daughter of the legation's counselor who had been invited according to protocol, since her father was a widower. The girl, brought up in the

Palestinian youth movement, felt that the wearing of evening dress and stockings would be a betrayal of her egalitarian principles and a surrender to the bourgeoisie. A quarter of a century earlier, many Russian boys and girls of the Revolutionary movement would have sympathized with the Israeli girl's scruples. Jael begged for a compromise costume of a long dress and white socks, but finally the needs of diplomacy prevailed.

Golda was received by Molotov in a room reserved for the heads of legations while the guests of lesser rank milled around in other rooms. After a few minutes Mrs. Molotov, accompanied by a secretary, came up to Golda in a friendly manner and said, "I have been looking for you." The two women began seeking a common language when Mrs. Molotov announced: "I speak Yiddish." Golda asked her, in Yiddish, whether she was Jewish. Mrs. Molotov answered: *"Ich bin a Yiddishe tochter,"* a phrase with warmer overtones than a merely factual, "I am Jewish."

Mrs. Molotov seemed to be genuinely affected by the meeting with Golda and made no attempt to conceal her emotion. She mentioned the high holiday episode: "I hear you went to the synagogue; that was good. Jews wanted so much to see you."

They discussed various matters, including the boundaries of the Negev which the United Nations was debating at the time. When Golda remarked, "I can't give up the Negev; my daughter lives there and she won't allow it," Mrs. Molotov, upon hearing that the girls were in the next room, said impulsively, "I must see them," and went out to talk to them. She was charmed and intrigued by the blond, blue-eyed girls who were practicing socialism in a utopian enclave in the Middle East. She was curious about the social organization of the cooperative farms and plied Sarele with questions about her kibbutz in the Negev. Of course, neither Jael nor Sarele could speak Yiddish. Native-born *sabras,* they knew only Hebrew, but Namir translated their replies into Yiddish. Mrs. Molotov seemed to be fascinated by the notion that Jews were in agriculture and that they had an army. When Sarele told her that at Revivim there was complete communal ownership of property, Mrs. Molotov shook her head. "That's not good," she said. "People won't go there if they have to share everything. We are against that."

As she heard Sarele describe the youth movement she commented: "Just like the *Narodniki* [Russian revolutionists who carried on propaganda among the peasants]; you go to the people the way we did." To which the usually shy Sarele replied in a matter-of-fact way, "We don't go to the people. We are the people." Mrs. Molotov advised Sarele to study the writings of Stalin, assuring her that they would make her very happy.

Finally the secretary reminded Mrs. Molotov that she had to get back to her guests. Those present report that she parted from the two young *sabras* with tears in her eyes.

When she returned to her official receiving line, she was still full of her discovery. She kept introducing Golda and referring to the girls, as if anxious to show them off. Her final words to Golda were: *"Soll eich sein gut. As eich wet sein gut, wet sein gut allen Yidden auf der welt"* ("May things go well with you. If all will be well with you, things will go well for Jews in the whole world").

Mrs. Molotov's public enthusiasm created a sensation. Various diplomats of the satellite countries came up to Golda and told her that they had Jewish wives. In any other country further expressions of friendliness would have followed naturally. But that was the sole contact. Golda never heard from Mrs. Molotov again. "That evening she was a Jewish woman," Golda said. (Subsequent reports from Russia indicated that Mrs. Molotov fell out of favor and was sent into exile, from which she was recalled after Stalin's death.)

On the basis of these experiences, the Israelis were convinced that the Soviet had not succeeded in eradicating Jewish consciousness among its Jewish citizens. The Russian authorities apparently came to the same conclusion.

Since 1919, Zionist activity and the study of Hebrew had been outlawed in Russia as bourgeois deviations. The Soviet formula, "national in form, socialist in content," according to which the languages and folkways of the various national minorities in the Soviet Union were sympathetically fostered, did not apply to Russian Jewry. Both Lenin and Stalin held that the Jewish problem would be solved by assimilation. In the meantime, as a temporary measure, the use of Yiddish, free from the religious and historic associations of Hebrew, was permitted. Jews could read Sholem Aleichem but not Isaiah.

Not all Communist leaders shared Stalin's view. President Kalenin urged the establishment of a territory in which "Jews would acquire all the attributes of a nation" and in which "Jewish culture would blossom." In 1934, Biro-Bidjan, a region in the Soviet Far East, beyond the Urals, was proclaimed an autonomous Jewish province. One reason for Stalin's change of heart was that a Jewish settlement in the Siberian wastes might prove a useful buffer against possible Japanese aggression and Chinese penetration from Manchuria. Therefore Jewish nationalist sentiment became ideologically correct if centered on Biro-Bidjan but criminal heresy if directed toward Palestine. However, Russian Jews showed little interest in colonizing Siberia, even if allowed to use Yiddish, and the experiment failed.

In the heart of Russia, Yiddish publications and the Yiddish theatre faithfully toed the government line, whatever that happened to be. The authorities had no complaints on this score. Yiddish journalists maintained a decent silence about the Jewish massacres during the Nazi-Soviet pact. The passionate lamentations of an Ehrenburg were heard only after Germany attacked its partner. Yet despite the good behavior of the few remaining Jewish bodies, government tolerance came to an end abruptly. In January 1949, the newspaper *Einigkeit*, the publishing press *Emes*, and the Jewish anti-fascist committee were shut down. By April the Yiddish theatre was closed. This ended the last vestiges of organized Jewish expression in Soviet Russia.

These steps took place within five months after the arrival of the Israeli legation. No one knows whether the measures were prompted by the demonstrations which greeted the Israelis or whether these merely speeded up the process. After thirty-one years of repression, masses of Russian Jews had hailed Golda as the symbol of Jewish renascence. That the demonstrations had taken place in the naive faith that Soviet recognition of Israel boded a new era, and had stopped as soon as government displeasure had been indicated, did not alter the fact that Jewish interest in the fate of the Jewish people outside the Iron Curtain was not wholly dead. Anything likely to foster the sense of Jewish identity had to go, even such faithful Communist tools as *Einigkeit* and *Emes*.

From the Soviet point of view, Russian Jewry had displayed abnormal interest in the Israeli legation. Contact with foreigners, evidences of "cosmopolitanism," were tantamount to treason. The kind of natural rapport which existed between

[233]

the Israeli legation and the Jewish community in the United States or other countries was out of the question in Soviet Russia. After the first two months, none but purely formal inquiries were received at the legation. Its work was no more and no less circumscribed than that of any other legation in Soviet Russia. There were a series of routine duties to be performed and little else. Of necessity, the Israelis led a self-sufficient existence, with social contacts limited to fellow diplomats of friendly countries. The Russians were polite but distant.

For a woman of Golda's temperament, the isolation in Moscow could hardly have been satisfying. The glamor of her position was inadequate compensation for absence from the young Jewish state in its crucial first year. In Israel, too, her energy and ability were needed. When Israel's first elected government invited her to join the cabinet, there was no question about her acceptance.

Golda left Moscow on April 20, 1949, to assume the post of minister of labor. The experience in Russia had had its inevitable frustrations but the Israeli legation had received exactly the same kind of treatment as the embassies of more powerful nations. In answer to rumors in the American press, Golda denied that she had been dogged by plain-clothes men and stated curtly that her legation had suffered "neither from excess nor lack of attention." And she was able to say with complete sincerity: "I shall always remember the profound understanding shown by the Russian authorities to the many problems of our young state. It was my endeavor to further friendly relations between the Soviet and Israel, and I hope I have succeeded." Her sorrow for the silenced Jews of Russia was another matter.

MINISTER OF LABOR

ISRAEL'S first elections were held in January 1949. The structure of the state was that of a democratic republic with a unicameral legislature, the *Knesset*, whose 120 members were elected on the basis of proportional representation by universal suffrage. Everyone over the age of eighteen had the right to vote. For the first time in history, Arab women joined their menfolk at the ballot box. Oriental Jews, recently arrived from feudal monarchies, were introduced to the unfamiliar workings of the democratic process. And a bewildering number of parties—21 in all—offered platforms and candidates. Proportional representation, no matter how ideally democratic in theory, resulted in a multiplicity of small parties which complicated the setting up of a tenable government. From the first, Ben-Gurion ruefully eyed the simpler methods of such countries as the United States which managed to get along with 3 or 4 parties at most. Despite this splintering of the electorate, Mapai, though not scoring a clear majority, received 35 percent of the vote—20 percent more than its closest rival. Ben-Gurion would form the coalition government.

The offer of the post of minister of labor was made to Golda in February. She flew to Israel, took her oath of office with the other members of Israel's first elected government on March 11, 1949, and returned to Moscow to make her formal farewells. Her new duties began on her return to Israel in April.

When Mapai announced its proposed appointment of Golda Myerson to the cabinet, the religious bloc was not happy with the choice. Despite her undeniable merits, Golda was a woman. Willy-nilly, the orthodox groups had been obliged to tolerate the many and varied activities of women in the development of Palestine, but a cabinet member seemed excessive. The ultraorthodox *Agudat Israel* had reservations about the equality of women. Some orthodox rabbis pointed to the Biblical injunction: "Thou shalt in any wise set him king over thee," and recalled the interpretation of Maimonides that, as the Bible had not mentioned queens, women "should not rule over Israel." These arguments were countered by citizens who offered pious precedents. One outraged reader wrote to the Jerusalem *Post*: "In regard to the controversy about women M.P.'s in the United Religious Bloc let me point out that the Bible mentions Deborah as a judge in Israel while at least two queens governed Judah and Israel respectively, Athalia, mother of Agaria, and the wife of the Hasmonean, King Alexander Yannai, who followed her husband to the throne. Why therefore should anyone object to Mrs. Myerson's being a minister in Israel?"

The first Israeli cabinet had to learn on the job: Fortunately its members did not come to their colossal tasks wholly untried. Some, like Moshe Sharett who became foreign minister, could step naturally into their posts. For others, like David Remez who was appointed minister of transportation, or Zalman Shazar, who became minister of education, the technical problems were largely unfamiliar. In these fields specialists had to be developed. Golda was as well if not better qualified than most of her associates. Her years of work in the Histadrut, where she had been in charge of labor problems, had given her an intensive preparation for her ministry.

In the Histadrut she had dealt with questions of employment, unemployment and social security. This was known territory. But the ministry of labor had more complex functions. The construction of public housing, road building and various types of public works projects, was also in its province. There was much to learn.

Golda's department had to provide work and houses for the thousands of newcomers who were daily pouring into Israel. The crisis was continuous and unrelenting. Fortunately Golda knew how to surround herself with competent assistants and how to inspire devotion in her staff. She chose men and women who had worked with her in the Histadrut, as well as new people with specialized skills. The technical aspects of her program would have to depend on them.

Golda's task was always threefold: she had to fight for the policy she advocated; she had to raise the funds to make implementation possible; and then she had to implement the policy. If it were a question of housing, she first had to win the approval of the *Knesset* for the budget she offered; then, as any minister, she became responsible for the execution of the program.

She might have been a novice when it came to building materials or engineering projects, but she had clear and determined views in regard to the basic questions of principle

which her ministry had to answer. One of her first public utterances was in her characteristic bold and uncompromising
style. Speaking to a Mapai conference, she raised the question of greater productivity on the part of the individual
worker—a very ticklish subject at a labor meeting. "We need
cheap housing quickly. Building workers are sitting here.
Shall I be told that four hundred bricks is the maximum that
can be laid? I do not want sweated labor but I am not afraid
of proposing contract labor. Our party has the courage to
say unpopular things when necessary. I say that if fixed
wages are holy, then the foundation of the state and the absorption of thousands of Jews are holier still."

The Left stormily repeated the old charge ("She is against
the workers!") so often hurled at her whenever she insisted
that there could be no cleavage in Labor Zionism. Her concept was single, with no division into the interests of
the workers and the interests of the country as a whole, for
these interests were identical. "There can be no Zionism except Socialist Zionism," the theoretician of the movement,
Nachman Syrkin, had said half a century earlier. The constructive activity of Mapai had been predicated on this idea
for decades. For Golda, as she had often declared, the
Histadrut was the chief instrument in the reconstruction of
the homeland rather than merely a trade union concerned
primarily with getting better economic conditions for its
members. Almost her first statement as minister of labor was
to put the goal of a Jewish state "established on the foundations of social justice" squarely before the public. During a
May Day celebration she provoked a storm from the Right
by expressing the romantic hope that perhaps it might be
possible soon to hail the ideal socialist Jewish state.

A social form like the kibbutz was both an ideal way of life and the most practical instrument for pioneering. The essence of the kibbutz lay in its national-economic synthesis. From the socialist Zionist viewpoint, the kibbutz would be meaningless if it were solely a utopian commune which for some mysterious reason had chosen the deserts of Palestine for its social experiment. The whole history of the Palestinian pioneer had shown, as Golda pointed out again and again, that what was good for the worker was good for Zionism and what was good for Zionism was good for the worker. The vision was one. Even all the qualifications and inevitable compromises did not lessen her faith in the eventual good world.

In the perpetual struggle with the Right and the Left, some of Golda's sharpest satirical thrusts would be centered on Mapam. Radicals who righteously waved the banner of social progress while accepting no responsibility for its realization by entering the government were particularly exasperating. In the role of opposition, Mapam sanctimoniously protested acceptance of an American loan as "selling out to the West," and shouted for bigger and better houses for immigrants.

Despite endless debates, there was nothing doctrinaire in Golda's approach to the multiplying practical problems with which she had to cope at once. The makeshift camps for immigrants were full to overflowing. At the same time, lines of unemployed were registering at the labor exchanges. The budget could not keep pace with both the new streams of immigrants pouring in and the requirements of the established population. Each ministry was bitterly aware of how meager was the allotment for its needs. The population had to be defended, educated, fed, transported, represented, housed—all inadequately. But there were certain minimums. Defense had to consume a sizable proportion of the income; otherwise the achievements of the young state might be destroyed by the perpetually threatened "second round." As for the rest—there was "austerity," a euphemism for an abundance of nothing except frozen fish and eggplant. Sometimes even the frozen fish was missing.

On May 24, a month after her return from Moscow, Golda presented to the *Knesset* the "Myerson plan" for the construction of 30,000 housing units. Throughout the subsequent months she kept fighting for an ampler housing program. By August, she had introduced an ambitious public-works program of which the construction of new roads linking all parts of the country was a major feature.

Many of the government's trained economists objected to a large-scale housing program as inflationary. The limited available funds, they claimed, should be invested in productive enterprises such as factories or agriculture instead of in housing for the immigrants or in the improvement of their living conditions. There was still another point of conflict. Many of the newcomers showed no enthusiasm for agriculture or other forms of productive work. They tended to congregate in towns and become peddlers instead of farmers. Since the immigrants were not idealists of the Second or Third *Aliyah,* amenable to ideological persuasion, the economists urged that public-works programs should not be expanded; only the pressure of unemployment would drive the immigrants to the land.

Despite the exacting standards by which Golda measured herself and her comrades, she was not in sympathy with this cold-blooded strategy. Moreover, she had a kindly understanding of the simple Yemenite or Moroccan and a realistic conception of what could justly be expected. In discussing these differences of opinion, she once said:

> My contention was that good citizenship and decent behavior cannot develop as long as people live in tents. There is no sense in talking about social responsibility and duty to the country as long as the immigrant lives in abominable physical conditions. [And she added with vehemence] I am always shocked by economists, themselves well fed, who concoct a theory according to which human beings cannot live with any dignity in the present. I do not believe that any ultimate good can come of this. When people are embittered, they will only become more demoralized. You cannot drive them to the land using hunger as a whip. Nor am I impressed by all this talk of delinquency among the immigrants. If my children had been hungry, I would have stolen bread for them. The economists forget that a man is a human being, not only a statistical figure.

In her fight for her housing program, Golda made much of the human element. Housing was not only a technical question of providing shelter for as many as possible as cheaply as possible. It was also a question of transforming the immigrant into a citizen of Israel. She advocated the building of permanent structures rather than the erection of cheaper units for temporary use.

Should the houses be built near urban centers where work was available, or should they be placed in those parts of the country which most required settlement? There were arguments for both courses. Golda insisted that housing be dispersed, excluding neither developed nor undeveloped sections. The spectacular growth of Beersheba is partly due to her planning.

In the debate over these issues Golda as usual was charged with being "emotional" and swayed by feminine feeling instead of cold logic, but she was undismayed. Whether she persuaded the *Knesset* by womanly passion or masculine reason, she secured the larger appropriation she demanded. At the same time it should be noted that her "emotionalism" differed from the usual variety, be it feminine or masculine. Most human beings are indifferent to the sufferings of anonymous masses but are touched by the pain of an individual. The reverse was true of Golda. She was little swayed by individual appeals. In that sense she was emotionally incorruptible. The significant achievement was not to change the lot of one immigrant who accidentally might tug at her heartstrings by a personal tale, but to feel for the thousands who had not managed to run up to her as she made her rounds of camps and villages. A momentary sentimental impulse was the easy way out; basic policy mattered.

The road-building program, too, was fought by many as a luxury. Is a road productive? Does it substantially contribute to the development of a new section? Could the money be expended more profitably elsewhere? Everyone agreed that a road through the desert to Sodom on the Dead Sea was essential if the possibilities of the region were to be exploited, but what about a little road to a border settlement in the Jerusalem hills? Was it economical to build a difficult road to a remote Negev kibbutz or should the collective be asked to wait another couple of years when financial pressure might ease? Could the new immigrants take root in a rural area if there were no connecting links of road? Would they have the stamina to exist in isolation? Fundamental questions of immigrant absorption and security, not merely of easier communication on pleasant highways, were involved in each branch of the network of roads for which Golda pressed.

Some of the opposition to the roads program was most vocally expressed by city people whose travel consisted of a comfortable taxi ride between Jerusalem and Tel Aviv. Their objections were finally overcome by the necessity for a public-works program that would take advantage of the large supply of unskilled labor that was available. The Oriental Jews had almost no technical training. They had to be given work adapted to their capacities and that would make possible the teaching of skills on the job. Ninety percent of the public housing was erected by untrained men under the direction of skilled foremen who taught the workers in seventeen languages. To vary the work on the roads, the ministry of labor launched the program of "Green Public Works," which involved reforestation, stone removal and terracing, thus making reclamation of the soil along the road part of the project. Delighted Israelis, accustomed to plowing through mud up to their knees in the rainy season or roughly jogging along over stone and sand if the vehicle could make it, called the roads, in tribute to the minister, *"goldene wegen"* (golden roads).

Though she had no knowledge of the professional and technical aspects of either housing or road construction, Golda was no absentee minister. Her assistants appreciated the conscientiousness which made her ride over the roads and inspect the housing for which she was responsible. One of her associates told me: "No minister has visited every part of the country as often as she. No matter how hard the trip may be, she insists on going along personally." Instead of being irritated or resenting her presence, her workers responded to this interest in the actual job.

[243]

Golda Meir: Woman with a Cause

I spent an exhausting three days with her when she went on one of her routine inspection tours of public-housing projects in the vicinity of Haifa. Each time she reached a new project she was greeted by workers, foremen and local dignitaries. These formalities over, she began going relentlessly from room to room. Often the buildings were half finished and she had to walk along narrow planks. In the broiling summer heat, a couple of houses, all pretty much alike, were enough as far as I was concerned. Unfinished houses in the noonday sun were no promenade for middle-aged ladies. But Golda, though everyone knew that she had never fully recovered from her taxi accident and was not in good health generally, walked up and down planks and rickety steps without a glance to indicate that the footing was treacherous or the ascent difficult. When I urged her assistants sotto voce to halt the killing pace, they answered: "We know but we can't stop her. She wouldn't like it."

Were the kitchen porch and other facilities so arranged as to provide the maximum of convenience under the circumstances? She looked with fresh delight at each group of small new houses, visualizing the families that would occupy them. One project was situated high in the hills, giving a glorious view of Haifa and the Mediterranean below. The loveliness of the place gave her a special satisfaction—low-priced houses that offered beauty; beautiful houses for workers. "Why not beauty for people who are not rich?"

The next day was spent in Haifa proper. There were press conferences, labor conferences with the Histadrut and receptions. It was presumably the normal day of a public official except that there seemed to be too much of everything.

On the third day, Golda dropped in at some of the offices of the ministry of labor. The first few hours she went from office to office pleasantly and efficiently, asking questions about the particular office. Her manner was informal and friendly; it was instructive to see how her simplicity and lack of airs in no way diminished her authority or the affectionate deference with which she was received. However, at the last building there was no elevator and five steep flights to climb. I and the other woman with her knew that our hearts, legs and blood pressures were unequal to the climb on a July noon in Israel. But Golda said, "They expect me," waved us into the automobile, and trudged upstairs.

On the way back from Haifa there were more houses to be inspected. Each time she saw the modest, pleasant little concrete houses, she was reconfirmed in her belief that in the long run it was more wasteful to keep repairing canvas huts, which could not stand more than one season of winter rains, than to erect concrete dwellings in the first place. At first—to empty the camps quickly—the government had built small concrete boxes measuring 290 square feet to lodge a family of four; this was soon discontinued. No matter what the drain on the treasury, Israel would not be transformed into a slum.

Each change from tent to blockhouse to roomier dwelling was bitterly debated in the *Knesset*. The Left advocated more spacious houses, and Golda, who was fighting for each additional square foot within the realms of the possible, commended them tartly for their "esthetic sense." The Right attacked the housing program because it did not encourage private enterprise; the Left objected that it did not go far enough on the road to a planned economy. To those who complained that Histadrut contractors were enjoying a monopoly in the public-housing construction, Golda pointed out that no private entrepreneur had been willing to undertake the work on terms the government could meet. Any offer to build good, cheap houses quickly would have been accepted, but private capital had imposed impossible conditions. It was an old story.

A large proportion of the funds for development, housing and roads were solicited from American Jewry. Within a few months of the acceptance of her housing program, Golda was already in the United States addressing UJA conferences and asking for the money to buy timber, building materials and pipes, just as a year and a half earlier she had asked for money for arms.

PLENTY OF JEWS

DESPITE the housing program, there was a sharp rise in unemployment. As transient camps were cleared, the immigrants ceased to be the responsibility of the Jewish Agency which had transported them and housed them in the immigrant centers. They merged into the general population where unemployment was already widespread. Work had to be found for an evergrowing number of inhabitants, and capital had to be attracted for the projects undertaken with government funds. The Mapai ministers had no doctrinaire qualms about private capital. From Ben-Gurion down, they stressed the view that private enterprise as well as public planning were essential to Israel's development. Part of Golda's task in the United States was to persuade businessmen to invest in the new state in the expectation of a reasonable profit. What was reasonable? A generous philanthropist who would give thousands of dollars to the UJA might become steely eyed as soon as the rate of profit would be discussed. That was business, a sphere with its inviolable laws where considerations of sentiment could not be operative. The former kibbutzniks turned practical statesmen had to orient themselves to an unfamiliar psychology quickly.

As the economic and social difficulties of absorbing the immigrants increased daily, doubts about the wisdom of Kibbutz Galyoth (the ingathering of exiles) began to be heard in and out of Israel. On the day that the British mandate had ended there had been fewer than 700,000 Jews in Israel. During the entire three decades of British rule (January 1919–May 1948) only 390,580 Jews had entered Palestine. Almost as many poured in within the first year and a half of Israel's existence. By the end of 1949, the 1,000,000 mark had been reached.

Whole communities in Western and Eastern Europe, in North and South Africa, in remotest Asia and the Arab lands of the Middle East, packed up and left for Israel. No corner of the dispersion went unrepresented: India and Afghanistan; Aden and Yemen; Turkey and Bulgaria; Shanghai and Capetown; DP camps and Buenos Aires villas; a small number of idealists even left New York apartments and Los Angeles bungalows. The great exodus was in full swing.

Nor was the end in sight. According to the government's four-year plan, the population was to be doubled within that period: Israel's goal was a second million. According to all indications, the figure was conservative. In 1949, a thousand newcomers entered each day. Even with a slackening of the pace, the hundreds of thousands still pressing toward Israel guaranteed a continued rapid growth of the population of the Jewish state.

The "ingathering of exiles" foretold in prophecy was taking place. For the unorthodox kibbutznik, as well as for the bearded sage in Jerusalem, these were messianic times. Even the socialist pioneers quoted the Bible in preference to more secular explanations of the phenomenon of the "return." The political slogan "Mass immigration" had rapidly given way to the inspired description "The ingathering of exiles." Socioeconomic terminology, despite its aptness, was rarely employed even by the leadership. Thirty years earlier, Ber Borochov, the socialist-Zionist theoretician, had promulgated a thesis called ponderously *"der stychischer prozess,"* which foretold an eventual tidal movement to Palestine on the part of the Jewish masses. Borochov had made use of a Marxist rather than messianic vocabulary. According to his thesis, the sharpening of the class struggle would make the situation of the marginal Jew politically and economically untenable in the capitalist world. Consequently Jews, impelled by historic determinism and directed by conscious desire, would inevitably stream toward Palestine.

While the thesis was borne out with devastating accuracy, the victorious disciples abandoned the disputatious terminology on which they had sharpened their wits. Ben-Gurion quoted Isaiah: "For a small moment have I forsaken thee, but with great mercy I gather thee." Whatever economic and political causes drove the immigrants to Israel, they disembarked to the trumpets of prophecy.

Many of the Oriental Jews came led by a childlike faith. An exquisite girl from Aden explained that she had left home and kindred to behold Jerusalem the Golden. "I imagined it was like a shining palace," she confessed naively in the drab reception center where she was interviewed. When asked if she was disappointed, she answered shyly, "A little." Then she added, "But bread and water in Jerusalem are sweeter than milk and honey in Aden."

[249]

This answer, with slight variations, was heard frequently: "It is written in the Bible that one day in the Land of Israel is worth one thousand in exile."

A child from India explained: "Gandhi was a good man; the Arabs killed him because he was kind to Jews, so then we all wanted to go to the land of the Jews." Her explanation of Gandhi's murder, despite its inaccuracy, reflected the radius of the impulse which had reached as far as the bazaars of India.

Primitive Jews from Morocco heard the call of the Messiah in their market places and squalid alleys. A youth with fierce black eyes and more than a touch of banditry in his manner explained in French: "We came to live in Jerusalem. If there is a Jewish kingdom once again, don't we belong there?"

The European Jews were more sophisticated. They did not speak of "Jewish kingdoms" and "shining palaces," but on them, too, lay the spell. The Jewish survivors had emerged from the Nazi terror with an elementary urge for revival as well as survival, and it was idle to inquire whether they rushed toward Israel because of Herzl, Hitler or Jehovah.

The ingathering was not artificially stimulated. The drive toward Palestine could not be mechanically produced by crafty propaganda, as anti-Zionists have charged. It was a natural force arising out of the agony of a people. But it could have been dissipated and permitted to peter out fruitlessly and tragically, leaving more wreckage in its wake. To channel the flood, to harness the reckless energy generated by the Hitler upheaval and to use it creatively for national redemption, became the task of Zionism.

The process could not be passive: "ingathering" is an active term; it does not denote drifting on the tides of chance. The dynamic of Zionism required what is palely called "mass immigration," just as it had required the creation of a Jewish state.

It was an open secret that Zionists had encouraged *bricha,* the flight to the shelter of the American Zone in Germany for the purpose of eventually reaching Palestine. In the terrible years of 1945-1946, when the population of the DP camps kept swelling and no reasonable expectation of a change in the White Paper policy could be held, more than one Zionist questioned the wisdom of the tactic which first encouraged the survivors to flee from Poland to Germany and then strengthened their will to endure the rigors of DP existence rather than return to the unhappy "countries of origin."

When the gates of the homeland were finally opened and the motley thousands began to fill the Israel reception centers during the winter rains, some asked whether the tempo of immigration should not be reduced. Could the immigrants be absorbed? Could the young economy of Israel stand the strain? Could the immigrants themselves stand the strain of further privation, inadequate housing and lack of employment?

All the questions and fears were legitimate—as legitimate as the hesitations which beset the war and the declaration of statehood. And as in the war, the affirmative answer was given by Ben-Gurion, who had perceived that the long immolation in the DP camps, the peril of the illegal journeys, the misery of the reception centers were all necessary hazards. At each stage there might be defeat. Everything was interlocked. Without a Jewish state, the DP's might have been doomed to indefinite imprisonment on German soil. On the other hand, without the DP's, the Jewish state might never have come into being. The Ben-Gurion policy viewed the Jewish problem as an organic whole which could only be resolved if treated as a whole. There could be no tentative or piecemeal solution.

The human suffering entailed was recognized; intuitively, the people gave it a name worthy of its magnitude. Again they used a religious term: these were the "birth pangs of the Messiah" foretold in prophecy. Under the disappointments, squabbles and irritations of daily living lay the knowledge that the labor was that of birth.

Nevertheless, as the messianic mood passed and the privations of "austerity" increased with each month's fresh thousands of immigrants, misgivings about the ingathering began to be voiced openly. The doubts were not only caused by an understandable longing for the fleshpots of Israel instead of its eternal eggplant and frozen fish fillet. Fears were felt for the character of the state swamped by the tribes of the Orient who shared neither the cultural background nor the aspirations of the settled population. What would happen to the idealistic vision of the pioneers now at the mercy of masses who understood neither its spiritual nor economic goals?

In the United States, too, as the requests for funds increased, big givers to the United Jewish Appeal worried about the tempo of immigration. At a United Jewish Appeal conference in Chicago, June 1950, Golda was already engaged in trying to lay the specter:

> Above all, nothing is so horrifying as the discussions in which we consider whether we can keep up this pace of immigration. You have heard that immigration will have to be curtailed. I don't believe it. Don't ask me how we are going to solve it if you don't help us. But I know that there is not a single man or woman among us who would want the title of minister or president or prime minister, who would want to live in the State of Israel, who would not rue the day the state had been established, if we have to reach the decision

that there is a Jew anywhere to whom we have to deny admittance. We don't want to live to see the day of illegal Jewish immigration into the State of Israel.

At the close of the long address in which she described without illusion the characteristics as well as the needs of the Yemenites, Iraqis and DP's, she declared: "Israel without them is not worth having."

Two months later she was fighting for rationing of clothes in Israel and for further austerity. She coined the slogans, "More immigrants or more shoes" and "Rationing of immigration or rationing of clothes," and promulgated her thesis up and down the land.

Her critics complained that such pronunciamentos sounded well but left the problem unsolved. The question of immigration became a major issue. Mapai made unrestricted immigration a cardinal plank in its election program of July 1951. Golda, in her straightforward fashion, stated bluntly: "Mapai does not promise a land of plenty if it wins. It promises only plenty of Jews and rationing to make that possible."

The insistence on "plenty of Jews" was not motivated by ignorance of the risks and difficulties. Ben-Gurion and his followers were well aware of the strains put on the new state and the danger that the structure might crack. It was a calculated risk, just as *bricha* and the war had been a calculated risk, but a failure to take the gamble would have been a guarantee of defeat. In each case it had been a question of choosing between possible victory and certain loss. Those with historic intuition understood that the impulse to reach the shores of the Jewish state was not something that could be choked off, held in reserve, and then turned on periodically when good times permitted. The hundreds of thousands had to be welcomed when the fever of the return ran high. Quotas according to economic absorptive capacity, the chill language of the mandate, could not be set by the new-born Jewish state. The notion that eventually there would be a neat, calm immigration in numbers large enough to matter was absurd. The historic moment had to be seized when it came. There would be no second opportunity. Only the survivors of Hitler's Europe and the Jewries of the Orient were likely to come. Western Jewry did not stir except for a handful here and there. No mass immigration could be expected from America in the foreseeable future. No doubt if conditions in Israel had been easier and the Israelis had devoted themselves to the problem of attracting the much desired American Jews with greater *savoir faire* instead of by prophetic proclamations, a few more Americans might have come and stayed. But the hope of enlarging appreciably the original nucleus of 700,000 could lie only in the hosts that came in the first years. Of itself the stream slackened so that by 1953 the population of Israel was almost static except for natural increase. It was idle to suppose that those who had entered could have been doled out to the state in digestible numbers over a period of years. They would have made their peace elsewhere.

Of course, another objection was raised: if Israel's increase depended on backward Oriental Jews with dubious table manners, perhaps the desire for growth should be abandoned. Here again it became a question of evaluation and of values. Golda's outcry: "Israel without these Jews is not worth having," was not a romantic outburst based on a hazy knowledge of the facts. No one knew better the immigrants as dwellers in the *maabaroth* (temporary camps for arriving immigrants) and as workers. On the basis of experience, she and those who thought like her viewed the exotic human material as rich in potential. These immigrants, and particularly their children, would be good citizens with as much to offer in their way as the Western Jews. Israel would be a synthesis of East and West. The Jewish state could not exist as a decorous select little center to be maintained for the delectation of respectable world Jewry. Israel had to be a living, fecund organism or die of anemia.

In a speech launching a drive for bonds in Washington, October 1950, Golda made a statement which sounded incorrigibly sentimental. In the midst of a staid, factual account of conditions and resources, she permitted herself the following extravagance. She offered as "security," "Thousands and thousands of children of Israel, our children, the children of the old-timers and the little Yemenite children and Iraqi children and the Rumanian children and children from all over the world, many of whom are bewildered because they can walk around free in the streets of the country."

The excerpt quoted was not typical of Golda's appeal to American Jewry for investment capital. The bulk of her speeches expertly and hardheadedly dealt with industrial potentials in terms of resources, exchange values, interest rates and costs. But the informing spirit of her words transmuted the charts and figures into a historical challenge as well as a business opportunity. This combination accounted for her success and marked the difference between her and the tear-jerker on the one hand and the cold statistician on the other. And of course she could salt her account of Israel austerity with homely details which no man would think of. When she mentioned that an immigrant mother in Israel received only six diapers for a new-born baby, she added:

"Every woman knows what that means." And she reduced a long discussion about deferred payments to its essence when she said: "You can't fry fish in July with oil that you will get in September."

In the campaign for funds, Golda became an early advocate of bonds for Israel. It was completely in character that this should be so. Quite apart from the fact that the UJA alone could not provide the stupendous sum of a billion dollars which had been set as a campaign goal over a three-year period, a bond issue with its pledge to repay carried the dignity of financial independence. The free dollars of the UJA donations were desperately needed, no matter what the success of the bond issue might be, but the role of pleading for contributions was becoming increasingly difficult for Golda.

She stressed the financial independence which a successful bond drive would achieve. To be the eternal object of philanthropy had its considerable demerits. At one point, she said: "This morning at a meeting a man got up and asked a question, 'What about packages to Israel?' Now, maybe this seems funny to you; it is not funny to me. I am a citizen of Israel, and I absolutely refuse to be classed as a person belonging to a people whose needs can be answered by packages. . . . I'm afraid I spoiled the meeting this morning because I said, 'We don't need any packages and don't send us any. . . .'"

Golda shared the *Yishuv's* profound disappointment at the failure of American Jews to join the immigrant tide to Israel. But her disillusionment was most bitter in regard to professed Zionists. At the 1951 Zionist congress in Jerusalem she minced no words. There was no crisis in Zionism but only a crisis among some Zionist leaders, she declared. "Had at

least ten American Zionist leaders packed and gone to settle in Israel the day after the state was declared, then
it could be said that they appreciated the significance of the
establishment of Israel."

This disillusionment impelled her to depreciate the importance of an organized Zionist movement in the United
States and to suggest limiting the scope of its activities.
Whenever the role of the American Zionist movement in re-
lation to the government of Israel would be under discussion, she would be likely to underestimate its influence and
political importance. On the other hand, the remarkable response that she had received from sectors of American Jews
who were not affiliated with the Zionist movement had convinced her that "friends of Israel" were friends in need. The
great mass of American Jews, she believed, were aligned
somewhere between the anti-Zionist Council for Judaism
and the Zionist organization. Of them she said hopefully,
"I don't give them up."

Her depreciation of the Zionists and her exaggerated estimate of American Jewry as a whole were unwarranted by
the facts. Without the motor power of a dedicated Zionist
movement, the sympathizers could not have been activated
and organized. But because American Zionism had proved
unequal to personal participation, she was impatient of its
claim and sometimes unjust to its contribution. She turned,
perhaps naively, to the great American Jewish public which
she thought could be persuaded to invest in Israel and free
it from the "generous shackles" of philanthropy.

The periodic tours in the Americas and Europe were a
tremendous physical and nervous drain on her energy. No
other member of the government devoted so much time to
raising funds for the state's work. Golda herself commented

on her anomalous role: "My ministry not only has to present a program and execute it. Into the bargain, it has to raise the needed capital."

During this period she suffered an unremitting series of personal misfortunes. In 1950, she returned from the United States to find her daughter, who was pregnant, critically ill. The doctor of the Hadassah hospital met Golda with the words, "I can give you no hope." Sarele survived but the baby was still-born. In 1951, while she was away on a campaign for bonds, she received word in New York of the death of Morris Myerson. Though they had been separated for years, she was deeply affected. She flew back to Israel at once to attend his funeral, which was delayed till her arrival. A close friend, David Remez, died within the same year.

In addition, there was a variety of physical ills. In St. Louis she fell and dislocated a shoulder, but as the local paper put it: "In spite of the accident, Mrs. Myerson continued her scheduled program." In the beginning of March, 1953, she was again at the Beilinson Hospital in Israel, where the doctors urged an immediate gall-bladder operation. But on March 13 she had to address the United Nations in New York about Soviet Russia's anti-Jewish policy as shown by the Prague trials. She refused to delay her trip, with the result that an emergency operation was performed in New York. Though the operation was performed in a great American hospital, it was not entirely successful, and some stones remained. Golda remarked ruefully and patriotically: "Everything is better in Israel. I should have done it at the Beilinson Hospital." There were the usual exhortations on the part of her physicians who assured her that it was dangerous to leave the hospital at this juncture, and as usual she had other plans. This time it was: "I have to present my budget to the *Knesset*." By June she was back in Israel.

A highly controversial subject on the *Knesset* agenda that summer (1953) was the bill for compulsory service for women which was being introduced by the ministry of labor. Few subjects had aroused so much excitement. For weeks the orthodox bloc had been inciting its followers against service for religious women no matter what the nature of the service. To understand the fury aroused, one must know something of the background.

Since the establishment of Israel the specter of a *Kulturkampf* had haunted the legislators and the public. *Kulturkampf* (cultural struggle) is a rather vague and comprehensive name for the specific conflict between religious orthodoxy and a modern state. The term implies not only Church versus State, a clash which can conceivably take place on the same plane of historic development, but an encounter between venerable church dogma, unrevised since antiquity, and the spirit of a new progressive state—hence a cultural conflict which transcends the classic struggle for power between Church and State but for which Church and State respectively have become the chief spokesmen.

The lack of clear limitations on the authority of the rabbinate had been a source of anxiety to most Israelis. The fact that there was no such thing as civil marriage and divorce in Israel and that only the rabbinate had the legal right to marry or divorce was accepted with misgiving by much of the population. The acceptance was due to the fear of precipitating the *Kulturkampf*. Circles far removed from the influence of the orthodox argued that Israel had so many economic and political difficulties that no measure likely to rouse the fury of religious fanatics should be taken. Though the orthodox bloc represented a minority of the population (some 16 percent), the population was prepared to understand that religion, by its nature, could not compromise, and that the clergy could not be expected to subject the validity of its position on a religious issue to the verdict of the ballot. The authority of the Torah could not be determined by secular electorates or by the force of numbers. Secular Israel understood, even if it did not sympathize, with this argument, and from this understanding sprang the forbearance shown by such liberal secular parties as Mapai. Since 1948, the internal history of Israel reflected a constant effort to avoid a flare-up on the religious issue. Such a course, despite the charges of "theocracy" often raised by the extreme Left, was dictated by good sense. Only irresponsibles more concerned with campaign slogans than with the vital interests of the state could suggest challenging the orthodox bloc to a showdown despite the almost certain victory of the secularists, for there was always the possibility that the fabric of the state might not withstand the strain of the triumph.

The debates about the service bill for women brought the central issue of Church and State sharply into focus, and in the process various elements of life in Israel which had previously been viewed as merely minor irritations suddenly began to appear as intolerable invasions of individual rights.

Under the stimulus of orthodox agitation against the bill, the watchfulness of the Sabbath observers reached such a pitch that private cars appearing in Jerusalem streets on Friday evening or Saturday would be surrounded by bands of zealots who threw themselves in the paths of the oncoming cars or stoned the vehicles. The Jerusalem public had always accepted the Sabbath stoppage of public transportation such as buses and most taxi services, but there had been some leeway for private vehicles and special taxis. Tourists generally smiled complacently as the "Watchers of the Sabbath" rushed through the city before sundown on Friday to announce the exact hour of the beginning of the Sabbath with a shrill blowing of a shofar, calling attention to the time in hours and minutes by their placards. But in the summer of 1953 these activities seemed less innocently quaint. More than one Israeli exclaimed bitterly: "We leave them alone: why don't they leave us alone?"

The wild demonstrations against the national service bill served to alarm and antagonize the general public as no previous acts had done. The excess of the orthodox bloc transformed what had often been good-natured indifference into active hostility.

The national service act for women, which called for a year's compulsory military service for girls, had at first almost no opposition, because the population as a whole appreciated the necessity for utilizing all available man and woman power. Many forms of service within the army could be performed by young women, thereby relieving young men for more dangerous or strenuous tasks. Even the religious parties did not protest the bill as a whole. The orthodox parties contented themselves with demanding that "religious" girls be exempted from military service on the grounds that such service was contrary to religious law. At first, as a temporary expedient, blanket exemption of girls claiming to be religious had been granted, but such blanket exemption led to numerous abuses—nonorthodox girls saw fit to claim the privileges of orthodoxy—and to a justifiable irritation on the part of the nonorthodox population who felt that some form of nonmilitary service could well be required from even the most pious daughters of Israel. Consequently a national service bill for religious women was drawn up, the provisions of which made it possible for religious girls to give a year of civilian service outside the military framework. All the professed objections of the religious groups were met: the girls would not live in barracks but would go home at night; they would not be in uniform; their service would consist of social work such as nursing or teaching in the immigrant camps. They would be under supervision of the ministry of labor, headed by a woman, Golda Myerson, instead of in the charge of the ministry of defense. Furthermore, the small number of Oriental girls who came from homes where a kind of purdah was still practiced—where unmarried females could not leave the home unaccompanied—would be wholly exempt. The bill showed extraordinary deference to extreme orthodox sentiment, and in fact had been drafted with the assistance of the moderate orthodox parties—Mizrachi and the Hapoel Hamizrachi. Therefore the hue and cry that attended the presentation of the bill served to enrage Israeli public opinion to an unprecedented degree, particularly when it was learned that the ultraorthodox *Agudat Israel's* campaign of vilification and misrepresentation had gone far beyond the borders of the country. It was bad enough to see in Jerusalem the handbills of the ultraorthodox parties warning orthodox parents that the Israel Government proposed to place their daughters in brothels. The knowledge that, thanks to the *Agudat Israel,* pious Jews were gathering in Brooklyn to lament this alleged threat to the virtue of the daughters of Zion was even worse.

In the ultraorthodox quarter of Jerusalem, Mea Shearim, the walls were plastered with posters calling on fathers and mothers to protect their daughters from "infamy" and "defilement." These appeals, backed by the authority of the rabbinate, were bound to frighten and excite ignorant and backward elements among the immigrants, many of them from Oriental countries where equal rights and privileges for women were unknown. As a result, disgraceful outbreaks of mob violence took place. Crowds of "pious" men and women marched on the *Knesset,* shrieking and attacking the police who tried to restrain them. The spectacle of orthodox kerchiefed women making public displays of themselves and attacking male police to prove that they were homebodies was sickening proof of the effectiveness of the opposition tactics.

Golda was at her polemical best in her defense of the bill. "You will not force your way of life on us," she told the orthodox bloc. "You will not terrorize a legislative body with demonstrations of hysterical women or by mob violence." She reminded the *Knesset* of the role that Jewish women had played in the revolt of the Warsaw Ghetto and at Kfar Etzion, and she asked whether no orthodox girls could be numbered among the heroines.

The charges that girls who served in the army would be corrupted was particularly offensive. *Knesset* members whose daughters were in the service rose at the insult in fury. Golda gave this aspect of the debate a sudden feminist twist. "Religious families have sons as well as daughters. If army life is degrading why are they not concerned for the morals of their sons?"

Men found an argument of this kind irritating rather than convincing. Once when the cabinet was discussing something new in Israel—a series of attacks on women—one of the members suggested a curfew for girls. Women should not be allowed on the streets after dark. Golda flared up,

"Men are attacking the women, not the other way around. If there is going to be a curfew, let the men be locked up, not the women." This was one of the occasions when her masculine associates deplored the irreproachable logic of the minister of labor.

Sometimes there were vexations of another kind. Once, on an inspection trip to a recently completed housing development, Golda was surrounded by disgruntled immigrants from Eastern Europe, who, disdaining preliminary courtesies, besieged her with angry complaints about the houses, the climate, the scarcity of work for professionals and the neighbors. They had expected an easier life. The small four-room cottages assigned each family were unfurnished except for essentials; the plot of land around each house was bare; a hot sun beat down on the treeless, sandy road; and appropriate employment was hard to find. Golda, proud of the well-designed houses with running water, electricity and good plumbing given to destitute immigrants for a few dollars a month, and aware of what it had cost to transport and settle these newcomers, reminded one of the impatient women that flowers and vegetables had to be planted. Why had she come to Israel? "Because I was afraid to stay in Poland. I don't care about Zionism," the woman answered unblinkingly. Her husband, standing nearby, nodded in agreement.

"Not one word of gratitude," said Golda bitterly to a companion as she left. But such episodes were the exception. Most of the time the sense of visible achievement—new houses in the stony hills, more paved roads to link the villages—made life as minister of labor deeply satisfying.

THE ROAD TO REVIVIM

As minister of labor, Golda had a spacious government residence at her disposal. She lived on the top floor of an old stone house on David Marcus Street in Talbyieh, a suburb of Jerusalem. From the windows there was a view of the austere expanse of the Judean hills stretching toward Hebron. At night on the wide balcony the brilliant stars of the Jerusalem heavens shone close. Enthusiastic guests, touched by the magic of Jerusalem and the beauty of the view, sometimes failed to note the exposed location of the house, within easy gunshot from the Jordan border.

Golda had a full-time maid who came in daily to clean and cook. She had conceded that much to the pressures of office. The apartment was too large to be cared for without assistance, and Golda had no time to stand in line with her ration card for the products due her as a citizen of Israel. But the old psychology of "self-labor" was hard to down. Her relations with her maid and her chauffeur were on the egalitarian basis dictated by ideology. Unless there were formal visitors present, it was taken for granted that servant and mistress ate at the same table. Many of the Labor notables continued this early pioneer tradition. In Golda's case it was carried out to an exaggerated degree. If a batch of unexpected visitors arrived—a constant occurrence—it was still temperamentally easier for her to get up and start serving tea or supper than to give the necessary orders. Fortunately her maid had as human an attitude to Golda as Golda had to her and would often insist on remaining to help.

Sometimes the demon of pioneer independence went too far. On one occasion two workers delivered a heavy table to her home. Golda at once started heaving the table to where she wanted it, while the two men stood watching. Why did the two workers let their female minister of labor move furniture unassisted? Presumably, the men were overwhelmed by the forceful great lady, unless of course they, too, were halutzim of the old school. Golda was behaving true to form. As a member of the kibbutz of Merhavia, she had made it a point of honor not to ask male assistance in a tough physical task, and she still found it hard to give orders in her personal household.

The habit of dropping in, a remnant from the days when nobody had a telephone, had not vanished completely. In addition, there was a steady stream of announced friends and acquaintances. Besides the Palestinian comrades of a lifetime, Golda had formed many warm ties with friends in America who arrived periodically for welcome visits.

Yet despite Golda's sociability—it was never too late for another cigarette and another cup of tea—hers was a fundamentally solitary life. Menachem occupied Golda's Tel Aviv apartment. Sarele was in Revivim. The moments of family warmth were best enjoyed in the cottage of Shana at

Holon, where Golda often spent the night when she had a late meeting in Tel Aviv.

About once a month she visited her daughter and grandchild: Sarele's second baby had lived. It would have been pleasant to see the young family more often, but the journey to Revivim consumed the whole day. A two-day trip for personal reasons was a luxury which Golda could rarely allow herself.

Revivim was one of the classic Negev settlements. "The wastes of the Negev" (the first line of a popular Israeli song) challenged the imagination of Israel pretty much as the swamps of the Emek had fascinated an earlier generation. The forbidding sands of the Negev were to be transformed like Degania or Ein Harod. The vision of a reclaimed "South" (Negev) probably found its most dramatic expression in Ben-Gurion's departure to live as a shepherd in Sdeh Boker.

It was not romantic extravagance which inspired the formidable dream of reclaiming some 3,800 square miles of desert and semidesert territory. The Negev represented approximately two thirds of the area allotted to the tiny Jewish state by the partition resolution. Desolate, practically uninhabited, with a total population of some 60,000, consisting mostly of Bedouin nomads, the Negev was the chief area available to Israel for cultivation and settlement.

Jewish pioneers had looked toward the barren south as their chief hope of colonization long before the passage of the partition resolution. On July 13, 1939, an agricultural settlement bearing the symbolic name of Negba (Southward) was founded. Though a little north of the Negev proper, it was the southernmost point then reached by Jewish colonization and marked the beginning of an epoch. By 1948 there were twenty-seven Jewish settlements in the Negev, despite the fact that the nine years since the establishment of Negba had included World War II, the struggle against the White Paper, and the Arab invasion.

In 1943, when the first three settlements—Gvulot, Beth Eshel, and Revivim—were established, nothing was known of the Negev, except that in antiquity it had been the seat of a highly developed civilization. Jews had dwelt there from the time of the patriarchs. Abraham's wells can still be seen at the entrance of Beersheba. King Solomon's seaport had been at Eilat, the ancient Hebrew name for Akaba; and Jewish communities had existed in the Negev as late as the sixth century A.D.

The problem of the three Jewish agricultural outposts was to determine whether the long deserted soil could again be made fruitful. Scientists analyzed the soil, measured the rainfall, and studied the water resources. On the basis of scientific research and the practical experience of the settlers, further colonization was encouraged. The findings were good: given adequate water and stout hearts, the soil could be restored. "Operation Negev," when eleven new settlements were established in one day, took place in 1946 in the midst of the struggle with the British.

The stout hearts were available; water was less abundant. Some of the young settlements were entirely without water during the first weeks of their existence, being wholly dependent on what could be carted by truck. Nevertheless, unromantic non-Jewish specialists agreed that the untapped water resources of the country would be adequate for an irrigation system.

When the Egyptians launched their invasion, they quite

sensibly expected that it would be a simple matter to reduce these small, remote settlements. They cut the water line, shelled the dams and reservoirs, destroyed the farms and seized the supply road. But the settlements, after evacuating their children by air, dug in.

Only two of the Negev settlements were occupied by the Egyptians. Even Beth Eshel, though situated less than two kilometers from Beersheba, the main Egyptian base, refused to surrender. The settlers burrowed underground while Egyptian shells systematically razed their homes. They did not emerge until the arrival of Israeli troops, sent to their relief. It was in such a settlement that Golda's daughter lived.

I accompanied Golda on one of her trips to Revivim. We left Jerusalem on the morning of a hot July day, stopping at Holon to pick up Shana, who was coming along with us. Since Sam's death the winter before, Shana had insisted on living alone in the cottage they had built. During the day she trudged about, doughtily inspecting kitchens in government institutions to make sure adequate sanitary standards were maintained, putting her training as a dietitian at Battle Creek to good use. But the evenings were long and melancholy, and no matter how tired she might be, she would awake at dawn to preserve some of the fruit from her orchard if there were enough sugar, or busy herself about the house and garden. A trip to Revivim was a distraction; on the way she could visit one of her farmer sons who kept her supplied with eggs and good white cheese, part of which was always sent to Golda to supplement the ration.

As far as Beersheba the road was good, the surrounding countryside green. We were traveling on one of the "golden roads" constructed under the state. Beersheba, the new city in the desert, no longer the cluster of mud hovels with a few solid stones houses that the Jews had captured in 1948 from the invading Egyptians, was fast becoming Ben-Gurion's dreamed "Capital of the South," with hundreds of modern dwellings and thousands of inhabitants engaged in industry and agriculture.

After Beersheba, the going was tougher. Part of the way lay along newly constructed roads which would eventually cross the entire Negev, but as we approached Revivim the sands grew deeper. The road which would link Revivim to the highway had not yet been completed. Occasionally Golda's car stuck in the sand, but each time we managed to plow through. By late afternoon we were in the settlement.

It was something of a shock to see Revivim. The kibbutz was over ten years old—middle-aged as Israel settlements go—yet the sands stretched desolately about the little houses as far as the eye could see. A patch of grass and a cluster of flowers grew here and there. The kibbutz had fields where it raised vegetables, but the heart-lifting sense of renewal apparent in almost every settlement in Israel was missing. The desert was being held at bay, not conquered.

The housing, on the other hand, was quite respectable. The married settlers who were *vatikim*, old-timers from the point of view of settlement not of age, had good-sized one-room units. Judging from the reading matter, the settlers had varied intellectual interests. In addition to Hebrew books and English and German works on economics, I noted Plato in Jowett's translation and considerable *belles-lettres*, as well as the inevitable Freud. The Plato room also had a picture book about Sambo, which meant that the couple had a child. The only negative feature as far as living quarters were concerned was the lack of tolerable toilet facilities. The outhouses were among the most primitive I had seen on my rounds of settlements.

Zacharia, Sarele's husband, received us while Sarele went to fetch the baby from the children's house, where the children of the kibbutz were lodged and reared. Naomi, ten months old, had her father's delicate dark features and dark eyes. The adults at Revivim, especially the women, looked tired and worn despite their youth, but Naomi, like other babies I saw later, was flourishing.

Sarele looked too tired for her twenty-six years. She and Zacharia were among the few of the original founders of the settlement who had remained. Understandably enough, there was a large turnover at Revivim. Sarele had her mother's stamina. During her tragic first pregnancy she had developed an acute kidney condition. When she became violently ill, no doctor willing to go into the Negev at night could be located. Despite constant seizures of convulsions, she was taken by truck to the Hadassah hospital in Beersheba, where her life was saved though the baby was lost. Naomi was born in Jerusalem, but as soon as she was able to travel, Sarele returned to Revivim.

I had brought chocolate, purchasable only with American currency, and Shana homemade cookies. We had tea in the privacy of Sarele's room instead of going to the general dining room. Then I learned something. The water contained salt. For over a decade, the settlers had drunk salt water; everything was cooked in salt water. I thought of Sarele's kidneys as she sipped the salt tea which I found undrinkable.

The salt water explained the aridity of the entire kibbutz. There could be no large-scale cultivation until irrigation with salt-free water could be introduced. Within the past year considerable sums had been spent on drilling for water; so far there had been no results. The only alternative was to pipe water into the settlement, which in view of the great distance was prohibitively expensive. In the meantime, the settlers had to endure the salt water.

When we went to supper in the common dining room, I was surprised to see that no notice was taken of Golda's entrance. I was accustomed to the welcomes and receptions which as minister of labor marked her arrivals. We sat down at the long tables usual in a kibbutz which has not yet abandoned simon-pure communal living in favor of the newer style of small tables for congenial groups. The food was poor. I would have felt honor bound to eat it if Shana had not declared that the same products could have been prepared in a more edible fashion, salt water, austerity and all. Shana's dietetic indignation made life easier.

The girl who was ladling out boiled potatoes was pregnant. Golda looked at her and whispered to me, "She's wearing the dress I sent Sarele last year." Revivim was rigorously communal in its ideology. Unlike many kibbutzim which had revised original conceptions to allow the private ownership of personal belongings like clothes, at Revivim everything still went into the common wardrobe. To each according to his need; from each according to his capacity. I had brought Naomi a charmingly embroidered dress from Wizo. I felt an unworthy pang of bourgeois regret when I considered that Naomi would get to wear the dress only when chance made it available.

When our party left the dining room, ignored upon its exit as upon its entrance, I commented on the extraordinary delicacy with which the young settlers had respected Golda's privacy; how deferentially they had refused to intrude upon her visit to her daughter by burdening her with a public awareness of her high office. My compliments were met with cynical amusement. Then light broke. Revivim was a Mapam kibbutz. Golda had been studiously ignored as an expression of resentment against a Mapai minister of labor.

Outside of this passive political demonstration, the kibbutz was hospitable. The several members of our party were accommodated for the night in the rooms of the settlers at considerable inconvenience to the occupants, and the settlers were individually friendly.

The next morning I saw the first sign of official cognizance of Golda's visit. A representative of the kibbutz appeared at Sarele's room, not to pay his respects to the minister of labor but to offer a list of grievances. He plunged into the question of water and of a road to Revivim that was under consideration. Golda listened patiently to the representative's protests, explained that the matter of water was not within her jurisdiction, but promised to discuss it with the proper authorities. The road would be completed as soon as possible. I later learned that Mapam believed that its kibbutzim received discriminatory treatment and that priority was given to the adherents of the ruling party.

Before we left Revivim the minister had an opportunity to play the role of grandmother: Golda, Sarele, Naomi—three generations, of whom two had been born in Israel, each representative of a different phase of Zionist pioneering. With Naomi, the process of taking root had finally become natural and unselfconscious. Even Sarele, born in Jerusalem, had been raised in a home which was fiercely trying to transform itself into a Palestinian family. For Naomi, child of a Western

and Eastern *sabra,* there would be no problems of adjustment. Naomi was at last free of the idea of Zion; she was part
of its hills, its sun and sand.

On the way back from Revivim, we stopped at the village
not far from Beersheba where one of Shana's sons had his
farm. Here was none of the grim heroism of Revivim. A pleasant village, a thriving small farm and lusty blond children
who were as unselfconscious Israelis as Naomi. Everything
was green and blooming. Sarele might say: "One day
Revivim will be like this."

THE FOREIGN MINISTER

B Y 1956, the political and temperamental differences between Ben-Gurion and Moshe Sharett, his Foreign Minister, were becoming increasingly acute. The two men were at odds, not so much about specific policies as about their implementation. It was all too easy for Sharett to deplore Ben-Gurion's activism as rash, and for Ben-Gurion to reject Sharett's moderation as unimaginative. With his wider experience in the field of international affairs, Sharett was more aware of the probable repercussions of a given course than his prime minister, while Ben-Gurion's messianic assurance rarely deserted him. The long partnership between the two men was over, to the regret of the whole country which valued their qualities as complementary rather than antagonistic. Sharett's successor would have to be a Mapai figure of national stature.

When Golda became Foreign Minister of Israel in 1956, history repeated itself. In 1946, when Sharett, head of the political department of the Jewish Agency, had been imprisoned by the British and sent to Latrun, Golda had been chosen to be acting head of the political department for the period of his detention. Exactly ten years later she was again viewed as the logical candidate to replace him. And, as a decade earlier, worried gentlemen both secretly and openly wondered whether the woman would be equal to her task. True, she had displayed unsuspected gifts on previous occasions when doubters had been vocal, but "this was different." Golda agreed that this was different, though not for the same reasons that troubled her male comrades. The ministry of labor had given scope to her talent for action, her love of concrete achievement—houses, jobs, roads; now she would be involved in the shadowland of negotiation, looking for slippery footholds in the world of diplomacy. The reluctance with which she accepted her awesome honor was real, not diplomatic.

Still another change would have to be made; her name had to be Hebraized. Since 1948, Ben-Gurion had battled for Hebrew names for the citizens of Israel. The alien appellations of the Diaspora should end with the exile. What was desirable for ordinary Israelis became *de rigueur* for members of the government. Not all Israelis shared Ben-Gurion's distaste. Men and women who had long borne distinguished Russian, Polish or German family names objected to surrendering them for freshly coined Hebrew ones. Nevertheless, one by one, the metamorphosis took place: Epstein became Elath; Rubashov, Shazar; Tchertok, Sharett; Lubianiker, Lavon. Ben-Gurion was saved the pangs of alteration, because he had providently shed his surname of Green when he arrived in Palestine in 1906. Golda had been one of the last holdouts. As foreign minister there could be no further delay. She would arrive at the United Nations as Golda Meir.

When Golda took office, Israel's relations with her neighbors were again reaching a critical state. In 1955, an arms deal with Czechoslovakia provided Egypt with huge supplies of modern arms, completely upsetting the power balance in the Middle East, and by the end of that year the Cairo radio had thundered: "The day of Israel's destruction approaches. This is our decision and this is our faith. There shall be no peace on the borders, for we demand vengeance, and vengeance means death to Israel."

During the same year, Nasser unleashed his *fedayeen* campaign against Israel. The *fedayeen* (armed infiltrators) crossed the borders at night and committed acts of terror and pillage: six children and their teacher were killed in an agricultural school; a wedding in a Negev village was bombed. The outrages kept mounting; neither village nor town was at peace. Heavy concentrations of *fedayeen* units recruited chiefly from the Gaza Strip were stationed in the Sinai Desert.

Although Egypt's nationalization of the Suez Canal in July 1956 created international complications that briefly eased the harassment on Israel's borders, the relaxation was temporary. Acts of violence continued to occur, and the anti-Israel campaign in Arab capitals increased in virulence.

During the summer of 1956, Israeli intelligence observed masses of Russian armor arriving in the Sinai. From all objective indications as well as from the bellicose pronouncements issuing from the Cairo radio, it was apparent that Nasser was readying his promised "second round." Israel's hope of survival against superior armaments and numbers lay in destroying the preparations.

On October 24, 1956, Egypt, Syria and Jordan announced the establishment of a unified military command

[277]

whose objective was the destruction of Israel. Egyptian and Jordanian spokesmen explained formally that the unified command represented "a supreme effort to tighten the death noose" around Israel. The portents were plain. Israel decided to strike on October 29.

Only key people in the country knew of the plan; one was Golda. Surprise was essential to success, and Israel woke up one Monday to find the campaign in full swing. Mobilization had taken place at night and in the dawn.

The Friday before, Golda, knowing what would occur on Monday, paid a visit to her daughter and grandchildren in Revivim. If the Egyptians should not be contained, Revivim would be one of the first points to be overrun. But Golda could not warn her daughter or under some plausible pretext take her to the greater safety of Jerusalem. In 1947, British High Commissioner Cunningham, discussing the probable disastrous results of Jewish intransigence, had counseled retreat. "You have a daughter in the Negev." And Golda had answered, "There are many daughters." Drinking the still brackish tea and playing with her grandchildren, she let no inkling of her tension reach her family. When she left for the long ride back, the youth in charge of kibbutz security approached her privately—he had learned of secret mobilization orders—and said, "I'm not asking any questions, but should we dig ditches?" Golda permitted herself to answer, "If I were you, I would."

Within six days, Israeli forces gained control of almost the whole of the Sinai Peninsula and of the Gaza Strip. The Egyptian bases were destroyed, thousands of prisoners were taken, and great stores of arms and equipment, chiefly of Soviet manufacture, fell into Israeli hands. Documents found on Egyptian commanders revealed detailed plans for an imminent attack on Israel. The rout of the Egyptian forces and the disruption of their military build-up had frustrated this design. The amount of Soviet intervention was apparent, not only from the type of armament but from Russian conversations between Soviet technicians and military advisers monitored by Israeli soldiers.

In addition to the swiftness of their victory, Israeli soldiers had another thrill. They stood at the foot of Sinai and some of the more energetic climbed the mountain on which the Law had been given to Moses during the Exodus from Egypt. This time the Egyptians were fleeing.

The Anglo-French move to seize the Suez Canal coincided with the Israeli attack. Britain and France acted for reasons of their own: Nasser's nationalization of the Suez Canal and the growing threat of Russian penetration into the power vacuum of the Middle East. But the reactions of their peoples differed sharply from that of the Israelis. In Britain, particularly, indignation at the use of force and "naked imperialism" ran high, with unhappy results for Anthony Eden. Worst of all, the United States, third party to the Tripartite Declaration of 1950—in which the three Western powers had pledged themselves to oppose any aggressive action in violation of the borders established by the Palestine armistice—took the side of Egypt. Only in Israel did government action enjoy complete popular support. The people, harassed daily by murder and sabotage, economically strangled by Egypt's blockade of the Gulf of Akaba, welcomed deliverance, untroubled by being branded "aggressors." They remembered Israel's solitary struggle against Arab invaders in 1948. Once again Israel had to defend her right to live with or without international approval.

The United Nations at once began debating the new threat

to world peace. On October 30, the United States submitted a resolution to the Security Council, calling for the immediate withdrawal of Israel's advancing forces. It was vetoed by Britain and France. On November 1, 1956, an emergency session of the General Assembly called for a cease-fire. Pressure against Israel kept mounting, and on November 8, Israel agreed to the withdrawal of her forces provided agreements were taken to ensure Israel's security against acts of belligerency by land or sea.

By the time Golda arrived to head the Israeli delegation at the United Nations, the Sinai campaign had taken place and the French and British had struck at Suez. From the first moment she was cast in a fighting role, called upon to defend Israel's "aggression" before a formidable tribunal. In a sense, the baptism of fire eased the transition into her new job. The urgency of the situation quickened and created contacts which might otherwise have developed more slowly. As always, she was at her best as the champion of an unpopular cause. As she saw them, the issues were clear cut: Israel had the moral right to defend herself against Egyptian infiltrators based in the Sinai Desert and against the blockade of her shipping through the Gulf of Akaba.

To the delegates of the General Assembly, Mrs. Meir was a not wholly unfamiliar figure. In 1953, when Stalin's anti-Semitic excesses had culminated in the notorious Moscow Doctors' Plot which charged well-known Russian-Jewish physicians with conspiring with Ben-Gurion and other "Zionist criminals" to assassinate Stalin, Sharett had sent her to present the Israeli case at the United Nations. Though Golda was minister of labor, her experience as minister in Moscow in 1948 made her the natural spokesman on this occasion. Then her task had been simplified by the general sympathy inspired by Stalin's monstrous accusations. In 1956, however, Israel was being branded as the aggressor, and no such sympathy could be assumed. The new foreign minister would have to take a stand in the face of widespread and powerful opposition.

Even the friends of Israel pronounced themselves disappointed. Israel's switch from target to attacker was an unlooked for occurrence. Had the young state already adopted evil ways? The foreign minister's first problem was to dissipate the semantic fog that beclouded the issue. Who was the true aggressor? She reminded the assembly that Egypt had defended her obstruction of Israel's shipping and her anti-Israel campaign by claiming "belligerent status." More than once Egyptian representatives had explained: "We are exercising a right of war."

In her first address before the Assembly she punctured this pretense. "A comfortable division has been made: The Arab states unilaterally enjoy the rights of war; Israel has the unilateral responsibility of keeping the peace. But belligerency is not a one-way street. Is it surprising if a people laboring under this monstrous distinction should finally become restive and at last seek a way of rescuing its life from the perils of a regulated war conducted against it from all sides?"

Among the outrages she described was the murder of a group of Israeli archeologists studying an excavation. No one except some members of the Israeli legation knew that one of these archeologists had been a veteran settler, father of Ayah, her son's wife. And the foreign minister naturally made no mention of her personal loss. But there was no mistaking her conviction when she stated: "If moral distinctions are to be made, then let me suggest that controlled military actions—with limited and well-defined military or police objectives—are less abhorrent, even to the most sensitive conscience, than wanton and indiscriminate murder which strikes, not at military targets, but solely at civilians."

How many times in past struggles had she said: "We have no alternative"? Now she said it again:

"We are a small people in a small barren land which we revived with our labour and our love. The odds against us are heavy; the disparity of forces is great, but we have no alternative but to defend our lives and freedom and the right to security. We desire nothing more than peace, but we cannot equate peace merely with an apathetic readiness to be destroyed. If hostile forces gather for our proposed destruction, they must not demand that we provide them with ideal conditions for the realization of their plans."

As a passionate girl, she had often moved her small circle of listeners with the justice of the cause she fervently pleaded; now the audience listening to the grave woman embraced the world. Quiet, controlled, neither nervous nor self-conscious, she expounded Israel's case. That was the easier part of her task, a role in which she excelled. But while the original hostility of the delegates lessened she had to do more than explain the compelling reasons that had prompted Israel's incursion into the Sinai. The Assembly had also to be convinced that Israeli forces could only withdraw on assurance that the *status quo* would not be restored. The purpose of the campaign had been security. Now Israel wanted a pledge that defeated Egypt would no longer interfere with her shipping and that the Gaza Strip would not be re-established as a base for aggression.

Throughout the deliberations, the representatives of Israel kept hammering at one point: the root of the trouble lay in

Egypt's claim to belligerent rights. As long as Egypt and other Arab states felt privileged to blockade and harry Israel, the powder keg of the Middle East would remain a powder keg. It was unrealistic to demand that Israel surrender the fruits of victory and retire within her borders if this meant that Egypt would promptly resume the blockade of Akaba and the launching of *fedayeen* from the Gaza Strip. Israel sought no foot of territory outside her borders; she had enough deserts. But she could not permit a return of the former situation.

Gradually the atmosphere in the Assembly became more favorable, though the delegates continued to deplore Israel's noncompliance with the decision of the UN. While the withdrawal of Israeli forces was steadily continuing, some units were still stationed at the Gaza Strip and on a strip of coast west of the Gulf of Akaba.

Since the beginning of November, American pressure on Israel to comply with the United Nations directive had been heavy. Golda Meir was constantly negotiating with John Foster Dulles and members of the State Department. United States amiability was wearing thin, and relations between the tiny country and its great patron were becoming severely strained. France and Great Britain had yielded, but Israel still stood her ground, demanding assurance that she had not fought in vain. Conceivably a more pliable foreign minister might have given way, but Mrs. Meir characteristically refused to be intimidated. When the American Secretary of State threatened to invoke sanctions against Israel, the wave of indignation that swept the United States and other parts of the world caused him to pause. Finally, after prolonged private negotiations, a compromise formula was hammered out. On March 1, 1957, Mrs. Meir announced the imminent withdrawal of the remaining Israeli forces on the basis of certain "assumptions": the right of free and innocent passage for Israeli shipping in the Gulf of Akaba would be protected by the United Nations, and Egyptian units would not be permitted to return to the Gaza Strip. "Assumptions" were less than assurances but they had been formally given. Mrs. Meir quoted from an address President Eisenhower delivered on February 20 in which he stated: "We should not assume that if Israel withdraws, Egypt will prevent Israeli shipping from using the Suez Canal or the Gulf of Akaba." And she added: "This declaration has weighed heavily with my government in determining its action today."

When Mrs. Meir completed her address, Henry Cabot Lodge, the American representative, rose to re-emphasize the international character of the Gulf of Akaba. But he altered the assumptions in regard to the Gaza Strip; its future should be worked out in the framework of the armistice agreements. In plain English this meant the return of the Egyptians. A surprise change vitally affecting the assumptions had been made without notice to the Israeli delegation. Whether the new interpretation stemmed from the State Department or was conceived in the heart of the United States delegation at the last minute, nobody knew, but it was obvious that someone—after the agreed formula had been devised—had yielded to the pressure of the Arab bloc.

Mrs. Meir, who had just made a public announcement of Israel's compliance, could not jump up and cry, "Double cross," as might have been possible in the hurly-burly of Israel politics in the chambers of the *Knesset*. Nor could she retract the pledge just given to complete the withdrawal of Israeli forces. She and her associates had to sit tight-lipped as the full extent of the damage became apparent. This was diplomacy; words were weighed, pondered, refined, and meant nothing anyhow. And "assumptions" were particularly vulnerable.

On March 2—to ease the sense of betrayal—President Eisenhower wrote to Ben-Gurion: "I know that this decision was not an easy one. I believe, however, that Israel will have no cause to regret having thus conformed to the strong sentiment of the world community."

There had to be something more definite. Conferences in Washington continued, at the close of which Secretary of State Dulles and Golda Meir issued a joint statement. It reiterated American support for Israel's expectations of UN responsibility in the Gaza Strip, free passage for Israeli shipping in the Strait of Tiran, and the operation of the Suez Canal.

Israel had fought as doggedly at the United Nations as in the Sinai. At crucial moments when the threat of sanctions loomed, the refusal of the foreign minister to be bludgeoned or persuaded by the fears of American friends had been decisive in preserving some if not all of the gains of the military campaign.

On October 29, 1957, on the anniversary of the Sinai campaign, a madman seated in the balcony of the *Knesset* threw a grenade at the table around which the members of the cabinet were seated. At the sound of the explosion, Golda, thinking it was a volley of shots, threw Ben-Gurion to the floor. Though Ben-Gurion and others were injured, the most gravely hurt was Minister of the Interior Shapira. In the excitement Golda at first did not realize that she had been wounded in the leg. The seats of her chief adversaries, the members of ultrarightist Heirut, were near her chair. When they helped her to the ambulance, they could not refrain from expressing their admiration at her not having screamed.

The injury to her leg meant several weeks in bed. That was one way of getting a rest. She shrugged off the plaudits for valor coming to her from unexpected sources. Tears might flow from her eyes under stress, but she had never been given to what she contemptuously described as "yelling." She had borne her children without benefit of soporifics or drugs; Shana and Morris, standing outside the room, had heard no sound until the babies cried. Childbirth was more painful than grenade splinters in a leg. If she had not screamed then, why should she start screaming now, the foreign minister wanted to know, in response to the inquiries of solicitous friends.

The immediate results of the Sinai campaign were considerable. The Russian-supplied arsenals had been destroyed or captured. The *fedayeen* units were disorganized, and Egyptian guns at Sharm esh Sheik no longer menaced Israeli shipping through the Gulf of Akaba. A respite had been won, but no one had any illusions about its permanence.

Military defeat made the Arab states press all the harder for the economic and political isolation of Israel by means even more far-reaching than boycott and blockade. In the course of a global struggle in which the Middle East was both a potential prize and battlefield, the Arab-Israel conflict could not remain a local dispute. Soviet Russia and the United States had replaced Britain and France as the prime contenders for influence in the Middle East. Russia, one of the champions of Israeli independence during the struggle with Great Britain, with characteristic opportunism switched to the Arab side and whetted Arab intransigence with lavish arms deals and Security Council vetoes of all efforts to resolve the Arab refugee problem.

The problem of the Arab refugees was one of the major political questions that Golda had to face in the UN. The territorial partitions and upheavals of the postwar world had resulted in vast movements of peoples. A population transfer of 15,000,000 refugees took place between India and Pakistan. West Germany resettled 9,000,000 refugees from East Germany. Four hundred thousand Karelians in Finland were absorbed by the Finns, and 350,000 *Volksdeutsche* by Austria. Only the Arab states refused to permit the integration of the Palestinian refugees into the economies of their huge lands.

Approximately 500,000 Arabs had originally fled from Israel in 1948. Maintained by UNRWA (the United Nations Relief and Works Agency) in refugee camps, their numbers grew through natural increase and through the padding of relief rolls. In the Geneva Assembly, Arab spokesmen called for the return of 1,000,000 Arabs to Israel, which already had an Arab minority of 250,000 consisting of 100,000 Arabs who had not fled, their children and refugees who had returned immediately after the armistice under special arrangements for the reunion of families.

The Arab states made no secret of their purpose in blocking every constructive proposal for the resettlement and rehabilitation of the Arab refugees. "Any discussion aimed at a solution of the Palestine problem which will not be based on ensuring the refugees' right to annihilate Israel will be regarded as a desecration of the Arab people and an act of treason," read a resolution adopted by a conference of refugees in 1957, and official pronouncements from Cairo, Beirut, Bagdad, Amman and Saudi-Arabia, reiterated this thesis with unflagging violence.

The sacred right to destroy Israel was obviously one which

no Israeli could grant. Some good liberals sympathetic to Israel urged the Jewish state to respect the desire of refugees to come home. Golda pointed out that Arab strategy called not for repatriation but for reinvasion by a hostile fifth column, coming not to be loyal citizens of Israel, but pledged openly to its destruction. "This is an army," she declared.

Objectively the Arab refugee problem was the easiest of all refugee problems to solve. A population transfer had already been effected through the immigration of 500,000 Oriental Jews from the Arab countries into Israel. The resettlement of Palestinian Arabs among their fellow Arabs involved no change in language, religion or landscape—adjustments which had to be made by Jewish and other refugees. There was even no specific Palestinian nationalism to cherish. In the Arab world, Palestine had been called Southern Syria until World War I. The Arab refugee problem had been artificially created and was artificially maintained as ammunition against Israel, whatever the fate of the individuals involved.

Once during a discussion on Arab refugees, after Mrs. Meir had marshaled an impressive array of arguments against the continued exploitation of the refugees as tragic pawns in the Arab fight against Israel and had contrasted the Arab refusal to resettle their kinfolk with the Jewish state's acceptance of hundreds of thousands of Jewish refugees from Arab lands, one auditor asked her when she thought the problem would at last be resolved. Mrs. Meir answered: "When the Arabs love their children more than they hate us."

If Israel's attempted neutrality in the cold war, hopefully begun under the aegis of the joint American-Russian sponsorship of the partition resolution in 1947, gave way in the face of active pro-Arab Russian intervention it was because neutrality, like peace, could not exist unilaterally. Yet Israel's identification with the West brought no assurance that the growing imbalance between her defensive capacity and Arab striking power, steadily replenished by the East, would be altered in Israel's favor. American policy in the Middle East vacillated between a genuine friendliness for the small democracy which looked to the United States for help and an eagerness to appease the Arabs. The Arabs had oil, large populations and huge, unused territories. Israel could offer no such attractions. The marshaling of public opinion within the United States to act as a brake on the pro-Arab enthusiasts in the State Department was a task Israeli diplomats could not ignore for a moment.

Within the wide circle of global rivalries, Israel had still other problems. Ringed by foes and cut off from normal contacts with her neighbors, she could not solely rely on remote friends in Europe and the Americas. A part of Asia, she had sought acceptance from Asian countries since her establishment. There had been a few notable successes such as Israel's warm relations with Burma, but by and large the combination of Moslem solidarity and Russian-Chinese Communist influence served to nullify her efforts. The Asian-African Conference of Bandung in 1954, a conference in which theoretically every independent state of Asia and Africa was to participate, had excluded Israel, though Prime Minister U Nu of Burma had urged that Israel be invited. Nehru, too, had favored admission but had been overruled.

Except for a few non-Moslem states, Israel's isolation seemed complete. The effort to break through the Moslem-

Communist cordon became the foreign minister's chief activity after the Sinai campaign. Golda's several journeys to Africa could not be dismissed as routine goodwill tours.

Relations with Africa had originally been established during the ministry of Sharett, who was keenly aware of Israel's need to create ties wherever possible in Asia and Africa. First contacts had been made in the early fifties by representatives of the Histadrut who met representatives of indigenous African labor movements at international conferences. Since African trade-union leaders were also closely allied to the nationalist movements of their countries, these encounters resulted in a greater understanding of Israel's political aims and acted as a useful antidote to the vilification emanating from Cairo.

Golda introduced a new element. Instead of seeking out Africans in order to discuss the question of Arab refugees or the status of Jerusalem, her prime objective became practical assistance to the developing states. Israel, a small, poor state, had just solved or was in the process of solving the very problems facing other countries barely over the threshold from colonialism to independence. Israeli engineers, teachers and sanitation experts went to cities and villages in Africa, and Africans who wanted to study cooperative farming in the kibbutzim or road construction in the towns came to Israel. Just because Israel had been obliged to discover solutions under conditions of hardship and scarcity, she was a more useful model than a rich, powerful country with unlimited resources.

The thesis made sense, and many Israelis applauded it as an astute move to break through Arab encirclement. But Mrs. Meir's success in her enterprise came because she appraised the situation more simply. Insofar as possible, it was

Israel's duty to assist struggling young states. This was halutziut (pioneering) on an international scale. When President Kennedy established the Peace Corps, he was undertaking something that Israel had already begun.

Golda's great virtue—that people believed her—stood her in good stead on her African journeys. The fledgling statesmen she encountered were no political innocents; they knew exactly how advantageous their friendship might prove to Israel, but thanks to Golda they also perceived how genuine was the friendship Israel offered.

On her first African trip in February 1958, Mrs. Meir visited already independent Liberia, Ghana and Nigeria, and the French Ivory Coast, soon to receive independence. The journey took place only a few months after her recovery from the *Knesset* shooting, and the usual fears were expressed about her physical ability to stand the pace she set. But her amazing energy as she flew over mountains and jungles, emerged at humid, makeshift airports, and went through steaming day after day of meetings and receptions, showed no diminution. In Liberia, she was made an honorary paramount chief of the tribe of Gola. Since the chief is the equivalent of the king of the tribe and "Gola" happens to be the Hebrew word for Diaspora, this honor gave rise to witticisms that Golda was now the king of the Diaspora. She was not made queen mother, but a paramount chief because she was a "man important in her own right." No feminist could have asked for more.

After the ceremony in a little village of the Gola, Mrs. Meir, attired in tribal robes, was admitted to the Zoe society, composed of the women of the tribe—the first foreigner so honored. The secret initiation took place in a small, white, round building with no windows and only one door through which Golda entered accompanied by twenty women of the tribe.

The Israeli members of her party watched Golda's departure with some trepidation. Eggs and a chicken had been brought in by the members. Music and chants could be heard from within. It was a fearfully hot day, and the crowded room was obviously unventilated. At length Golda emerged, draped in colorful robes, serene and smiling. And she offered no disclosures about the nature of the secret rites. The festivities concluded with dances by Grigri bush girls and two female devils.

In Accra, at a party given for her by the Ghana Minister of State on the roof garden of the Ambassador Hotel, she was agreeably startled by the familiar strains of the *horah*, Israel's traditional folk dance, played by the orchestra. In no time at all she became part of a whirling circle of dancers consisting of members of the Israeli Embassy and Ghanaians, including two ministers who had learned the dance on visits to Israel. Though nearly sixty years old, Golda danced with the spirit if not celerity of the days when she had gone with her comrades to celebrate the founding of a new kibbutz in the desert. The formal reception thawed into spontaneous friendliness.

In Nigeria, the local *Eastern Outlook* acclaimed her arrival on March 20 as that of the first foreign minister to visit the country: "Wearing a white coat over a snow-white frock her white buck shoes first tapped on the soil of the region shortly after noon. She looked resplendent and eager in her towering height." This was probably the only time that her stature of five feet five inches had been hailed as "towering."

Even to one familiar with the exotic charm of the Middle East, the allure of Africa was bewildering in its variety. But throughout the dazzle of strange scenes and novel customs Mrs. Meir missed no chance to get closer insights into the serious strivings of the people she met.

In Ghana, at the home of Minister of State Kojo Botsio, Nkrumah's Number Two man and chief ideologist, she had an opportunity to address a private gathering of Students of Socialism, a closely guarded inner circle of the ruling party. She brought the example of Israeli socialism to bear on the needs of Ghana. Despite its ideological roots, Israel had not sought to adopt socialistic dogma mechanically; the particular circumstances of Israel had dictated the development of several kinds of social forms ranging from strict communal ownership to private initiative. While doctrinaire Marxists from the Soviet Union came to Ghana and other African states with their gospel of revolution, the Foreign Minister of Israel could point to the peaceful models of kibbutz and moshav, as well as to the central role of the Histadrut, as effective ways of social change.

Mrs. Meir's conversations with Nkrumah were frank as well as cordial. Both agreed that friendship between Israel and Ghana was desirable and possible despite other pressures to which each country might be subject. Ghana as part of the Asia-African bloc might subscribe to anti-Israel resolutions. (In 1961, for example, at a conference of African heads of state at Casablanca, Ghana voted to brand Israel as imperialist.) Israel, on the other hand, had her special interests such as her alliance with France. However, these separate involvements were not inevitably antagonistic. If the will was there, a basic friendship could exist even under such stresses.

This qualified amiability could not be dismissed as too tepid to be meaningful. Since Nasser's objective in Africa was the nonrecognition of Israel by the new states, the fact that only two—Somalia and Mauretania—failed to establish diplomatic relations with Israel on gaining independence became a measure of the difference between active Arab enmity and African goodwill. Mrs. Meir was wise enough not to press for unrealistic commitments.

Everywhere, she met with educated African women anxious to discuss the status of women in societies emerging from tribal organization into the political freedoms of the twentieth century. Here, too, Israel's intimate experience of the problems of social and cultural absorption posed by the influx of Jews from Yemen and other parts of the Orient gave authority to Mrs. Meir's comments. One point she never tired of repeating. While the transition might mean an impossible leap across centuries for the elders, the children, if given the chance, could be born into the present. Such was the lesson of Israel.

A danger that Mrs. Meir noted was the estrangement of Africa's educated youth from its ancestral villages. If a young man went to town for schooling, he turned his back on the primitive village from which he sprang. In Israel, idealistic young men and women had rejected their intellectual past and made a cult of physical labor, because manual work had been disdained in the Diaspora. In the African countries the contrary was true. There had been too much physical work. Now the boy from the bush and town had to be given the chance for secondary education, and if possible university training. To be independent, Africa had to develop its own technicians, professionals and teachers. This was primary. At the same time it was essential to avoid a situation in which anyone with secondary schooling permanently abandoned his village.

Discussions with African statesmen conscious of the danger of creating an alienated caste of the educated, who instead of acting as a leaven in the population would remain isolated, reached the conclusion that: "We must change the village." There was no point in moralizing about the unwillingness of high school graduates to be farmers under the primitive conditions they had known. A kind of farming had to be developed to which these young people might return. At this point, on more than one occasion, a direct request for specialists from the kibbutzim was forthcoming. Golda agreed and added a countersuggestion: "Send your young people to our kibbutzim and moshavim for six months or a year. When they come back, they will if necessary be accompanied by Israeli experts, but in the meantime they will have themselves learned how to establish and run a cooperative farm."

This was diplomacy at its most agreeable. For the first time since she had become foreign minister, Golda had a sense of concrete achievement. The fostering of good relations with undeveloped countries was not an abstract phrase. Every African who learned something about agriculture or administration in Israel, every Israeli who went to work in an African country offering the one thing in which Israel was rich—practical and theoretical knowledge—represented a contribution to Africa's real independence. And though the foreign minister was not so quixotic as to ignore the benefits resulting from African-Israeli friendship, the woman for whom independence and equality had been lifetime goals was deeply and purely stirred by the spectacle of the emergent continent.

When she drank Assis tomato juice in a hotel in Accra and saw other Israeli products in the stores, this was the best evidence that the Arab boycott had failed to seal off the new countries from Israel, despite Nasser. More than mutual compliments had been achieved.

In 1960, Mrs. Meir was in Africa to participate in the Independence Day ceremonies of the former French Cameroons. For over a month she traveled to new African states at whose head stood men who realized that political independence was not a goal in itself but only a means for creating a modern society.

In September 1960, an international conference on the role of science in the advancement of new states was held at the Weizmann Institute in Rehovot. Of the forty nations represented at the conference more than half came from Africa and Asia.

African leaders, habitually suspicious of the white man's largesse, were completely won by Golda. "You are like a mother to us," one of them touchingly said to her in a public greeting at a dinner; another quipped, "You should change the name of your ministry to the Friendly Ministry." When a sophisticated auditor commented later, "How corny," Golda silenced him. "No," she said, "seed corn."

The most significant political result of her African policy became apparent at the Addis Ababa conference of African heads of state held in 1963. Though Nasser kept pressing for the passage of an anti-Israel resolution, he could not duplicate the success he had enjoyed at Bandung or Casablanca. In the face of certain assurance that his proposed resolution would be defeated, he was obliged to retreat. He explained his withdrawal by stating that he had not come "in selfishness to discuss the problem which we consider the gravest of all, namely, the problem of Israel."

Golda was less successful in establishing warm personal ties with the statesmen of Asia. While the basic human and

political needs of the young African peoples appealed to her
innate simplicity, the ancient, complex civilizations of Asia
were harder to fathom. Subtlety and ambiguity were virtues
which Mrs. Meir neither admired nor cultivated. In deference to the intransigence of Arab nationalism, India refused
to establish normal diplomatic relations with democratic
Israel. Though many Indians individually came to study the
cooperative settlements of Israel, Nehru—while privately
promising Israeli representatives to exchange ambassadors—
still hesitated.

Already existent bonds had to be strengthened. When
Golda became foreign minister, the Franco-Israeli friendship
was at its height. It was no secret that Israel was getting arms
and planes mainly from France. Through personal meetings
with French diplomats from De Gaulle down, these ties grew
still closer.

In her visits to countries she had once toured as a propa-
gandist from Palestine, the foreign minister was received by
heads of state. She still found time to address ecstatic thousands in Buenos Aires or Mexico City, but the real work was
done in conference with the world's leaders—often in delicate and unpublicized negotiations. These were conducted
with less melodrama than her famous secret meeting with
Abdullah, but sometimes with no less at stake. The outcome
of a conversation could determine a crucial vote at the United
Nations.

In the Scandinavian countries, she saw the possible future
of the African experience. These small democracies, with
their magnificent social-welfare programs, represented a
hope achieved, just as Africa was challenged by potentiali-
ties as yet unrealized. When she watched a parade of school
children celebrating Norwegian Independence Day without

a single plane or tank, the Foreign Minister of Israel prayed for the day when Israel, too, could celebrate its independence, not with processions of tanks and guns but simply with singing lines of school children. And seeing the vast forests of Norway, she was able to joke about Israel's "intimate" forests where every tree had a donor's name and every grove its benefactor.

One thing that still came hard was the need to read a prepared text at her public appearances at the United Nations. At her best as an extemporaneous speaker, she felt cramped by a written speech. On one occasion she startled her auditors by a dramatic departure from the prepared script by turning to the Arab delegates with a direct plea for the peace which would give all the peoples of the Middle East a chance to co-operate for mutual well-being instead of mutual destruction. No speech of hers ever omitted this theme. Expositions of the virtue of peace were safely routine at the United Nations, but Mrs. Meir managed to invest the trite phrases with emotion. When Golda spoke of peace, she was not only a foreign minister making a political offer but also, perhaps unconsciously, the halutza—the pioneer who had worked in a swamp in Merhavia and for whom the challenge of creation would always be more exciting than any military victory. Peace was the great human chance. It gave man's incalculable energy the chance to transform all the wastelands of his life—on the soil, in the economic structure, in social relations—into something valuable. To one for whom Israel had meant a new society as well as a new land, it was doubly precious.

At the same time, as long as the plea was rejected, she unblinkingly strove to strengthen Israel's defensive position. The dread of physical extinction by the encircling Arab millions did not terrify her into compromise. Survival had more than biological meaning. Once when discussing the future of American Jewry with American friends who were deploring their children's trend to intermarriage and assimilation, she announced startlingly: "My American friends worry about their grandchildren. My grandchildren are in the Negev in a frontier kibbutz, but I don't worry about them. They are safe." Of course she knew better than anyone to what risks grandchildren in Revivim—or for that matter grandchildren in Tel Aviv or Jerusalem—were exposed, but they were safe in the way that seemed to her most significant. Whatever else in their lives might be problematic, it would not be their Jewishness. In this regard their destiny was assured.

Sometimes she clashed with Ben-Gurion in domestic questions, notably in the Lavon affair. In 1955, Defense Minister Pinhas Lavon resigned from office under a cloud. It was rumored that he had ordered a seriously bungled security operation whose nature was never disclosed to the public. Lavon, claiming that the order in question had been given by a senior army officer without his knowledge, steadfastly denied responsibility. A committee of inquiry, set up by Sharett at Lavon's request, held secret hearings but reached no conclusion as to which of conflicting witnesses told the truth.

Though elected secretary general of the Histadrut in 1956, Lavon, alleging that he had been framed by political enemies in the army, continued to seek vindication. In 1960, new evidence indicating that Lavon's supposed order had been forged came to light. A cabinet committee, appointed to examine what had burgeoned into the "Affair," cleared him, but Ben-Gurion, considering the verdict an attack upon the honor of the army, denounced it as a "gross miscarriage of justice," and resigned. The passions engendered by the Lavon scandal led to the dissolution of the government and new elections in which Ben-Gurion was again returned to office.

Without admiring or agreeing with Lavon, Golda was one of the few Mapai leaders who fought for his vindication. A question of principle was involved—the right of a man to be judged solely on the evidence. Her measured opposition troubled Ben-Gurion more than the untrameled attacks of his adversaries, for he could not contemptuously dismiss her as a politically inspired opportunist. Golda's purity of motive, her loyalty to Mapai, could not be questioned.

On a later occasion, her disagreement with Ben-Gurion was less overt but equally unmistakable. The disclosure that German missile experts, many of them ex-Nazis, were in Cairo developing rockets whose avowed target was the Jewish state, roused Israel to furious indignation. In a passionate address to the *Knesset,* the foreign minister attacked the German experts "whose aim is to expose to destruction the State of Israel in which the remnants of our people who have survived the Nazi holocaust have gathered," and called on the German Government "to put an immediate end to this dangerous activity of its citizens" in Egypt. To the argument that Bonn had no jurisdiction over German nationals outside its territory, Golda cried out: "Men make laws, men can change them!" Should Nazi scientists in Nasser's employ be allowed to complete Hitler's program of annihilation? Without a dissenting vote, the *Knesset* passed a resolution demanding that the Adenauer Government take action.

Ben-Gurion sought to quell the outburst of anti-German feeling in the country. Primarily concerned with Israel's security, he feared the mushrooming of a campaign that might jeopardize Bonn's continued economic and military aid to Israel. The threat of Nazi scientists hired by Egypt would not be lessened by the disruption of friendly relations with West Germany. According to Ben-Gurion, Israel had to come to terms with the "new Germany" and not forever hold it responsible for the sins of the old. His policy prevailed, the storm abated, and Mapai closed ranks as in the Lavon affair. But such realism rankled.

In the Eichmann case, on the other hand, there were no divisions of opinion. Mapai and Israel were virtually unanimous in their approval of the action of the Israeli volunteers who seized Eichmann in Argentina and brought him to stand trial in Israel. Outside of Israel, however, the rights of Israel's position were not universally apparent, and Golda had to make explanations at the United Nations.

In June 1960, Argentina, charging that its laws and sovereign rights had been infringed, brought the matter before the Security Council. Mrs. Meir expressed her government's regrets; at the same time she urged that this isolated violation of Argentina's laws be seen "in the light of the exceptional and unique character of the crimes attributed to Eichmann on the one hand, and the motives of those that acted in this unusual manner on the other hand." After a documented review of Eichmann's major role in the Nazi extermination program, she asked the Security Council: "Is this a problem for the Security Council? This is a body that deals with threats to the peace. Is the trial of Eichmann by the very people to whose physical annihilation he dedicated all his energy a threat to the peace, even if the manner of his apprehension violated the laws of Argentina? Or did the threat to peace lie in Eichmann at large, Eichmann unpunished, Eichmann free to spread the poison of his twisted soul to a new generation?"

Argentina accepted Israel's apology, and the matter was closed as far as formal representations before the Security Council were concerned. Neither West nor East Germany challenged Israel's right to try a German national. No international tribunal to whose jurisdiction Eichmann might be surrendered existed, though the delegation of Israel had repeatedly and vainly advocated the creation of a permanent international criminal court at the United Nations. Eichmann was in the hands of the only country interested in bringing him to book for his crimes.

At the United Nations, Golda spoke with diplomatic restraint. However, like most Israelis, she took it for granted that—except for inveterate Nazi sympathizers—world opinion would view the trial of Eichmann by the Jewish state as a supreme act of poetic and historic justice. This proved to be a naive assumption. While legalistic arguments about Israel's jurisdiction had to be answered with suitable quotations of precedents, the sanctimonious hullabaloo that ensued was unexpected. The argument that Eichmann, who had repeatedly asserted, "I will jump into my grave laughing, because the fact that I have the death of five million Jews on my conscience gives me extraordinary satisfaction," was only a small cog in a machine, a conscientious servant of Hitler, whose orders he punctiliously obeyed, appeared to her shocking as well as absurd. Assuming even that the record of Eichmann's activities in the implementation of the Nazi extermination program could be disregarded, the little-man theory of conduct provided no extenuation. To Golda and other stout believers in the dignity of the individual and the authority of his conscience, no excuse seemed more abject.

Some practical souls wanted to know why the Israeli agents who discovered Eichmann had not killed him quietly in a dark alley and avoided the international fuss. This gross misconception of Israel's purpose had to be clarified. The capture of Eichmann was not a private vendetta. Through the trial, Israel sought a moral examination of the social forces that had made Eichmann possible. For nearly twenty years the world's collective amnesia had consigned what had taken place in the heart of Europe to a willed oblivion. Israel insisted on a confrontation of the past for the sake of the future.

Such bitter re-arguing of the obvious was one of the difficult aspects of being a nation's spokesman. Nor could Golda escape the unhappy reflection that many of the most voluble pleaders for justice for Eichmann showed the least concern for the fate of his victims.

Her successes on the international scene were not immediately paralleled by the kind of recognition that mattered on the home front. At no stage did Ben-Gurion relinquish the direction of foreign policy nor was he likely to do so whoever his foreign minister might be. As long as he was at the helm, the prime minister's central role in the shaping of policy was not likely to be challenged seriously. However, Ben-Gurion had as close associates in the defense ministry a group of younger Mapai members such as Moshe Dayan and Shimon Peres, who sometimes arrogated authority. Delicate negotiations, properly belonging to the foreign ministry, were on occasion initiated by representatives of the defense ministry without previous consultation with the foreign minister. If there had been any notion that Mrs. Meir would tolerate any division of control in regard to her ministry, it was soon dissipated. While it would be inaccurate to speak of a power struggle within the higher government echelons, lines of authority long blurred by the strong light of Ben-Gurion's paramount influence had to be demarcated.

In addition, there was the lesser problem of self-appointed spokesmen for Israel. Representatives of the Jewish Agency, members of other ministries and leading Zionists presumed to speak in Israel's name on urgent international questions. The bringing of discipline into the easygoing atmosphere that had for years characterized Israeli and Zionist affairs required firm action on Mrs. Meir's part. Any group cherishing the expectation that she might accept the role of figurehead in any sphere of her rightful activity was quickly disabused. After the election of 1961, when she was again appointed foreign minister, there was no longer any question of divided authority. Mrs. Meir held the conduct of foreign affairs firmly in her hands, and Ben-Gurion gave her unequivocal praise. "I consider her one of my two best statesmen," he said, adding emphatically, " 'statesman' not 'stateswoman.' "

The silent, not always explicit, internal struggle was over. The crass exponents of *Realpolitik* among some of the up-and-coming younger men of Mapai had learned how much firm will remained in the "ineffectual romanticism" of the older generation and how tightly declarations of principle could be tied to their implementation. No trace of the half-cynical, half-affectionate assumption that had greeted her original appointment—she would prove a convenient yes woman on the inside and an effective mouthpiece for the Ben-Gurion line on the outside—remained. The forcefulness with which she had battled for the Israeli position from the Sinai campaign on, and the forthrightness with which she had conducted diplomatic negotiations, were characteristically her own, as the more timorous and conventional members of her department were obliged to learn.

In questions of major policy, Golda continued to see eye to eye with Ben-Gurion, but the notion that she saw through his eyes, as skeptics had once alleged, was thoroughly exploded.

AT HOME

IT is not name-dropping or a coy attempt at misplaced familiarity for an Israeli to call Her Excellency quite simply "Golda." That is how she is known. *"Golda Shelanu"* ("Our Golda") an Israeli citizen may cry out in a moment of exuberant patriotism. It is perhaps an anachronistic reminder of the romantic egalitarianism of the prestate pioneer period when any title was disdained. Within a particular historic context, the name is both tender and matter of fact.

The newcomers can be differentiated from the old-timers by the name they use. If someone strolling past the handsome stone villa shaded by olive trees on 9 Perez Smolenskin in Jerusalem casually informs a companion, *"Golda po"* ("Golda is here"), the chance is good that he is long a dweller in the land. If he says, "the foreign minister"—and in the sex-conscious grammar of Hebrew the feminine ending never lets you forget that the minister is a ministress—he is probably a recent arrival to whom official distinctions come more easily. But both old-timer and newcomer are likely to stop and look a moment if Mrs. Meir should be getting out of her car while the soldiers on guard before her residence snap to attention. Her Excellency returns the salute smartly, as though this is how it has always been.

Yet one old-timer bumbling along in the rose-gray Jerusalem twilight is irked by the salute. This protocol, these quasi-military trappings—empty forms, dangerous forms, false to the original vision of a new society in a new land. Was it of this that the early pioneers dreamed when they set out on their task of redemption in the marshes of the Emek? And Golda, who had been among the most valiant of the valiant first? What was she doing with this hocus-pocus? Just like any ordinary little state, with uniforms and brass buttons!

Whatever cause for worry about declining values the old-timer may rightfully have, that of corruption by too much spit and polish need not be one. As soon as the doors have closed behind Her Excellency, the soldiers promptly slouch back to their previous informality. They resume their interrupted occupations—reading a paper, sipping tea, or lounging in the garden. Not that they lack deference for their august charge. A minor Mapai functionary—this being in the midst of an election campaign—enters the soldiers' booth with a message: "Here is Golda's voting card; be sure to tell her where to vote." The young dark-eyed soldier, a Yemenite, is shocked into expostulation. "Tell her! I don't tell her anything; I just salute."

Yet that, too, is not the whole truth. The soldiers know something about the minister which would give the old-timer heart. Jerusalem nights are cold, not only in the winter when gusts of rain and wind make even the protected booth chilly and dank, but even in the pure clear air of summer. Every night, long after the housekeeper and staff of servants have left, Mrs. Meir works late over state papers not completed during the day. Often the soldiers see the lights burning in bedroom or study till daybreak. Sometime during the long cold night Mrs. Meir is likely to appear at the back entrance, carrying a steaming pot of tea and a plate of cookies for the men on watch. The soldiers are touched and grateful. In what other country does a cabinet minister make tea for a common soldier in the middle of the night? A minister who works so hard, who is tired, no longer young, a woman? As she stands there in her dressing gown, carrying a tray—kindly yet undiminished in dignity—she is again the Golda who forty years earlier in her kibbutz would gaily hurry unbidden to bring a big kettle with hot, sweet tea to comrades standing on guard in the moonlit fields of Merhavia.

Inside the house, too, the threads mingle, separate, and join again. Downstairs in the admirably appointed drawing rooms where diplomatic receptions are held, all is cool elegance, from the damask sofas to the silk draperies. Before a formal dinner, Mrs. Meir will come down early to check on the flowers in the huge vases, the crystal and silver, and the seating plan—particularly the seating plan. Two secretaries have already indicated which dignitary will sit to the right and which to the left and in what descending order, but Mrs. Meir will personally examine the cards at the table anyhow. It may be a dinner for Japanese members of Parliament or Turkish ministers or the American Ambassador. Whoever the guests—and they are varied and numerous—all punctilio will be decorously observed. Her Excellency will receive her array of notables with gracious assurance, and certainly no one would suspect that Mrs. Meir had rarely worn a long dinner dress before 1948.

Upstairs in her private apartment another world emerges. Sitting room and study are rich with mementos from every continent—African masks, elaborately carved elephant tusks from Ghana, Royal Copenhagen china, figurines from Burma or Argentina—each marks a high moment in this immensely energetic and imaginative life. The closets in the hallways bulge with scrolls, plaques, keys of cities, honorary degrees—in recognition of service to "the Jewish people and mankind." The phrasing of the tributes is repetitious: "Modern Deborah," "Greatest woman of our time," "Heroine of the Jewish renascence," "Founding Mother of Israel."

The private dining room is rarely used. Upstairs Golda eats in the large modern kitchen equipped with the latest electrical appliances, a gas stove and a dinette. The green vinyl-covered table and chairs at one end form a pleasant dining section for her and her household. When children and grandchildren come, the table can be extended. Most of the time Golda is alone, though she rarely eats alone even when there are no guests. Yehudith, the housekeeper who came to Palestine from Germany with Youth *Aliyah*, naturally sits down with her mistress. So does Esther, the twenty-year-old girl from Iraq who does the cleaning. Should Itzhak the chauffeur, originally from Rumania, happen in at mealtime, he, too, will be urged to sit down at the table. With Golda, once from Milwaukee, at the head, the table offers a cross-section of the Israeli ingathering of all the tribes of the dispersion. The grumbling old-timer would find this daily scene deeply reassuring, though a stranger might well be puzzled. Must the little cleaning maid sit with Madam Minister? Golda is not trying to upset any traditional apple carts. On the contrary, she is devoutly practicing her particular pieties.

This respect for the individual regardless of status is not merely doctrinaire—an ideological form to be mechanically observed as the forms of diplomacy are rigorously observed below. One trifling incident is more illuminating than a dozen discourses on the brotherhood of man. Itzhak has walked into the kitchen where coffee is being served to a number of guests who would ordinarily visit in the sitting room but for some reason have landed in the dinette. An American visitor has been entrusted with the pouring. As the cups are passed, Golda suddenly whispers in English, which Itzhak does not understand, "Give him a white cup." In the midst of a complex discussion in which she is the central figure, she has not failed to note the number of cups already passed, the number of each color remaining in the closet, and the probability that with the white cups coming to an end the pourer might well hand Itzhak a pink plastic cup, since he has arrived last. Whoever in that distinguished company is to get the plastic cup it must not be the chauffeur, who might suspect a slight in an act of chance.

On the bedroom walls hang samples of the usual kindergarten art fond grandmothers display—crayon drawings of Revivim and an unevenly lettered Hebrew calendar. Menachem's children are still too young to bring their offerings. And there are many photographs of children and grandchildren taken at various ages. The only other personal photograph is an old picture of Morris on the bedroom table.

All morning, members of her staff confer with her in regard to the abiding thorny problems with which Israel is beset. Preparations must be made for the forthcoming session at the United Nations where the Arabs are seeking to draw the emergent African nations into their anti-Israel camp: ways must be found to counter this hostility. In addition, a constant stream of diplomats and distinguished visitors must be welcomed as they come to pay their respects. Each one is a possible friend and must be brought to an understanding of Israel's needs and hopes. To each, Mrs. Meir tries to convey Israel's longing for peace in the Middle East. At some point in her conversations with the representatives of various countries who file before her, she finds a way to return to her constant, consuming concern.

One visitor provides a pleasant break—a Persian princess from Iran who has come on a brief visit to Israel to learn what women's organizations are achieving there. The two women form a piquant contrast: the princess, slight, dark, fashionable, wearing white sandals with gold spiked heels and open toes which show her coral-tinted toenails; Mrs. Meir, heavier of frame, dressed in a straight-lined blue linen dress bare of ornament except for a silver pin, her wavy chestnut hair with traces of gray at the temples severely parted in the middle and coiled at the nape of her neck in the austere halutz style of forty years ago, and of course without a trace of make-up on her strong, resolute face—even face powder is taboo. The princess, though an admitted grandmother, is still pretty. Few would guess that Golda had been a wonderfully attractive girl. Her features are still clear and firm, though the straight nose seems more prominent than in girlhood, but the dominant impression is one of power. Yet this woman has not withered or faded; rather, before the decay of old age, this is her permanence. As she sits at her desk, grave and motionless, she might be her own statue. When she speaks, her warm smile dispels the illusion, but in repose her face for a moment assumes finality without hardness. The princess, on the other hand, is still mobile, still to be changed.

The conversation is curious. The princess is a highly intelligent modern woman, anxious to discuss women's problems with this prime exemplar of emancipated womanhood.

"You are a young, energetic country," she says. "We are old and indolent." She complains of her country's backwardness and of masculine indifference to female progress. The ladies discuss polygamy, illiteracy, and the general tendency of men everywhere to hold women down. Mrs. Meir is tactful and sympathetic. She encourages the princess with the information that Yemenite Jewesses came to Israel unable to sign their names; now they are literate. As to polygamy—the younger Yemenite men are learning to appreciate the charms of one wife. Both ladies marvel that Swiss women are apparently reconciled to their lack of suffrage. With mild amusement, Mrs. Meir recalls the slight self-consciousness of the Swiss Ambassador when he had to present his credentials to a woman minister.

After the princess leaves, it is time for lunch—Metrecal and coffee. The Metrecal is a lost cause. There are too many dinners at which Mrs. Meir is either hostess or honored guest for the sporadic diet to be of much use.

In a subtropical climate like that of Israel, sensible people rest after lunch in the summer. Even in cool Jerusalem the noonday sun beats too hotly for activity. But Golda must drive down from the green terraced hills to humid Tel Aviv, steaming by the sea. There is a campaign speech to be made in the late afternoon and another in the early evening. After Ben-Gurion, Golda is the speaker most in demand; thousands will gather whenever she is announced. Large audiences cannot be taken for granted during this dreary campaign which follows the Lavon scandal. People are apathetic and disenchanted; even the magical figure of Ben-Gurion is tarnished in the popular mind. And Mapai, the Labor party at the helm since the creation of the state, feels the waves of discontent and distrust welling up throughout the land.

The oratory of the regular party hacks—solid workers though they be—makes little dent. For the Mapai faithful themselves have grown skeptical. For the first time, loud, ugly charges have been raised: corruption, personality cult, one-man rule and the like. Even if they cannot be substantiated, the disaffection is pervasive. That is why Golda is called upon to campaign at this nerve-shattering pace which everyone delicately agrees "would kill a horse." For in this hour of waning confidence she is one of the few who is trusted completely. The people believe her. She is not a charismatic figure like Ben-Gurion, who runs the danger of every messiah—he may be rejected. She has her own homelier aura, a mother figure, heroine not of one high moment but of decades of struggle; indigenous not to the physical Palestine to which she came in youth but to the Israel she helped fashion. Her listeners, the few who came with her in the twenties, the many who came later, are aware of her both as creature of their common history and as creator. When she stands on the open-air square, surrounded by the surging crowd, her moral authority expunges some of the doubt.

Ben-Gurion has stubbornly demanded a new vote of confidence from the electorate, and Golda again has rallied behind the "old man." Whatever the errors and failings of man and party, Israel's best hope lies with the Mapai and B.G. This she believes and of this she has to convince her listeners, even though some sharp-tongued opponents taunt her with supinely bowing to the party machine.

Despite her physical exhaustion and inner misgivings, the huge, intent throng works its usual alchemy on her. As soon as the chairman finally ends his catalogue of plaudits and she steps forward, she becomes the expositor whose straightforward clarity—never chill or academic—at once involves the multitude even to the far edges of the crowd where people stand and move about.

The finely chiseled faces of the Oriental women in her audience, unmistakable even without their characteristic headdress and silver bangles, turn attentively to the strong, dominant figure which lacks their delicate grace. The deep voice, amplified by loud-speakers, fills the square and adjoining streets, the surrounding balconies and open windows. Aware of the gleaming faces before her, the speaker uses homely images drawn from domestic lore to make her point: A party is like a cake. It is not only the ingredients but their proportion that matters: too much salt or too much sugar are equally bad; you want the right mixture.

The listeners nod appreciatively and smile at some telling shot, like their less exotic Western sisters in this working-class audience. It is obvious they take a novel pleasure in this woman who is a *sarat ha-hutz*, a foreign minister—whatever that is—who so seriously discusses men's affairs with them and asks for their vote. Those who have the courage to churn around her with the men when she makes her way to the car, touch her dress like a talisman.

Her ability to respond to immediate contact with her audiences never grows stale. The harassments of minor functionaries are another matter. At the close of the mass meeting, Mrs. Meir is informed that a group of devoted party workers has arranged a little reception for her in the nearby headquarters. This time Her Excellency is furious. Why had the date not been cleared beforehand? She has to be present at a gala celebration for French Independence Day later that night; it is impossible to sandwich in still another meeting. To the tired bystander, the solution seems simple; the unscheduled affair—a piece of rude thoughtlessness at best—

can be skipped. Of what importance is this reception by hum-
ble rank-and-file members whose chairman had not even wit
enough to make proper arrangements?

Just for that reason perhaps, Golda climbs up three flights
of stairs to a hot, crowded meeting room. The chairman
makes his glum announcement: because of unexpected de-
velopments, Her Excellency will only greet them briefly and
depart. She cannot stay for an evening of planned tribute.
But Golda, looking at this gathering, chiefly of Oriental Jews
from Salonika, forgets her vexation. In the excitement, the
chairman fumblingly has introduced her as minister of labor
—her office before she became minister of foreign affairs. The
error delights her; the role of minister of labor was closer to
her heart than her present eminence. As minister of labor you
worked for tangible results—roads, houses, social-welfare
laws. These were the fruits of your own wrangling and striving. Better still, as minister of labor you were the initiator of
action. You might be defeated, but in a basic sense you were
—and here you come to the most precious and characteristic
word in the Meir vocabulary—independent. As foreign minister you must negotiate, consider, decide, not only in the
terms of your own views but in the light of other peoples' con-
sciences and desires. Warily you must find your footing in
a web of others' weaving. In short, you are dependent.

Not that Golda says all this to her shining-eyed listeners.
Instead she recalls the primary role of Salonikan Jews, skilled
shipyard workers, in building the port of Haifa. Warmly, immediately, she is again Golda—one with those before her in
their common labor for the land. Where would the ships fleeing with the doomed from Hitler's charnel house have an-
chored, if not for the port they built? The memory of the
great days has been summoned, and there is nothing per-

functory in her greeting, as the emotion of her hearers testi-
fies. And Her Excellency will not be late to the formal reception. The change of dress may be hurried, there will be no
moment of rest, but Mrs. Meir will arrive on time, gracious
and apparently unruffled. Fortunately it is the French Ambassador who is delayed a few minutes.

There are also the amazing American tourists; no matter
how preoccupied the stately woman walking from her car
may be, they will dart up, blissfully impervious to propriety.
"Mrs. Meir, I must shake your hand. . . ." "I heard you in
Poughkeepsie, Boston, El Paso. . . ." Mrs. Meir extends her
hand without enthusiasm and smiles courteously. These man-
ifestations have long stopped pleasing her, and the violent
intrusions on her privacy are sometimes offensive. Israelis are
more discreet. They keep their distance save on occasions
when they have a rightful claim on her attention—when she
goes to them, her constituents. But these Americans! Every
contributor to the UJA has a proprietary interest, not only in
Israel, but in its leaders. "Bought and paid for," mutters an
Israeli. However, this view is needlessly harsh. The American
fan is offering tribute, not getting a receipt—this is one of
Golda's blind spots. She does not understand vicarious
thrills: "If they think us so wonderful, why are they not here?"
The chasm between the doer and the well-intentioned spec-
tator is deep, and Golda, like Ben-Gurion, finds it difficult to
bridge.

At last the long night ride back up the winding road to
Jerusalem, city of quiet and stars. Small wonder that when
she finally sits down, unwound, before the portfolio on the
kitchen table of her hushed mansion, she looks completely
spent. Her eyes do not light up at the papers as they do at the
sight of an audience whom she must arouse and challenge.

Now something else keeps her going—a dogged will which admits weariness only after the job is done, and a shrewd intelligence determined to grapple personally with the intricate problems the day's cables have brought. Tomorrow she will consult with the specialists on her staff; first she will get her own bearings in the complexities before her. Only the soldiers on guard who see the bedroom lights extinguished know at what hour her day ends.

Despite the relentless tug of the campaign, one evening of this week in the summer of 1961 has been reserved for a festivity free of politics and international goodwill. It would mark a very personal anniversary—forty years since a group of nineteen young Americans arrived in Palestine after leaving New York together on the S.S. *Pocahontas.*

Now, exactly forty years later, Golda was giving a party for the companions who had come with her to the desert and marsh of Palestine. The Israeli newspapers carried an intriguing announcement: "The Foreign Minister invites all members of the *Pocahontas* contingent to an evening at her home; not only the original dwindling group but husbands, wives, children and grandchildren."

The press picked up the item with delight. What an opportunity to editorialize on the fiber of one batch of American Zionists who actually carried out their professed beliefs in the harsh years long before the state. Though journalists begged for permission to attend, the foreign minister refused to be lured into acquiescence despite the hypothetical salutary effect of such publicity on the much desired *Aliyah,* immigration from America. The original press announcement had been the only means of communicating directly with scattered individuals and families whose addresses were unknown even in this small land, but no correspondents would be present to capitalize on the occasion.

Only 8 of the original 19 came: some were dead, others ill; one had returned to America. A handful of aging men and women ranging from sixty to seventy years of age posed for the inevitable photograph and tried to remember how each had looked forty years earlier. But youth filled the rooms: children and grandchildren of various ages; blond, blue-eyed *sabras* of European and American origin; dusky Yemenites whose presence testified to the mingling of East and West in the authentic melting pot of Israel. They moved about the parlors admiring Her Excellency's mansion, yet in typical Israeli fashion, were not overawed. Some of the more curious leafed through the leatherbound guest book in the hall, in which so many of the world's great had inscribed their names. As they chattered in Hebrew, stopping occasionally to make polite conversation in their stilted high school English with an American visitor, they were already in appearance and manner a different breed from the parents and grandparents who had left the haven of America for the remote wastelands of Palestine.

Golda's own grandchildren highlighted the contrasts: the blond, blue-eyed babies of Menachem and the dark beauty of the children of Sarele. Here were the husky farmer sons of Shana, and there the trim college-trained daughter of Regina. And this sturdy young matron was the girl born to Dinah Kaplan ten days after arrival in Palestine—she had been called a free passenger by the triumphant but anxious group who had worried whether Dinah would hold out till the voyage was over. Now old Mrs. Kaplan chuckled at the memory.

A few farmers, a plumber, a storekeeper, a housewife, a retired secretary—no one had done anything spectacular,

[318]

except of course Golda. Disregarding lamentations of relatives and warnings of prudent friends, they had set out in all the heedless gallantry of youth to begin building "a homeland for the Jewish people on the principles of social justice." Yet none in his rash optimism had believed that the amorphous vision would take such concrete form: that they would live to be contentious citizens of a Jewish state and that the gray-eyed girl with the thick lashes who had studied Hebrew on the deck of the *Pocahontas* would be among its chief statesmen.

At the tables they reminisced. Let their vivid, confident Israeli offspring—so alien to the experience of the Diaspora —try to understand the spirit of their parents—why they had left the goodness of America for the hazards of an uncertain yet unfashioned homeland. Somehow the anecdotes did not come off. The weather-beaten veterans had too long been a part of the land's reality to be able to indulge in belated Zionist rhetoric. And their children could not share the pang of severance or be amazed at their daring. What could be more matter of fact than for a Jew to be born and live in Israel?

The forty years that stretched from the first hot night in the bedbug-infested hotel on the sandy outskirts of Tel Aviv to this starlit evening in Jerusalem among the olives and pines of the patio called for even more grit than the romantic exaltation of youth envisaged. Each of them knew it now, tasting the victory in the savor of the home-grown peaches on the platters or in the crispness of the apples from Galilee. Not that anyone voiced anything so smug. In the contentment of the common recollection, briefly oblivious of the latest threat from Cairo or Moscow and of the impending election headache, they returned to one note. "We came."

[319]

Golda Meir: Woman with a Cause

This was the achievement which rose from the dredging of the past—not border battles or famine in besieged Jerusalem but the conquest of hesitation long ago in free America.

Mrs. Kaplan, still speaking Yiddish more fluently than Hebrew after forty years, shrugged her shoulders and said simply, "We came. So what? Let somebody else make speeches."

Later, when the talk was over, the young folks gathered around a singer in their midst. They listened avidly, not to the familiar songs of Israel but to intriguingly strange cowboy chanties and Negro spirituals from America.

Golda, in the plenitude of fulfillment, stood in the doorway watching her guests depart. "*Shalom*," she kept saying. "*Shalom*."